NATHANIEL HAWTHORNE

The Man,
His Tales and Romances

Edward Wagenknecht

A Frederick Ungar Book
CONTINUUM • NEW YORK

1989

The Continuum Publishing Company
370 Lexington Avenue
New York, NY 10017

Copyright © 1989 by Edward Wagenknecht

Printed in the United States of America

Library of Congress Cataloging-in-Publication Data

Wagenknecht, Edward, 1900–
   Nathaniel Hawthorne : the man, his tales, and romances / Edward Wagenknecht.
      p. cm. — (Literature and life series)
   "A Frederick Ungar book."
   Bibliography: p.
   Includes index.
   ISBN 0–8264–0409–X
   1. Hawthorne, Nathaniel, 1804–1864. 2. Novelists, American—19th century—Biography. I. Title. II. Series.
PS1881.W32 1989
813′ .3—dc19
[B]   88–18146
                                                                  CIP

For my daughter-in-law
ELIZABETH ANN MARTIN
wife of
Dr. Walter C. Wagenknecht
July 27, 1985

Contents

Preface

Nathaniel Hawthorne, Man and Writer was published in 1961 as the first of the nine books about American writers that I wrote for the Oxford University Press. Like its successors, it was a straight psychograph or character portrait, the writings being drawn upon only to portray the man. This book is different. Chapter 1 is a biographical survey of Hawthorne's life experience, and chapter 5 ("The Man") is a very condensed summary of the findings reported in 1961. But the heart of the book is the critical study of Hawthorne's fiction contained in the three intervening chapters. Chapter 2, with its important appendix, is devoted to the tales, chapter 3 to the romances, and chapter 4 to the books Hawthorne attempted to produce during his last years but never succeeded in bringing to completion. Professor Edward H. Davidson, of the University of Illinois, is the supreme authority on this period, and I wish to thank him for his kindness in reading this chapter.

At this date, nobody can pretend to study Hawthorne in a vacuum. I am aware that this is attempted from time to time, but the results have not been generally enlightening. As in my other books in Frederick Ungar's Literature and Life series (*Henry Wadsworth Longfellow: His Poetry and Prose; The Novels of Henry James;* and *The Tales of Henry James*), I have here chosen to view my subject in the light of modern criticism and research, though I have certainly not attempted any comprehensive survey or digest such as Lea Bertani Vozer Newman has offered in her *Reader's Guide to the Short Stories of Nathaniel Hawthorne* (G. K. Hall, 1977). Wherever they seemed called for, I have been frank to indicate either my agreement with or my dissent from other writers, but for the most part I have left such evaluation to my readers, using my notes not only to indicate my indebtedness but also to point the way to further elaboration of the ideas thrown out in my text, whether or not these are in harmony with my own approaches or interpretations.

Though I had assembled most of my own references independently before I encountered Lea Newman's study, I should not wish to allow either this or the fact that I am not always in entire agreement with this writer's views to obscure the fact that I heartily admire her work. From now on, any reader of Hawthorne's tales who does not avail himself of the generous help that has been provided here will merely be selling himself short.

Edward Wagenknecht

West Newton, Massachusetts
October 1987

Chronology

1804   July 4. Nathaniel Hawthorne born, Salem, Massachusetts.

1808   Father dies.

1813   Temporarily crippled by injury to foot and spends part of his boyhood near Raymond, Maine.

1825   Graduated, Bowdoin College.

1828   Publishes *Fanshawe* anonymously, at own expense.

1830   "The Hollow of the Three Hills" published in Salem *Gazette;* publication of other tales and sketches follows in various media.

1836   Edits *American Magazine of Useful and Entertaining Knowledge.*

1837   Publishes *Peter Parley's Universal History* (with sister Elizabeth Hawthorne) and *Twice-Told Tales* (enlarged edition, 1842).

1839   Becomes engaged to Sophia Peabody.

1839–40   Employed in Boston Custom House.

1841   Lives at Brook Farm, West Roxbury, Massachusetts. Publishes *Grandfather's Chair,* stories from New England history for children, followed by *Famous Old People,* and *Liberty Tree.*

1842   July 9. Marries Sophia Peabody and goes to live with her at the Old Manse, Concord, Massachusetts (until 1845). Publishes *Biographical Stories for Children.*

1844   March 3. Una Hawthorne born at the Old Manse.

1845   Edits *Journal of an African Cruiser*, by Horatio Bridge.

1846–49   Employed in Salem Custom House.

1846   June 22. Julian Hawthorne born in Boston.

1846   Publishes *Mosses from an Old Manse* (revised 1854).

1849   Mother dies.

1850   Publishes *The Scarlet Letter*.

1850–51   Lives at Lenox, Massachusetts. Rose Hawthorne born, Lenox, May 20, 1851.

1851–52   Lives at West Newton, Massachusetts.

1851   Publishes *The House of the Seven Gables, The Snow-Image and Other Twice-Told Tales, True Stories from History and Biography*.

1852   May. Moves to The Wayside, Concord, Massachusetts.

1852   Publishes *The Blithedale Romance, A Wonder Book for Girls and Boys, The Life of Franklin Pierce*.

1853   Publishes *Tanglewood Tales for Girls and Boys*.

1853–57   Serves as United States Consul, at Liverpool, England.

1857–60   Lives in Europe, largely Italy and England.

1860   Returns to The Wayside, June 28. Publishes *The Marble Faun*.

1863   Health breaks. Publishes *Our Old Home*.

1864   May 19. Dies at Plymouth, New Hampshire, May 23. Buried on Author's Ridge, Sleepy Hollow Cemetery, Concord, Massachusetts.

1

The Life

Nathaniel Hathorne (later, by his own choice, Hawthorne), was born in Salem, Massachusetts, on July 4, 1804, the second of the three children of Nathaniel Hathorne (1780–1808) by his wife, Elizabeth Clarke Manning (1780–1849). His elder sister Elizabeth had been born in 1802; the younger Mary Louisa, would follow in 1808.

The Hawthornes traced back to an English yeoman family who were supposed to have taken their name from Hawthorn Hill, overlooking Bray, Berkshire. The earliest direct ancestor of the writer who has been definitely identified is Thomas Hawthorne, of East Oakley in the hundred of Bray, who was born about the time of the discovery of America. During the lifetime of the first William (born about 1545), the preferred spelling came to be Hathorne. The first ancestor in the new world was the third William (1607–1681), who came over with his brother John between 1630 and 1633, settling first in Dorchester and later in Salem. Both he and his son John Hathorne (1641–1717) were involved in the persecution of Quakers and alleged witches.[1]

Hawthorne's father followed the sea and married the daughter of a neighboring blacksmith whose family had emigrated in 1689. He died, at twenty-eight, when his son was only four years old, on a voyage to Surinam (Dutch Guiana), interestingly enough the scene of one of the very earliest English romances, Aphra Behn's *Oroonoko* (1688). Since his death left his widow practically destitute, she moved from the Union Street house owned by her husband's family to the Manning residence on nearby Herbert Street. Here Nathaniel grew up, in his "chamber under the eaves," in "Castle Dismal," an indulged, somewhat spoiled child, in a rather crowded, heavily feminine household.

When he was nine, an accident to his foot reduced him for over two years to a state of invalidism that probably contributed toward developing his taste for reading. This was nicely balanced by the fact that from about 1816 he was able to spend considerable time on land owned by the family in a heavily wooded area on Lake Sebago, near Raymond, Maine, where he savored all the delights of field and stream. Among his early schoolmasters and tutors was Noah Webster's archrival among American lexicographers, Joseph Emerson Worcester.

In 1821 his uncle Robert Manning, a man of substance and authority, sent him to Bowdoin, then a small, rural, freshwater college (founded 1803) near Brunswick, a lumbering village, some thirty miles from Portland, Maine. There were 114 students, among them Henry Wadsworth Longfellow and Franklin Pierce. The faculty included some distinguished men, such as the scientist Parker Cleaveland and the philosopher Thomas Cogswell Upham. Tuition was only twenty-four dollars the year, but Hawthorne was often fined for breaches of discipline and sometimes for academic shortcomings, and Uncle Robert was not overprompt in paying his bills.

Hawthorne may have written some stories and sketches while still in college, from which he was graduated in 1825, and we hear of a collection called "Seven Tales of My Native Land," which he recalled from a prospective publisher who had angered him by keeping it too long. His sister Elizabeth thought she remembered tales about witches, pirates, and privateers, and his future sister-in-law, Elizabeth Palmer Peabody, said that before publishing *Twice-Told Tales*, he destroyed more manuscript than he would publish afterwards; moreover, Hawthorne himself wrote much about authors burning their manuscripts. We hear also of "Provincial Tales" and "The Story-Teller," which latter made use of the author's travels in and about New England in the early 1830s. Arlin Turner rightly describes it as possessing "a tighter frame" than the other contemplated collections, "with the Story-Teller serving as both narrator and character." These all failed of publication in their original form, but some of their contents, which included a number of Hawthorne's finest short pieces, appeared individually in such magazines and annuals as *The Token, The New England Magazine,* and *The Democratic Review,* from which they found their final abiding place in

Twice-Told Tales (1837, 1842), *Mosses from an Old Manse* (1846), and *The Snow Image and Other Twice-Told Tales* (1851). Before any of these however, Hawthorne had published anonymously, at his own expense, in 1828, his first experimental romance, *Fanshawe: A Tale,* which he never acknowledged or reprinted.

In 1836 Hawthorne went to Boston to edit a few numbers of *The American Magazine of Useful and Entertaining Knowledge* for Samuel G. Goodrich and the Bewick Company. He was responsible for selecting or improvising the contents, his stipend was often in arrears, and his engagement was terminated upon the company's bankruptcy. He remained on good terms with Goodrich however, and it was for him that with the aid of his sister Elizabeth, he turned out *Peter Parley's Universal History* (1837), a long popular compilation for young readers. In 1838 there was consideration of a plan that came to nothing of collaborating with Longfellow on a book for children, which was intended to "make a great hit, and entirely revolutionize the whole system of juvenile literature." In 1841 however, Elizabeth Peabody published for him a successful collection of tales from New England history called *Grandfather's Chair,* which was shortly followed by *Famous Old People* and *Liberty Tree.*

Meanwhile, however, in 1838, he had been involved in the most insane action of his life, when he virtually challenged his friend John O'Sullivan to a duel in behalf of Mary Crowninshield Silsbee (later Mrs. Jared Sparks), with whom Hawthorne seems to have fancied himself in love, and who either believed or pretended to believe that O'Sullivan had wronged her. Fortunately the latter kept his head, Hawthorne accepted his explanation graciously, and their friendship was not interrupted. Shortly thereafter, Jonathan Cilley, then a newly elected congressman, who had been at Bowdoin with Hawthorne, was killed in a duel by a colleague from Kentucky. It has been both asserted and denied that Cilley was encouraged to accept a challenge he might with "honor" have avoided by Hawthorne's example; if there is any truth in this, it must have laid another burden on the writer's sensitive conscience.

Perhaps Hawthorne might have missed Mary Silsbee more if he had not by this time have found himself falling in love with Sophia Peabody. The Peabodys and the Hawthornes had lived near each other in Salem since Nathaniel's childhood, but he never called at the

Peabody house as an adult until November 1837, when Sophia, who had gifts both as a writer and an artist but who was plagued with severe headaches, was in her chamber. At the earliest opportunity, her older sister Elizabeth, one of the pioneer Transcendentalists and a close associate of Emerson, Bronson Alcott, and William Ellery Channing, ran upstairs to urge her to come down and greet a visitor who was more handsome than Lord Byron. Sophia only laughed and said that if he had called once, he would call again. He did, and it was upon that occasion that the two first stood face to face. Their mutual attraction was instantaneous, but he looked at her so intently that he frightened her. The evening ended with Elizabeth's promise to call at the Hawthorne house, but Sophia declined the invitation on the ground that she never went out at night. "'I wish you would,' he said, in a low, urgent tone. But she smiled and shook her head, and he went away."

They soon progressed beyond this however, and it was not long before each understood how the other felt. It was Elizabeth who had established the adult connection between the two families through her discovery and praise of Hawthorne as a writer, and for some time observers seem to have been in doubt as to which sister Hawthorne was interested in. If Elizabeth was disappointed, nobody ever found it out, for she was one of the great saints and one of the great intellectuals, as well as one of the great eccentrics of early American culture, and she went through a somewhat-similar experience with Horace Mann before he made it clear that he meant to marry her sister Mary.[2]

Two other barriers remained between the lovers. One was Hawthorne's poverty, and the other was Sophia's health. The latter they agreed to leave to God. If it was His will that Sophia should marry Nathaniel, He would relieve her of her headaches. God graciously vouchsafed the sign. There is no record of their having asked Him for money, but in November 1838, the historian George Bancroft, now Collector of the Port of Boston, prompted by Elizabeth, offered Hawthorne a place in the Custom House, and in January 1839 he accepted it, though he wrote Longfellow that he was about as well qualified for the post as Sancho Panza had been for his governorship. He did his work well nevertheless, asserting himself without difficulty, and on at least one occasion spectacularly, over the rough men with whom he had to deal. But he felt "hampered and degraded" by it, and in January 1841 he was happy to be relieved of his duties.

There followed another highly uncharacteristic action. From April to November 1841 this solitary, introspective man lived and invested and lost some of his hard-earned money in the Brook Farm Institute of Agriculture and Education, a Transcendentalist kind of cooperative community that George Ripley and others were trying to establish in West Roxbury, Massachusetts, and which Elizabeth Peabody hailed in *The Dial* as offering "Leisure to Live in All the Faculties of the Soul" and affording "A Glimpse of Christ's Idea of Society." The explanation was that, eager to be married, Nathaniel and Sophia hoped thus to solve their economic problem and secure a home of their own at the farm at an earlier date than they might expect to acquire it elsewhere. Again Hawthorne did a man's work and did it manfully, also becoming one of the officers of the institution, but neither he nor the enterprise itself thrived, and by November it was all beginning to look like a dream behind him: "the real Me was never an associate of the community." Labor might be "the germ of all good," as Elizabeth Peabody had proclaimed, but shoveling manure and feeding swine did not inspire literature, and even when it left leisure for it, it did not leave strength.

On July 9, 1842, Hawthorne and Sophia ventured upon matrimony nevertheless, the ceremony being performed by the Reverend James Freeman Clarke, at the West Street house in Boston where the Peabodys were now living. The groom was thirty-eight, his bride thirty-three. No member of the Hawthorne family attended. Elizabeth Hawthorne had written Sophia that she hoped their future intercourse would be agreeable, especially since they did not need to meet often if they did not "happen to suit each other."

From Samuel Ripley the newlyweds rented for a hundred dollars a year the Old Manse beside the battleground in Concord, a house that had been built by Emerson's grandfather in 1765 and where Emerson himself had once lived. Hawthorne never shared his wife's enthusiasm for either Emerson ("that everlasting rejecter of all that is, and seeker for he knows not what") or the Margaret Fuller whom Emerson regarded as a supremely great woman, and when Margaret suggested that her sister and the latter's husband Ellery Channing might be received as boarders at the Old Manse, he firmly declined. He had no more intention of sharing Eden with another Adam and Eve than with the Serpent. Thoreau he liked better, for though he was as "ugly as sin," he was a "healthy and wholesome man," with "real poetry in him," and "a keen and delicate observer of nature."

Though the Hawthornes were blissfully happy in each other during their residence in the Old Manse, they had no income except what he could earn with his pen. He edited and improved the *Journal of an African Cruise* (1845) by his friend Horatio Bridge, and "The Birthmark" and "Rappaccini's Daughter" were among the "mosses" he produced while living there. On March 3, 1844, their first child, the lovely Una, was born there (Mrs. Hawthorne had had one previous miscarriage). By March of the following year they knew that the owner wished to reclaim the house, and they left Concord in October. This meant temporary lodgings in Salem and Boston, sometimes with in-laws and apart from each other. Their second child and only son Julian was born in Boston, on June 22, 1846.

Hawthorne's friends with political connections or influence now set to work to pull every string that could be pulled to get him back on the public payroll. For a time the Salem postmastership was the prize eyed, but what finally materialized in April 1846 was the surveyorship of the Salem Custom House.

This solved the financial problem, but it did not stay solved long. By June 1849 political machinations, involving prominently "that smooth, smiling, oily man of God," the Reverend Charles W. Upham, and other locally influential Whigs succeeded in depriving Hawthorne of his office. The result was a local sensation and a newspaper scandal which, as Hawthorne said, "caused the greatest uproar . . . since witch-time," and it flared up anew after the publication of *The Scarlet Letter,* with its introductory sketch, "The Custom House." The familiar story that when Hawthorne told Sophia he had lost his place, she said, "Good, then you can write your book," is probably not literally true, though it well indicates the spirit of both parties. Nevertheless, Hawthorne longed for "some stated literary employment"; even an application for work at the Boston Athenaeum was considered.

After "your book," *The Scarlet Letter,* appeared on March 16, 1850, the worst of the Hawthornes' poverty was over, but meanwhile there was a period to go through when they were so pinched that they were even obliged to accept contributions from friends. Sophia used her artistic talents to decorate screens and lampshades for sale, and Hawthorne minded the children after spending a nine-hour day at his desk. He was now completely out of sympathy with Salem (his mother had died, tended by Sophia, in the summer of 1849): "I detest this town so much that I hate to go into the streets, or to have the people see me. Anywhere else, I shall at once be entirely another man."

"Anywhere else" turned out to be Lenox in the Berkshires. They rented a little old farmhouse there, "as red as the Scarlet Letter," in April 1850, but it was not available until the end of May, and this meant another period for Sophia and the children with her family in Boston and for Hawthorne in lodgings. The red house was in full view of what is now the Stockbridge Bowl and of much natural beauty, and Hawthorne's outdoor life there was much like what he had enjoyed at the Old Manse. There were literary neighbors too, of whom the most important was Herman Melville, Hawthorne's response to whose exuberant confidences were less eager than the younger man could have wished. Yet Sophia thought Melville's "Hawthorne and his Mosses" in *The Literary World* the first really adequate appreciation of her husband's genius that had appeared, and when *Moby-Dick* was published in 1851, Hawthorne was the dedicatee. He began work on *The House of the Seven Gables* soon after arriving in Lenox, and it was published on April 9, 1851. On May 20, his last child, Rose, was born, and in November the Hawthornes left Lenox for West Newton, Massachusetts, to spend the winter in a house on Chestnut Street, owned by Horace Mann and his wife, Sophia's sister Mary, who were leaving temporarily for Washington.

In West Newton, Hawthorne wrote his most realistic novel, *The Blithedale Romance,* making use of his memories of Brook Farm, ten years before; it was published on July 14, 1852. Meanwhile, in December 1851, he had learned that Bronson Alcott's "Hillside," in Concord, was for sale. In February 1852 he bought it and renamed it "The Wayside," paying fifteen hundred dollars for the house, together with nine acres of land, later increased to thirteen. They moved in June, and this was the only house Hawthorne ever owned.[3]

All in all, 1852 was an eventful year in Hawthorne's life, both for good and for evil. After his friend Franklin Pierce was nominated on the forty-ninth ballot as Democratic candidate for the presidency, Hawthorne was enlisted to produce his campaign biography, which came out in early fall and led to his consular appointment and determined the pattern of the rest of his life. But in the summer, on her way to visit the Wayside, his sister Louisa was drowned in the *Henry Clay* steamboat accident, and he took it hard. Within four years inclusive (1851–53), he published seven books (*True Stories from History and Biography* had also appeared in 1851, and *A Wonder Book* and *Tanglewood Tales* followed in 1852 and 1853). These were indeed his wonder years, marking the only period in which Hawthorne could have been called a truly prolific writer. After *Blithedale* he would not bring out another novel for eight years, and this would be the last to appear during his lifetime.

Having won the Election of 1852, Pierce honored his biographer and their long and devoted friendship by appointing him United States consul at Liverpool, which was considered the most lucrative post in the foreign service. As soon as the election was over, Hawthorne was much involved in advising Pierce about other appointments, an activity in which he displayed considerable sagacity. With members of the Peabody family occupying the Wayside during their absence, the Hawthornes sailed on the Cunard steamer *Niagara* on July 6, 1853, arriving at Liverpool after ten days at sea. On August 1, the new consul took up his duties.

As a public official, Hawthorne was drawn at once into many functions, even embracing speech making, which, until now, he had regarded as utterly outside the range of his capacities. There was also more social festivity than he had ever experienced before. Both American visitors and English celebrities sought out the distinguished author who was in government service, and the family explored historic sites and literary shrines in "our old home" whenever his consular duties granted him leisure. Hawthorne responded fervently to Gothic cathedrals, though not to the Anglican service. The family took a pew at a Unitarian church in Liverpool, whose pastor was an American clergyman, William Henry Channing, but it was generally occupied by Sophia and the children.

Hawthorne was not born for government work, and it did not take him long to begin to be thoroughly sick of his job and to long for his hillside and "what I thought I should never long for—my pen!" Nevertheless it should be stated with emphasis that this dreamer made one of the most faithful, efficient, humane administrators on record. One communication to the secretary of state comprises 108 pages in his own handwriting, with numerous enclosures (one wonders if it was ever read). What he saw of English poverty and the causes that produced it appalled him, as all readers of *Our Old Home* will remember. He could not do anything about that, but, having learned that there was "nothing in this world so much like hell as the interior of an American ship," he did his best, though without avail, to effect reforms in the merchant service. When he tried to interest the great antislavery advocate Charles Sumner in this matter, Sumner did not even bother to answer his letter, which must have strengthened his conviction that reformers are blind as bats to everything except their own particular cause.

In assisting Americans in distress, even when he knew their troubles had been justly earned by their own folly or wickedness, he went far beyond not only the call of duty but even beyond what most persons would have considered reason, for he had always agreed with Hamlet that if men were used according to their deserts, few would escape whipping. When money was needed, and not provided for out of government funds, he supplied it from his own meager resources. Sometimes, as with the "Poor, Reverend Devil! Drunkard! Whoremaster Doctor of Divinity!" who had been in a brothel for a week, he had to become father confessor and disciplinarian to boot, and his adventures with the "Bedlamite" Delia Bacon, who wanted to open Shakespeare's grave in search of evidence that Bacon wrote his plays, and for the publication of whose book Hawthorne paid without accepting her heresy (or getting any thanks for his kindness), left him feeling that "this shall be the last of my benevolent follies, and I never will be kind to anybody again as long as I live."

What finally triggered his resignation however was that Mrs. Hawthorne could not stand the damp, cold English climate; indeed she and the girls spent one winter in Portugal, leaving Hawthorne desolately alone once more. He resigned on February 13, 1857, but was not relieved until October 12, and the Hawthornes were not free to leave England for the Continent, which they had determined to visit before returning home, until January 1858. After a brief visit in France, they moved on to Italy, mostly Rome and Florence (Hawthorne thought there was no other place where life could be "more delicious for its own sake than in Florence"). There they enjoyed the society of the Brownings, W. W. Story, Hiram Powers, and others, and there Hawthorne's education in art proceeded apace, as *The Marble Faun* shows. But on November 2, 1858, Una came down with a grueling, six-months siege of malaria, during which her life was nearly despaired of, and from the strain of which Mrs. Hawthorne believed neither the girl nor her father ever really recovered. Sophia herself did not get to bed for a fortnight nor have a chance to enjoy a good night's sleep until about a month after that.

Hawthorne wrote the first draft of *The Marble Faun* in Italy, but did not finish it until after having returned to England in June 1859. Their original plan, to go back to America in summer, was frustrated when Fields arranged with Smith and Elder for an English edition of the *Faun;* to protect the English copyright, they were obliged to stay over until the book had been published in London. They reached home on June 28, 1860. Fields and Harriet Beecher Stowe and her husband had been fellow passengers. Hawthorne had enjoyed the voyage so much that he thought he "would like to sail on forever" and had been in such good spirits that he had amused himself teasing Fields, who was seasick, by talking about various exotic and imaginary foods.

Their old Concord neighbors welcomed them home, and Hawthorne was elected to the Saturday Club, which met once a month at the Parker House in Boston, and which most of the illuminati of the New England "flowering" attended. But the sociability that had been forced upon the author by his consular duties did not carry over, and he soon fell back into his old solitary ways.

For this, however, there were several good reasons not under his control. In September, Una had a relapse, which, though fortunately short-lived, was harrowing while it lasted, for it affected her mind, and she had to have electrical shock treatment to recover. Her father's differences of opinion with his "patriotic" Concord neighbors over the first imminent, then engrossing and omnipresent Civil War did not help either; neither did his article, "Chiefly about War Matters," in the July 1862 number of the *Atlantic Monthly* nor his dedication of *Our Old Home* (1863), the only book he published after his return to America, to Franklin Pierce, who was extremely unpopular in the North.[4] "Chiefly about War Matters" was written after a visit to Washington and the war zone (he called the *Monitor,* pride of the North, a "gigantic rat-trap"). Because Fields objected to his reference to Lincoln as "Uncle Abe," he cut the entire account of his interview with the president (who had obviously never heard of him), but reserved his right to restore it should the article be reprinted. Harriet Beecher Stowe's reaction to the dedication to Pierce is a good example of the hysteria to which patriotic women are subject in wartime ("What! patronize such a traitor to our faces!"). As for Hawthorne, Fields had warned him that the dedication would hurt the sales of his book, and he was never more admirable than in his reply:

My long and intimate personal relations with Pierce render the dedication altogether proper, especially as regards this book, which would have had no existence without his kindness; and if he is so exceedingly unpopular that his name is enough to sink the volume, there is so much the more need that an old friend should stand by him. I cannot, merely on account of pecuniary profit or literary reputation, go back from what I have deliberately felt and thought it right to do, and if I were to tear out the dedication, I should never look at the volume again without remorse and shame. As for the literary public, it must accept my book precisely as I see fit to give it, or let it alone.

From the beginning of 1863 at the latest Hawthorne, not yet sixty, was obviously a very sick man. Of late years there has been a great deal of speculation about this, much of it silly, and all of it inconclusive. We hear of impaired eyesight and locomotion, deafness, chills, indigestion, loss of weight, one terrible attack of nosebleed that lasted for twenty-four hours, assorted aches and pains, and an overwhelming weariness. Anyone who compares his penmanship during the last years with what he had previously produced will find it difficult to avoid feeling that he had all of a sudden become a very old man. Hawthorne "looks gray and grand," wrote

Longfellow, "with something very pathetic about him." When he returned from Philadelphia in April 1864, Sophia was "frightened out of all knowledge" by the sight of his face, "so haggard, so white, so deeply scored with pain and fatigue."

Except for Oliver Wendell Holmes's report of his last talk with Hawthorne, we have only, by way of diagnosis, the guesses of Mrs. Hawthorne and Fields, and Franklin Pierce's conjecture that his friend's brain and/or spine must be affected because he walked and used his hands with difficulty. That his brain might go was the hideous fear that had plagued Hawthorne himself, and when Sophia heard that Holmes had suggested this, she was almost beside herself; her penciled scrawl to Fields about it, so utterly unlike her usual handwriting, still affects the reader like a moving cry of distress. Of course even Holmes had no opportunity to make a proper examination of Hawthorne. He had "refused all along to see a doctor," but when his wife "discovered that it is only to a homeopathic physician that he has an objection," Una at once got a letter off to Mrs. Fields asking her to arrange to have Holmes encounter her father "accidentally on purpose," as the saying is. The Peabodys were all passionate homeopaths, and when Mrs. Hawthorne and the children were sick, they were treated by homeopaths, though once, in London, in 1856, Hawthorne had called an allopath for his wife, being "inclined to put faith in what is tangible." Yet he was so horrified by the allopathic treatments to which he saw Ticknor subjected in Philadelphia that his special antipathy to homeopathy at this particular time is not without its surprising aspects.

Dr. Holmes found nothing "that gave warning of so sudden an end" as soon appeared, but he could not regard Hawthorne's general "aspect" as other than "very unfavorable."

There were persistent local symptoms, referred especially to the stomach,— "boring pain," distension, difficult digestion, with great waning of flesh and strength. He was very gentle, very willing to answer questions, very docile to such counsel as I offered him, but evidently had no hope of recovering his health. He spoke as if his work were done, and he should write no more.

A psychologically (or pseudopsychologically) oriented age has naturally not been content to leave it there, but so far the results of these lucubrations have not been especially impressive. Critics have tied up Hawthorne's physical breakdown with his unhappiness about the Civil War and the failure of his powers as a writer, as supposedly manifested in his inability to finish *Dr. Grimshawe's Secret* and *Septimius Felton*. Both these factors must indeed have had a depressing effect. Even Jane Addams, whose estrangement from World War I was certainly far more firmly grounded ideationally and philosophically than Hawthorne's from the Civil War, afterwards testified that she sometimes "secretly yearned to participate in the folly of all mankind." And what could possibly have a more depressing effect upon a writer's health than the fear that his powers had failed him?

One good critic, Hyatt H. Waggoner,[5] has even seen fit to introduce a hypothetical Oedipus complex into the picture, along with "lifelong restlessness, unease, and sense of guilt or estrangement." But there is simply no evidence that during his last years Hawthorne lost any of the anchors his ship had carried since childhood, and, as for the "typical liberal views" of the period, which Professor Waggoner saw him as having finally relinquished, the only thing that needs to be said is that he had never held them. In his last conversation with Melville, it was not faith and immortality that Hawthorne found "dismal" subjects but rather what he regarded as Melville's own life- and energy-paralyzing attitudes toward them.

Moreover, there was a great deal in Hawthorne's behavior toward the close of his life to refute the notion that he had lost the will to live to any greater extent than would be reasonable for a man who was physically as sick as he was. His son Julian writes that he never seemed old to his family, "even to the last. There was a primitive freshness in him, that was always arching his eyebrow and twitching the corners of his mouth." He continued to dress for dinner. He kept at his work, passionately desiring to produce one more important work, perhaps his greatest. He seized upon every favorable symptom as marking the turning of the tide back towards health. Even in the year he died he did not give up hope. To the old man in "The Dolliver Romance" he attributed an inability to believe health gone forever or himself grown old. Bernard Cohen, I think, is fully justified when he complains that critics have been so busy with the aesthetic shortcomings of *Septimius Felton* that they have forgotten its philosophical content, which is sound and sane and deeply Christian. "If Hawthorne had been able to fuse form and content in the same way that he had done in *The Scarlet Letter, Septimius Felton* might have been ranked as his greatest novel." All in all, we do not know why Hawthorne's health broke down as it did early in the sixties. We do not know whether the causes were wholly physical or whether some psychosomatic factor was also involved, and it is highly unlikely that we shall ever find out. Unless and until we do, we shall gain nothing by being fanciful or melodramatic about it.

When the end came, it was with surprising suddenness. In the spring of 1864 he was sent on a trip from which it was hoped he might derive benefit under the care of his publisher, William D. Ticknor. But in Philadelphia, Ticknor died suddenly, leaving the invalid to cope single-handed with all the consequences. Hawthorne rallied, as he always did under challenging circumstances, did what needed to be done with amazing efficiency, and dragged himself home to Concord, only to be packed off again to the White Mountains with Franklin Pierce. During the night of May 18–19, he died in his sleep at a little hotel in Plymouth, New Hampshire.

On May 23, they buried him on Author's Ridge in Sleepy Hollow Cemetery. The classical description of the day comes from Longfellow, who was one of the pallbearers:

HAWTHORNE

May 23, 1864

How beautiful it was, that one bright day
  In the long week of rain!
Though all its splendor could not chase away
  The omnipresent pain.

The lovely town was white with apple blossoms,
  And the great elms overhead
Dark shadows wove on their aerial looms
  Shot through with golden thread.

Across the meadows, by the gray old manse,
  The historic river flowed;

I was as one who wanders in a trance,
  Unconscious of his road.

The faces of familiar friends seemed strange;
  Their voices I could hear,
And yet the words they uttered seemed to change
  Their meaning to my ear.

For the one face I looked for was not there,
  The one low voice was mute;
Only an unseen presence filled the air,
  And baffled my pursuit.

Now I look back, and meadow, manse, and stream
  Dimly my thought defines;
I only see—a dream within a dream—
  The hill top hearsed with pines.

I only hear above his place of rest
  Their tender undertone,
The infinite longings of a troubled breast,
  The voice so like his own.

There in seclusion and remote from men
  The wizard hand lies cold,
Which at its topmost speed let fall the pen
  And left the tale half told.

Ah! who shall lift that wand of magic power,
  And the lost clew regain?
The unfinished window in Aladdin's tower
  Unfinished must remain!

Sophia Hawthorne survived her husband by seven years. She edited the only editions of his notebooks the world was to have until our own time, and in October, 1868, after a very unhappy quarrel with his publishers over Hawthorne's royalties,[6] she moved with her children to Dresden. In 1870 they came to London, where she died in February 1871. Una, who had become a devout Anglican, devoted to good works, died in 1877 at the age of thirty-three. Twice engaged, she died unwed. After the end of her unhappy marriage to George Parsons Lathrop, Rose, now a Roman Catholic, made a golden name for herself as Mother Alphonsa, the guiding saint and presiding genius of homes for cancer patients in New York City and Hawthorne, New York. She died in 1926. Julian, author, businessman, and father of many children, lived on until 1933.[7]

2

Tales

Hawthorne published three collections of short pieces: *Twice-Told Tales* (1837, 1842), *Mosses from an Old Manse* (1846), and *The Snow-Image and Other Twice-Told Tales* (1851). There were thirty-nine selections in the first, twenty-six in the second, and fifteen in the third. In 1852 and 1853 he published two volumes—*A Wonder Book for Girls and Boys* and *Tanglewood Tales for Girls and Boys*—each containing six tales in which he retold Greek myths and other classical stories. Besides these, the section of volume 11 in the Centenary Edition devoted to "Uncollected Tales" embraces thirteen more items.

Obviously not all this material can be considered seriatim in this chapter. Since *A Wonder Book* and *Tanglewood Tales* do not contain original material, they require only a general comment. Moreover, each of the other collections contains a number of items that, properly speaking, are not stories but sketches or even essays,[1] and since this book deals only with Hawthorne's fiction, these are excluded here. This however still leaves a considerable array of tales.

My procedure therefore will be as follows. After my general consideration of *A Wonder Book* and *Tanglewood Tales,* I shall proceed to eight stories based on New England history which, it seems to me, gain through being considered together. Then I shall close the chapter by seriatim consideration of the five outstanding tales which seem to me most imperatively to demand and most clearly promise to profit by such detailed study. Following the precedent set by my book, *The Tales of Henry James* (Ungar, 1984), I shall then consign the remaining stories to the Appendix, where they are arranged, for convenient reference, in alphabetical order, with, wherever practicable, at least one reference for each.

A *Wonder Book* and *Tanglewood Tales*

Hawthorne was considering a book of stories for children, to be done in collaboration with Longfellow, as early as 1838, but nothing came of this idea. In 1843 he was thinking of writing "one or two mythological books," and as late as the year he actually wrote *A Wonder Book* he was toying with the notion of a volume in which "classic myths modernized and made funny" should appear side by side with both fairy tales and "stories of real life." *A Wonder Book,* as we have it, was written in seven weeks of June and July 1851, while the Hawthornes were living in the Berkshires, and in March 1853 the author wrote R. H. Stoddard from the Wayside that he had completed *Tanglewood Tales.* The six stories in the former are "The Gorgon's Head," "The Golden Touch," "The Paradise of Children," "The Three Golden Apples," "The Miraculous Pitcher," and "The Chimaera." In the latter we have "The Minotaur," "The Pygmies," "The Dragon's Teeth," "Circe's Palace," "The Pomegranate Seeds," and "The Golden Fleece." Describing *A Wonder Book* in advance to James T. Fields, the author said that it would contain "The Story of Midas, with his Golden Touch, Pandora's Box, The Adventures of Hercules in quest of the Golden Apples, Bellerophon and the Chimaera, Baucis and Philemon, Perseus and Medusa," but he was more lazy when he described *Tanglewood Tales* to Stoddard merely in terms of "the Minotaur, the Golden Fleece, the story of Proserpine, etc., etc., etc."

His principal source was Charles Anthon's *Classical Dictionary* (1842), which is based on Lampière's work of the same title, supplemented by other sources, such as the *Odyssey* for "Circe's Palace."[2] He worked rapidly, perhaps more firmly in control of his talent than he would ever be again, nor does he seem to have viewed anything else he ever wrote with more complacency or fewer qualms: "I never did anything else so well as these old baby stories." He also wrote Washington Irving that the *Wonder Book* seemed more successful than his writings for adults, and Richard D. Hathaway has pointed out that in his letters to Ticknor there are more references to *Tanglewood Tales* than to *The Scarlet Letter, The House of the Seven Gables,* and *The Blithedale Romance* combined.[3] Certainly Julian Hawthorne, to whom, with his sister, Una, their father read the tales as he finished them remembered the time of their composition as a halcyon period.

Hawthorne knew perfectly well that he had substantially altered his materials, but he had done this deliberately, and though he allows the classicist Mr. Pringle to criticize the putative teller of the *Wonder Book* stories, Eustace Bright, for it ("the effect is like bedaubing a marble statue with paint"), it seemed to him that he had effected an improvement. Eustace himself describes his tone as "in some degree Gothic or romantic, or any such tone as may please myself instead of the classic coldness which is as repellent as the touch of marble" and goes on to justify his alterations on the ground that since "no epoch of time [could] claim a copyright in these immortal fables," they were "legitimate subjects for every age to clothe with its own garniture of manners and sentiment, and to improve with its own morality."[4]

This last point was very important to Hawthorne himself, for he saw "these old legends [as] brimming over with everything that is most abhorrent to our Christianized moral sense,—some of them so hideous, others so melancholy and miserable, amid which the Greek tragedians sought their themes," but he tried to convince himself that these "objectionable characteristics" were only "a parasitical growth, having no essential connection with the original fable" and that therefore Eustace (that is, Hawthorne) really did "appear to have overcome the moral objection." Hence he plays down sex and violence throughout, the most striking example being that in "The Minotaur," where we read that "some low-minded people, who pretend to tell the story of Theseus and Ariadne have the face to say that the royal and honorable maiden did really flee away, under cover of the night, with the young stranger whose life she had preserved. They say, too, that Prince Theseus . . . ungratefully deserted Ariadne, on a solitary island, where the vessel touched on its voyage to Athens."[5]

In *A Wonder Book*, Eustace Bright, a Williams College student, tells the stories to a group of child relatives known as Primrose, Periwinkle, Sweet Fern, Dandelion, Blue Eye, Clover, Huckleberry, Cowslip, Squash-Blossom, Milkweed, Plantain, and Buttercup, "during his vacations [in the Berkshires], sometimes at the fireside, sometimes in the woods and dells," and there are introductions and interludes. At the end too there are amusing comments on Hawthorne's brother writers, including his Berkshire neighbor Herman Melville, and on himself, as well as an interesting discussion of the differences between nature in the Berkshires and in Concord. In *Tanglewood Tales* however, this machinery is abandoned. Eustace Bright, now a writer, visits Hawthorne at the Wayside and brings him the stories *in manuscript*.

It is not possible for one who loved the stories of Ceres and Proserpina, Pandora's box, and Philemon and Baucis in childhood as much as the present writer did to be completely objective in his judgment of them now. Hawthorne's favorite character in Greek mythology seems to have been Hermes or Mercury, whom he calls Quicksilver, for he introduced him into four of the *Wonder Book* stories and two more in its successor. Certainly he allows himself some great liberties. King Midas "had a little daughter, whom nobody but myself ever heard of, and whose name I never knew, or have entirely forgotten. So, because I love odd names for little girls, I choose to call her Marygold." To the best of the narrator's belief, the breakfast set before these two "consisted of hot cakes, some little brook trout, roasted potatoes, fresh boiled eggs, and coffee."[6]

But there are striking virtues too and much charm. Hawthorne's generally overlooked humor is at its best in Baucis's housewifely fear that she lacks the wherewithal to do justice to the appetites of her divine guests, and the story of Jason in his quest for the Golden Fleece and the description of Bellerophon's fight with the Chimaera, so different from the author's usual subject matter, show that he did not read Scott devotedly throughout his lifetime without learning anything from him. Though he does say of Atlas holding up the sky in "The Three Golden Apples" that "this does really seem almost too much to believe," I think the only outright rationalizing comes in the passage where he conjectures that the half-equine schoolmaster Chiron was only a genial soul who carried his scholars about piggyback. Naturally there is much moralizing, on war and other subjects, but children would not object to this, and much of it might be good for them. To my way of thinking the only really serious faults are the use at times of a somewhat rhetorical or exclamatory style and, more rarely, a kind of coy condescension: "My stars, how it roared, and hissed, and bellowed!" "Now, who do you imagine those voyagers turned out to be?" And again, "And, on that island, what do you think he saw? No; you will never guess it, not if you were to try fifty thousand times."

Both *A Wonder Book* and *Tanglewood Tales* have of course been illustrated many times. Howard Pyle did the pictures for the volume devoted to them in the Old Manse Edition. The paintings Maxfield Parrish did for the Duffield edition of 1910 have been beautifully reproduced, but there are only ten of them. Of *A Wonder Book* there are memorable editions illustrated by Walter Crane (Houghton Mifflin, 1892) and Arthur Rackham (Hodder and Stoughton and George H. Doran, 1922). With Crane the book itself, like the individual illustrations, is a work of art. Rackham used several media, and his pictures have the additional distinction of being the only ones I know that are faithful to Hawthorne's text, for he has shown us Pandora, Epimetheus, and the other children of the Golden Age naked as God made them, clothing being a nuisance that had not yet come into being.

New England History in Fiction

The eight stories based on New England history that I have chosen to consider together in this section are "The Gray Champion," "Endicott and the Red Cross," "The Maypole of Merry Mount," "The Gentle Boy," and the four "Legends of the Province House," comprising "Howe's Masquerade," "Edward Randolph's Portrait," "Lady Eleanore's Mantle," and "Old Esther Dudley." The first appeared originally in the *New-England Magazine* for January 1835 and the next three in the *Token and Atlantic Souvenir* for 1838, 1836, and 1832 respectively, while the "Legends" were serialized in the *United States Magazine and Democratic Review* for May, July, and December 1838 and January 1839. All eight items were collected in *Twice-Told Tales*.

The brief, simple action of "The Gray Champion," with which Hawthorne chose to open the *Twice-Told Tales* collection, is staged on an April afternoon in 1689, when the hated royal governor of Massachusetts, Sir Edmund Andros, musters his troops to overawe the restless people of Boston. "O Lord of Hosts," cries a voice, "provide a Champion for thy people!" As if in answer to this prayer, an ancient man appears, "walking by himself along the centre of the street, to confront the armed band." Nobody knew who he was, whence he came, or what was his errand. "When scarcely twenty yards remained between, the old man grasped his staff by the middle and held it before him like a leader's truncheon."

"I am here, Sir Governor, because the cry of an oppressed people hath disturbed me in my secret place; and beseeching this favor earnestly of the Lord, it was vouchsafed me to appear once again upon earth, in the good old cause of his saints. And what speak ye of James? There is no longer a Popish tyrant on the throne of England, and by to-morrow noon, his name shall be a byword in this very street, where ye would make it a word of terror. Back, thou that wast a Governor, back! With this night thy power is ended—to-morrow, the prison!—back, lest I foretell the scaffold!"

Sir Edmund and his myrmidons quailed and fell back, and the Gray Champion's prophecy was fulfilled; the Glorious Revolution had occurred in England, and William III had replaced James II. As for the Gray Champion himself, perhaps he was one "of that stern Court of Justice which passed a sentence, too mighty for the age, but glorious in all after-times," which sent King Charles I to the block. But it is still held that "whenever the descendants of the Puritans are to show the spirit of their sires," he reappears. "In the twilight of an April morning, he stood on the green, beside the meeting-house at Lexington," and "should domestic tyranny oppress us, or the invader's steps pollute our soil," he may appear again, "for he is the type of New England's hereditary spirit."

In this tale Hawthorne has transferred the "Angel of Hadley" legend of 1675 to Boston in 1689 and imbued the incident with the Revolutionary spirit that was not to mount to its crest for nearly a hundred years. In 1675, during King Philip's War, while the people of Hadley were at church, a mysterious figure, conjecturally that of the regicide judge, Goffe, who had been in hiding there, appeared, rallied them to repulse attacking Indians, and then disappeared. The incident is recorded in Governor Thomas Hutchinson's history of

Massachusetts, which Hawthorne knew. He may also have seen Ezra Stiles's *History of Three of the Judges of King Charles I* (1794), and he had certainly read Scott's *Peveril of the Peak* (1822), in which the Hadley incident is related in chapter 14, and where Major Bridgenorth's "perhaps his voice may be heard in the fields once more, should England need one of her noblest hearts" has the same tone as Hawthorne's conclusion. The story had also been used before Hawthorne by American writers, by James McHenry in *The Spectre of the Forest* (1823), by James Nelson Barker, in a rather famous play, *Superstition* (1824), and, most importantly, by the great Cooper himself in *The Wept of Wish-ton-Wish* (1822).[7]

The flaming American patriotism invoked in the very first paragraph of "The Gray Champion" persists throughout and is passionately reaffirmed at the end, where the mysterious figure is identified with a kind of mythical semideity, guarding the people of New England and personifying their noblest spirit. Except for what a few critics have determinedly conjured up, there are no particular problems involved in interpreting this story, and though, as we shall see, Hawthorne's American patriotism had its limitations in its martial aspects, the only such passage in this tale is that in which, without clear relevance to the theme of the story itself, he pointedly reminds the reader that among those who confronted Sir Edmund's troops "were the veterans of King Philip's war, who had burned villages and slaughtered young and old, with pious fierceness, while the godly souls throughout the land were helping them with prayer." The author's handling of the Champion himself however seems characteristically ambiguous. Probably only very credulous readers would opt for him as a supernatural being, but the author does go out of his way to surround him with an aura that suggests he might be something more than human.

Though "Endicott and the Red Cross" is constructed quite as simply as "The Gray Champion," its emotional impact is more complex. "At noon of an autumn day, more than two centuries ago, the English colors were displayed by the standard-bearer of the Salem trainband, which had mustered for martial exercises under the orders of John Endicott." The people were uneasy because "the bigoted and haughty primate, Laud, Archbishop of Canterbury, controlled all the affairs of the realm," and they feared for both their civil and religious liberties. In the midst of the muster, Roger Williams, the minister at Salem, returns from Boston, with news, freshly arrived from England, to the effect that a governor-general is about to be sent over and "the idolatrous forms of English Episcopacy" established in Massachusetts Bay. Roughly rejecting Governor Winthrop's advice in the direction of caution and conciliation, Endicott cuts the Red Cross out of the English banner. "What have we to do with this mitred prelate,—with this crowned king? What have we to do with England?"

Endicott defaced the King's banner on November 5, 1634. Both Winthrop and Hutchinson record the incident, but Joseph B. Felt's *Annals of Salem* seems to be generally accepted as Hawthorne's most likely source. Historically Endicott's act was not politically motivated. To the Puritans the cross was a "Papist" symbol, and, as Cotton Mather says, Endicott's zeal was directed against "the continuance or application of a superstition." The order from England had been received by Governor Winthrop in September, but Hawthorne postdates its reception in order to widen the significance of Endicott's defiance. Moreover, Endicott was only an "assistant" in the government at this time, and so far from being regarded as a hero for what he had done, he was "censured and debarred from holding public office for a year." Finally, Roger Williams was far from being "an elderly gentleman" in 1634, and though he was soon to fall from favor and be banished from the colony, at the time he encouraged rather than disapproved of Endicott's action.[8]

The problem is to arrive at a correct interpretation of Hawthorne's attitude toward Endicott. He is assigned a heroic role in the tale and allowed to declaim eloquently on the Puritan virtues, and, as Neal Frank Doubleday has remarked, the concluding paragraph, here as in "The Gray Champion," is "blatantly nationalistic" and foreshadows the Revolution: "forever honored be the name of Endicott." Yet earlier in the tale he had been called "intolerant, sacrilegious, and traitorous" by persons who had been punished, and writers like Frederick C. Crews and Frederick Newberry have made the most that could have been made of this.[9] Certainly the punishments portrayed are cruel enough to horrify the modern reader even without Freudian rhetoric. At the very beginning we are told that "the whole surrounding scene had its image in the glittering steel" of Endicott's breastplate, where, first of all, we see "the grim head of a wolf . . . nailed on the porch of the meeting house," with "the blood still plashing on the doorstep." The whipping-post, the pillory, and the stocks stand in close proximity to the meetinghouse, with an Episcopalian and "a suspected Catholic" even now enjoying the benefit of their discipline. The young woman with a scarlet A on her bosom will be dully noted elsewhere in this volume, and a man who had "dared to give interpretations of Holy Writ unsanctioned by the infallible judgment of the civil and religious rulers" wears the label of A WANTON GOSPELLER. A woman wears a cleft stick on her tongue "for having wagged that unruly member against the elders of the church"; worse still, there are branded cheeks, cropped ears, and slit nostrils on view. Nor does Endicott fail to vaunt the superiority of Puritan weapons against "the few stately savages [who], in all the pomp and dignity of the primeval Indian, stood gazing at the spectacle," apparently quite unregardful that his boast itself testifies to the essential harmlessness of the Indians.

We shall meet Endicott again in a moment in "The Maypole of Merry Mount," where he seems a more complicated character than here; he does not appear in "The Gentle Boy," but it is clear that he has a share in the persecution of the Quakers about which that story revolves. In Hawthorne's paper on "Mrs. Hutchinson" however, he is harshly described as one "who would stand with his drawn sword at the gate of heaven, and resist to the death all pilgrims thither except they traveled his own path." Putting all references to him in Hawthorne's work together, it is undeniable that the reader must be left with a somewhat divided sympathy, but the suggestion sometimes offered that Hawthorne praised the Puritans while at the same time deliberately undercutting his praise by making subtle suggestions of villainy to the reader's mind is absurd. The real explanation is simply that his own mind was divided. There were some things about the Puritans that, like most of us, he admired, and there were others by which he was revolted. Perhaps we come as close as either he came or we can hope to come when he writes in the sketch "Main Street": "Let us thank God for having given us such ancestors; and let each successive generation thank him not less fervently, for being one step further from them in the march of ages."

"The Maypole of Merry Mount" goes back further into colonial times than either of the stories so far considered.

Bright were the days at Merry Mount, when the Maypole was the banner staff of that gay colony! They who reared it, should their banner be triumphant, were to pour sunshine over New England's rugged hills, and scatter flower seeds throughout the soil. Jollity and gloom were contending for an empire.

This anti-Puritan settlement was established by Captain Wollaston, at what is now Quincy, Massachusetts, in 1623 and at first named after its founder. It was renamed by Thomas Morton, who tried to establish "revels and merriment after the old English customs" there. In 1628, John Endicott, commanding a party from the Bay Colony, raided the settlement and cut down the Maypole. A previous raid under the command of Captain Miles Standish of Plymouth had already arrested Morton and sent him back to England. Hawthorne's tale merely describes the revels, Endicott's raid, and the arrest of the revelers, ending with Endicott's surprising lenity toward the young lovers, Edith and Edgar, who had just been married by an Anglican priest, decked out in what the Puritans regarded as profane attire. Touched by the obvious unselfish devotion of the young couple upon whom "the troubles of life have come hastily," and discerning the makings of good Puritans in both, Endicott contents himself with ordering Edgar's hair cropped, after which he "lifted the wreath of roses from the ruin of the Maypole, and threw it with his own gauntleted hand, over the heads of the Lord and Lady of the May."

For the historical basis of his tale Hawthorne had access to such of "the grave pages of our New England annalists" as were available in his time.[10] The historical accuracy of his story is something else again. He himself warns the reader not to regard it as authoritative when he calls it "a sort of allegory." There is a note in which he rather coyly and halfheartedly apologizes for having Endicott call the Anglican priest Blackstone (it was Claxton in the first printing): "The Rev. Mr. Blackstone, though an eccentric, is not known to have been an immoral man." What is more to the point is that neither was he a part of the Merry Mount settlement. Hawthorne does not mention the accusation that the Merry Mounters were supplying the Indians with guns either, which, if true, would have given Endicott and his party more justification than anything else for what they did. Some writers speak of the contrast between the austerity of the Puritans and the "sensuality" of Merry Mount. None of the latter is actually shown, as may be seen by comparing even the extract from Governor Bradford's journal quoted by Daniel G. Hoffman[11] with the story. The revels about the maypole are frivolous and the costumes worn are silly, but the presence of the Anglican priest performing a binding marriage ceremony for sincere and unselfish lovers does not support the accusation that Morton "became Lord of Misrule" who set up "a School of Atheism."[12] Why Hawthorne shifted the May Day celebrations to Midsummer Eve has also exercised critical craniums, and various explanations have been attempted: he wanted summer flowers; summer provides the better setting for a love story; since the abandon and fertility of summer dies with the coming of autumn, the later date better suggests the shadow of mortality hanging over the settlement. All in all, Gary Williams sums up well when he writes that "on a superficial or 'antiquarian' level . . . Hawthorne's rendering of the episode at Merry Mount is full of historical inaccuracies," but he is "intensely historical" in creating "a *symbolic* confrontation between the Puritans and their adversaries."

Whatever may be said of the extravagances in which certain anthropologically and mythically minded scholars have engaged in connection with "The Maypole,"[13] two other things at least are clear about sources: Hawthorne did make good use of Joseph Strutt's *Sports and Pastimes of the People of England* (1801), and he freely employed his knowledge of Milton. He himself mentions "Comus" in connection with the masquers,[14] but *Paradise Lost* is far more important. The last sentence relates of Edith and Edgar that "they went heavenward, supporting each other along the difficult path which it was their lot to tread, and never wasted one regretful thought on the vanities of Merry Mount." Not only do these words remind us of the end of Milton's epic, but the young lovers, expelled from their Eden, face the future in much the same spirit as Adam and Eve themselves. Only, to quote Gary Williams again, not having, like Milton's pair, been created sinless, they "fall upward into grace."

All this has a direct bearing upon Hawthorne's intent in telling this story or what the narrative *means*. It has been interpreted as if the author stood evenly poised between Puritanism and anti-Puritanism or, to put the contrast more gently, between "L'Allegro" and "Il Penseroso," and superficially it is not difficult to find evidence to support this interpretation. Merry Mount's history is "a poet's tale"; should the attitude it represents prevail in New England, "sunshine would break upon the hills, and flowers would beautify the forest, and late posterity do homage to the Maypole." The Puritans, on the other hand, are "most dismal wretches," who always keep their weapons handy "to shoot down the straggling savage." Their idea of a maypole is a whipping post. As the tree around which the Merry Mount festivities had centered falls, "the evening sky grew darker, and the winds threw forth a more sombre shadow."

Endicott himself is "the Puritan of Puritans." "The whole man seemed wrought of iron." Except for Edith and Edgar, the revelers who have been arrested are to be set in the stocks, there to await further consideration of branding and ear cropping. A particularly repellent touch is his ordering the bear who has had a share in the festivities shot: "I suspect witchcraft in the beast." Yet even though we need not go along with Gayle L. Smith, who sees him at the end performing the same function toward the lovers that Christ performs toward Adam and Eve in *Paradise Lost* ("he has progressed from Satan figure to Christ figure"),[15] the fact remains that Endicott *has* shown himself possessed of sufficient moral and spiritual sensitiveness to be aware of what it is that sets the lovers apart from the fribbles by which they have been surrounded and that his kindness toward them represents the closest approach the tale makes to a reconciliation between two worlds or ways of life.

Imperfect as they are therefore, Hawthorne opts finally for the Puritans and expects his readers to do so. As I have already noted, he omits all the uglier aspects of the Merry Mounters's moral and spiritual condition. But if these people are not evil, they are not only spiritually immature but apparently incapable of moral and spiritual growth. They have sought to detach themselves from human destiny. Though they think they are living in the Golden Age, they are really only playing at it. The Golden Age, like Eden before the Fall, has passed and can never be recovered. The only choice now is whether to fall back or press on to something higher. Having lost "the heart's fresh gayety," the people of Merry Mount have merely "imagined a wild philosophy of pleasure," living in a day dream and attempting to turn even a funeral into a festival. ("But," asks Hawthorne significantly, "did the dead man laugh?") As Sheldon Liebman puts it, "they have been 'maddened . . . into a gay despair,' by their refusal to accept life on its own terms, both good and ill."[16]

"The Gentle Boy" deals with a special topic in New England history—the Puritan persecution of Quakers. It opens on the evening of October 27, 1659, the day Marmaduke Stevenson and William Robinson were hanged in Boston, and Tobias Pearson finds the homeless Quaker boy Ilbrahim[17] mourning upon his father's grave and takes him home in spite of his own anti-Quaker prejudices and the anticipated certain disapproval of his friends and neighbors, and it ends in the autumn of 1661, when King Charles II, having been informed that a vein of blood had been opened in his dominions, to his everlasting honor replied, "But I will stop that vein." The king's order was actually received in Boston on September 9, but Hawthorne puts it later in the year, thus allowing more time for the story to develop and making it possible for Pearson to receive the news as the boy is dying and his mother Catharine arrives in the midst of a winter storm.

What happens between the two dates is simple but harrowing. Not only do the Puritans refuse to accept Ilbrahim, but as time passes, Tobias and his wife Dorothy, a faithful, loving woman, who gladly lavishes upon the outcast boy all the affection she had previously bestowed upon the children of her body, of whom death had robbed her, are forced to share his isolation. They are shunned when they try to take Ilbrahim to meeting, and the Puritan children behave like little fiends, treating the boy even worse than they treat Hester's Pearl in *The Scarlet Letter.* Hungry for childish companionship, despite all Dorothy's tenderness, Ilbrahim finally tries to make a friend of a particularly repulsive and, as it turns out, evil Puritan child who is being nursed by Dorothy after an accident. Yet, when partially recovered, this young devil calls Ilbrahim to his side by pretending that he wishes to protect him and then strikes and injures him cruelly. This turns out to be more than the Quaker child can bear. His faith in life and his zest for it wither away and he dies just as a better day for those of his persuasion is dawning.

Hawthorne acknowledges his debt to William Sewal's history of the Quakers; he also of course made use of some of the Puritan historians. Though no character seems to be a portrait of any single Quaker, Mary Fisher, Catharine Evans, Catharine Chatham, and others have been considered by way of comparison with the activities of Ilbrahim's mother. We even hear of one Quaker child, Patience Scott, who was "interrogated" by Puritan authorities, and who, we may be happy to know, "confounded" them by her answers. There are also recorded cases of Puritans who, repelled by the persecutions, went over to the persecuted sect, as Tobias Pearson does. Biblical quotations and allusions abound in the story, and Frederick Newberry speaks of the relations between Cromwell and a soldier named Pearson in Scott's *Woodstock* as having possibly suggested Tobias's quitting the army when Oliver's ambitions were manifested and his cause could no longer be regarded as holy, while Catharine's eloquence reminds Neal Doubleday of both Meg Merrilies in *Guy Mannering* and Ephraim Macbriar in *Old Mortality*.[18]

Since the Puritans appear in "The Gentle Boy" as persecutors and the Quakers as the persecuted, and since even the worst vagaries of the latter are harmless to society compared to the outrages society perpetrates by way of punishment, the sympathies of every decent reader are almost automatically enlisted by the Quakers. This is far from making "The Gentle Boy" "a Quaker story" however. Quaker fanatics actually challenge and court martyrdom, and Agnes Donohue is not far wrong when she speaks of "sadistic Puritans and masochistic Quakers." Ilbrahim's mother Catharine, "a woman of mighty passions," in whom "hatred and revenge . . . wrapped themselves in the garb of piety," dresses herself in sackcloth and usurps a Puritan pulpit to give vent to a "flood of malignity which she mistook for inspiration." God's voice within sends her forth on her mission as a "witness"; it does not occur to her that if God gave her a child, He must have expected her to take care of him. And the old Quaker who tries to comfort and counsel Tobias in the end can still rejoice that he was given grace to go out "in peace and joy toward the wilderness" when the voice came bidding him to desert his daughter on her deathbed and "go forth a wanderer." In other words, the choice the reader is asked to make in "The Gentle Boy" is not between Puritanism and Quakerism but between insanity and

common sense, between cruelty and a decent humanity. Celebrated
as he is for his ambivalence, Hawthorne could not have made this
more plain than he does when he goes to the length of actually
naming his allegory as Catharine and Dorothy stand beside Ilbrahim in the meetinghouse: "The two females, as they held each a
hand of Ilbrahim, formed a practical allegory: it was rational piety
and unbridled fanaticism contending for the empire of a young
heart."

"The Gentle Boy" is one of the longest of Hawthorne's tales, and
in his own time it was always regarded as one of the best; Longfellow indeed called it "the finest thing he ever wrote." The author does
not seem to have quite agreed. It was the only tale he ever revised,
and though he was ecstatic about the Flaxman-like drawing that
Sophia Peabody, not yet Mrs. Hawthorne, made for it, this enthusiasm seems to have been awakened more by her work than by his
own.

For his own part, he would willingly have supposed that a more practiced
hand and cultivated fancy had enabled him to excel his first inartificial
attempts; and there are several among his Twice-Told Tales, which, on repe-
rusal, affect him less painfully with a sense of imperfect and ill-wrought
conception than The Gentle Boy.

Nevertheless he had enough respect for his readers so that he was
willing to grant the possibility that this time "Nature had led him
deeper into the universal heart than Art has been able to follow."

In our own time few have put the tale thus high, the general
objection being that it is too "sentimental." But the line between
sentiment and sentimentality is at best a wavering one, and it may
be that a generation which nourishes its youth on films and television
shows reeking with sex and violence is not the best possible judge.
However this may be, the story is certainly not without its realistic,
nonsentimental aspects. "Ironically," says Agnes Donohue, "the
story of a gentle boy is a cruel and barbarous tale." Surely Frederick
C. Crews is right in finding Tobias "a peculiarly neurotic Good
Samaritan," who finds no more spiritual rest in Quakerism than
in Calvinism, and Ilbrahim himself "morbid as well as angelic,"
and realistically portrayed in the sense that one could hardly expect
Catharine's child, with his background and conditioning, to be

anything else. Indeed, Edwin Haviland Miller goes the whole way, denying that the boy is sentimentalized at all. "He is confronted with a task that defeats those older in years and wisdom—how to cope with abandonment or rejection."[19]

The "Legends of the Province House" are less substantial tales than those already considered here, and they have attracted much less comment. But it is easy to understand why they must have interested Hawthorne. As a fledgling writer, he had made three abortive attempts to produce a series of tales bound together by a frame, but this was the first such project he was ever to get published.

The Province House, he tells us, stands in Boston, almost directly across Washington Street from the Old South Church, but can now be reached only through a narrow passageway between the storefronts that have been erected before it. Built as a private residence in 1679, this building was purchased by the Province of Massachusetts in 1716 and served as the home of the colonial governors from 1718 to 1776; then, after having been used briefly by the new state government, it passed into private hands. From 1835 to 1851 it became a tavern, operated by Thomas Waite, who appears in Hawthorne's frame. It burned in 1864.[20]

The first three tales are communicated to Hawthorne or his persona by Mr. Bela Tiffany, a habitué of the bar, and the last by an unnamed old loyalist, but the writer makes it clear that since Mr. Tiffany "professed to have received [his information] at one or two removes from an eye-witness" and since "this derivation, together with the lapse of time, must have afforded opportunities for many variations of the narrative," he has himself "not scrupled to make such further changes as seemed conducive to the reader's profit and delight" and that, especially since it was not being transmitted "through the medium of a thoroughgoing democrat," the old loyalist's story required even more revision.

The narrator makes his first visit to the Province House and hears the story of Howe's masquerade in midsummer, but he does not hear the second tale until a stormy night during the following January. The last two stories are related upon a third, not precisely indicated occasion, but enough time must be allowed to permit Thomas Waite, grateful for the increased patronage directed to his house by the publication of the first two narratives, to invite Mr. Tiffany and the writer to an oyster supper. And when the writer leaves after the supper, he makes it clear to the reader that he has no intention to come again. As for the actions related in the four tales, "Howe's Masquerade" takes place during the siege of Boston in the winter of 1775–76; "Edward Randolph's Portrait" precedes the so-called Boston "Massacre" of 1770; "Lady Eleanore's Mantle" leads up to the terrible smallpox epidemic of 1721, during which Dr. Zabdiel Boylston, under heroic difficulties, introduced inoculation into Boston; while "Old Esther Dudley" opens when the last royal governor, Sir William Howe, is forced to leave the Province House, and ends when John Hancock comes to take possession after his election as governor of Massachusetts under the new state constitution in 1780.[21]

The neglect formerly accorded the "Legends" has been somewhat remedied during recent years, and a surprisingly large percentage of this commentary has been devoted to the series as a whole; there are still very few studies of the individual tales. Some of this criticism, like much that has been written about "The Custom House" in *The Scarlet Letter*, seems oversubtle or imaginative. I am not sure all readers will be able to go the whole way with Julian Smith when he says that Hawthorne "gives us the basic conflict between colonial and loyalist factions in the first story, develops the reasons for that conflict in the next two stories, and shows us the outcome in the last," nor yet with P. L. Reed's view that everything conjoins "to focus a life view in the American present," but surely the notion that the frames are only "casual fragmentary sketches" that merely serve to introduce unrelated tales will no longer do.[22] Edward Randolph (1632–1703), who had been largely responsible for the colony's loss of her original charter, and who had been introduced into "The Gray Champion" as "a blasted wretch" and "our arch-enemy," is revived in the second tale to warn Governor Hutchinson of the danger of turning Castle William over to the royal troops, and old Esther Dudley, about whom the final narrative revolves, is believed by the superstitious to have entered the Province House in the time of Colonel Shute, the first governor, who was the uncle of Eleanore Rocheforte, the wearer of the infected mantle in the third tale.

"Howe's Masquerade" is perhaps the best example in Hawthorne of the "explained supernatural" in the tradition of Mrs. Radcliffe's novels. It is also the slightest of the "Legends." There is only one touch of true supernaturalism, where it is suggested at the end that "on the anniversary night of Britain's discomfiture, the ghosts of the ancient governors of Massachusetts still glide through the portal of the Province House," and this is quickly dismissed. The forced atmosphere of the ball, held during the siege of Boston "under an ostentation of festivity," is broken into by a funeral march and a weird procession, in which the regicide judges, the provincial governors, culminating in the image of Sir William Howe himself in humiliating guise, and caricatures of General Washington "and the other principal officers of the American army" all appear. This is promptly interpreted by Colonel Joliffe, who, though of "known whig principles," is unaccountably present with his niece. "Now were I a rebel," reflects that pert young lady, "I might fancy that the ghosts of those ancient governors had been summoned to form the funeral procession of royal authority in New England."[23]

It is explained supernaturalism again in "Edward Randolph's Portrait," and though this time we may get a few more shivers, we are not really entitled to them. The source is Governor Hutchinson's history, and the tale revolves about the difficulty he faced in 1770, when he was ordered to remove the provincial troops by which it had hitherto been garrisoned from Castle William in Boston Harbor so that they might be replaced by soldiers directly responsible to the Crown. Hawthorne's nonfictional account of the matter in *Grandfather's Chair* is much more sympathetic toward the reluctant governor than the story. The mysterious portrait is a stock property in Gothic fiction, and Mrs. Hawthorne's statement that Alice Vane's restoration of it was suggested by what she herself had done with "that picture of Fernandez" makes her a kind of model for Hutchinson's niece in the story. This Alice Vane was "a pale, ethereal creature, who, though a native of New England, had been educated abroad, and seemed not merely a stranger from another clime, but almost a being from another world."

The portrait had blackened in its frame until nothing but blackness could now be seen, and many conjectures had been offered as to its origin, "one of the wildest, and at the same time the best accredited" being that it was "an original and authentic portrait of the Evil One, taken at a witch meeting in Salem." It had also been said that it was inhabited by "a familiar spirit or demon" who "had shown himself, at seasons of public calamity, to more than one of the royal governors," but Hutchinson himself insists that it was merely a portrait of Edward Randolph. "When the rulers feel themselves irresponsible," says Alice, "it were well that they should be reminded of the awful weight of a people's curse," and, being sure that it is now time for the "dark and evil Shape" to "come forth once more," she uses the arts of restoration she has learned abroad to cause Randolph's image, "with the terrors of hell upon his face," to manifest just as Hutchinson is about to sign the order required by the king's command. "Be warned, then! He trampled on a people's rights. Behold his punishment—and avoid a crime like his!" But while the reader might be able to stretch his credulity to the extent of believing that the girl could have restored the painting, that it should have reappeared only temporarily, just when it was needed, and then again have retreated "behind a century's obscurity" is a bit too much to swallow even in such a tale as this. And since Hutchinson *does* sign the order, the whole exercise seems pretty much ado about nothing.

"Lady Eleanore's Mantle" is more of a story than either of its predecessors and much richer in symbolism, though many find this obvious and mechanical, objecting especially to Eleanore's own exposition of the moral before she dies: "The curse of heaven hath stricken me, because I would not call man my brother, nor woman sister. I wrapped myself in PRIDE as in a MANTLE, and scorned the sympathies of nature; and therefore has nature made this wretched body the medium of a dreadful sympathy."

Certainly, the embroidered mantle is one of Hawthorne's most elaborate symbols. Reportedly responsible for much of the charm of Eleanore's appearance, it is supposed to be "invested with magic properties so as to lend a new and untried grace to her figure each time she put it on."[24] It threw an awe around Eleanore, "partly from its fabled virtues, and partly because it was the handiwork of a dying woman, and, perchance, owed the fantastic grace of its conception to the delirium of approaching death." The dying woman had indeed contributed more than her skill as a seamstress to the garment, for she was dying of smallpox, and the mantle communicated the disease to its wearer and through her to the whole city. When the funeral bell of the Old South Church tolls just as Eleanore approaches the Province House, Captain Langford thinks it outrageous, but Dr. Clarke, "a famous champion of the popular party," reminds him that "King Death confers high privileges" and that "a dead beggar must have precedence of a living queen," and when, later, Helwyse begs her to cast "the accursed garment" from her and "give it to the flames," he is exhorting her both to purge her body from contagion and her soul of pride.[25]

Both Hutchinson's and Caleb Snow's histories could have given Hawthorne the information he needed about smallpox in Boston. Various passages in his notebooks suggest the use he made of this knowledge, and two articles published in the *American Magazine of Useful and Entertaining Knowledge* while he was its editor, deal directly with the communication of a disease through infected garments.[26] He may well have drawn upon the properties and traditions of the Gothic novels also, and certainly nobody who knew Spenser as well as he did could have created Lady Eleanore without thinking of Lucifera and the House of Pride. The "belief" suggested in the last paragraph "that in a certain chamber" of the Province House, "a female form may sometimes be darkly discerned, shrinking into the darkest corner and muffling her face within an embroidered mantle" is not vouched for by the narrator nor anybody else, and it is anybody's guess whether the cessation of the epidemic after Jervase Helwyse had paraded through the streets with Eleanor's effigy and "waving the red flag of the pestilence," after which the mob burned the effigy and the garment in which it was wrapped, "and a strong wind came and swept away the ashes," was due to natural or supernatural causes.

There is hardly any action in the last of the "Legends," "Old Esther Dudley." There has been speculation as to why Hawthorne brought in a new, loyalist narrator for this tale; the most likely guess is that he wished to insure sympathetic treatment for the old lady. Certainly she is lovingly handled, and at the end the narrator is almost overcome by his own emotion.

Esther holds an "office in the household" at the Province House, "with merely nominal duties, [which] had been assigned to her as a pretext for the payment of a small pension." She had been there longer than anybody could remember, and when the last royal governor, Howe, is forced to depart, she refuses to go with him to

Halifax, as he desires. Instead she elects to stay (so that His Majesty may still have at least one loyal subject left in Boston) until either Howe shall return or some other royal governor arrive. So she remains, custodian of the great key that Howe reluctantly consigns to her, attired gorgeously in the increasingly "mildewed velvets or brocades" of the splendid past and sometimes illuminating the house with a "blaze of light," and with every American victory in the war transformed, in her warped imagination, into a British triumph. The townspeople come to believe that she could bring the worthies of the past out of "a tall, antique mirror, which was well worthy of a tale by itself," or summon from the same a black slave and "send him in search of guests who had long ago been familiar in these deserted chambers" to attend her at a midnight feast. Her only actual guests however are the neighboring children, in whom her "kindly and loving nature" finds its only true outlet, and who are so "greedily attentive to her stories of a dead world" that they astonish their parents by talking about long-past worthies as if they had known them.

So life—or a kind of life—rolls on until at last, for some reason best known to herself, or perhaps least of all to her, old Esther gets it into her head that the war has ended with a British victory, and gets ready to welcome the new royal governor. "Receive my trust! take it quickly! for methinks Death is striving to snatch away my triumph. But he comes too late. Thank Heaven for this blessed hour! God save King George!"

But the new "royal governor" is none other than the newly elected governor of the commonwealth of Massachusetts under her new constitution, that aggressive democrat and modernist ("We are no longer children of the Past!") John Hancock. The shock of having bidden a "traitor" welcome is too much for the old lady, and she collapses at his feet: "I have been faithful unto death! God save the King!"

This incident, or rather Hancock's reaction to it, is the only thing in the tale that has inspired opposing views, and this disagreement involves not only "Old Esther Dudley" but all the legends. As late as 1972, when he published *Hawthorne's Early Tales: A Critical Study,* N. F. Doubleday could write, "The reader who finds the nationalistic conclusions of 'The Gray Champion' and 'Endicott and the Red

Cross' a little shrill will find passages in the 'Legends' strident" and conjectured that the tone might have been influenced by what we should now call the "hundred per cent Americanism" of the editor of the *United States Magazine,* John O'Sullivan; but few recent writers seem to share this view. Julian Smith finds Hawthorne "highly ambivalent toward and sometimes critical of the American Revolution" and thinks the legends leave "republican and loyalist forces . . . in a kind of moral balance." Speaking specifically of "Old Esther Dudley," Thomas F. Walsh, Jr.,[27] finds Hancock's closing words "dramatically appropriate" but feels that they were intended to be "taken satirically," to which Julian Smith adds that they constitute "a rejection of the past, not of aristocracy." P. L. Reed thinks the moral of the "Legends" as a whole is that both ignoring the past and lingering in it too long are dangerous, while Margaret Allen, concentrating on aesthetic rather than political aspects, suggests that Hawthorne's not reporting either Mr. Tiffany or the old loyalist accurately was intended to suggest both the inevitable unreliability of our knowledge of the past and the superiority of the artist, "who can imaginatively narrate the past in a living form," over the mere chronicler. Perhaps it is too much to expect complete uniformity of opinion on this point, but the least one can say is that Hawthorne's reference to John Hancock in "A Book of Autographs" as a "man without a head or a heart" supports the newer rather than the older interpretation of "Old Esther Dudley."

"The Birthmark"

In "The Birthmark," which was published in the *Pioneer* in March 1843 and reprinted in *Mosses from an Old Manse,* Aylmer, a daring and accomplished eighteenth-century scientist, marries the beautiful Georgiana, whose only physical flaw is a tiny birthmark in her left cheek, clearly visible only when she is pale. Jealous women have called this a "bloody hand," but her admirers have generally regarded it as a charm, and Georgiana herself had been tempted to share this view until she learned that to her husband it was "the visible mark of earthly imperfection" and the symbol of her "liability to sin,

sorrow, decay, and death."[28] His desire to create "one living specimen of ideal loveliness without the semblance of a flaw" becomes
such an obsession with Aylmer that it threatens to destroy the happiness of both husband and wife, and at last Georgiana becomes
willing to face any risk to have the birthmark removed.[29] Unfortunately it turns out to be so "deeply interwoven" not only "with the
texture and substance of her face" but with her whole being so that
though her husband's science proves equal to the task he has undertaken, the experiment costs her life. She dies urging Aylmer not to
repent "that with so high and pure a feeling, you have rejected the
best that earth could offer," and he is left alone.

Nineteenth-century critics come close to missing the whole significance of this tale.[30] Herman Melville was an important exception. At the close of his copy of the tale, he wrote, "The moral here
is wonderfully fine." Certainly there is no Hawthorne story whose
"moral" is more obvious or which drives home its point with more
emphasis. In the second paragraph the author informs us that the
marriage of his principals was "attended with truly remarkable circumstances and a deeply impressive moral," and he returns to his
text in his concluding words:

Yet, had Aylmer reached a profounder wisdom, he need not have flung
away the happiness which would have woven his mortal life of the selfsame
texture with the celestial. The momentary circumstance was too strong for
him; he failed to look beyond the shadowy scope of time, and, living once
for all in eternity, to find the perfect future in the present.

To be sure, one modern critic, Austin Warren, taking his cue from
two notebook entries, pronounces the moral "ambiguous or
bivalent."[31] The first: "A person to be in possession of something as
perfect as mortal man has a right to demand; he tries to make it
better, and ruins it entirely." And the second: "A person to be the
death of his beloved in trying to raise her to more than mortal
perfection; yet this should be a comfort to him for having aimed so
highly and holily." But Warren's is a better interpretation of the
notebook entries than it is of the tale, where Hawthorne has Georgiana express the latter view only to negate it with authorial comment. It is true, as Richard Harter Fogle has observed, that though

Aylmer is "shown to be wrong," he is still given "a remarkably good run for his money,"[32] but, as Rita K. Gollin's analysis of his dream has shown,[33] he knew full well that he was risking Georgiana's life. Moreover he is guilty of monstrous hubris. When his wife, fresh from reading his own record of the magnificent failures that have resulted from his past experiments, remarks that "it has made me worship you more than ever," he calmly replies, "Ah, wait for this new success, then worship me if you will. I shall deem myself hardly unworthy of it."

The historical setting of the tale becomes important in this connection. The Gothic properties in Aylmer's laboratory have been criticized as so much hocus-pocus, but though Hawthorne did have a weakness for this kind of Gothicism, they are still useful in pointing up the essential perversity of Aylmer's experiment. Sunlight is not admitted into the laboratory, and drugs and hallucinations are required to bring Georgiana into the proper frame of mind. As Alfred S. Reid has shown, Hawthorne "molded the tragic character of Aylmer out of the virtuoso-Platonist, Sir Kenelm Digby" (1603–64), who killed his wife in an operation not wholly unlike his.[34] To be sure, neither David M. Van Leer nor Shannon Burns are much impressed by Aylmer as an alchemist,[35] but we must not forget that the story is set in the late eighteenth century, when, though science had not yet wholly freed itself from the trappings of magic, the progress made during the Enlightenment had still created in many minds a euphoria that tempted some not only to usurp the historic functions of the priest but even to confuse themselves with God.[36]

It is a mistake therefore to be seduced by Aylmer's "idealism," or the fact that he is "spiritual," in contrast to the materialism of his laboratory assistant Aminadab,[37] into sympathizing with him more than he deserves. Anyone who has read *The Divine Comedy*, to say nothing of Saint Thomas Aquinas, knows that the sins of the soul are far more deadly than those of the body. Aylmer is an idealist because the story deals with a temptation that only an idealist could experience, and the harm that an idealist can do is what "The Birthmark" is about. If Aylmer is not a scoundrel, he *is* a fool of the first water, and fools do quite as much if not more harm in the world than scoundrels. To return to Melville, it might be observed that Aylmer refuses to recognize the distinction Plotinus Plinlimmon makes in

Pierre between chronological and horological time, thus demanding of time what only eternity can give. Like other muddleheaded idealists, he opts for all or nothing, and like most of them he ends up with the latter. Finally, then, though he is wrong in seeing her birthmark as a sign of moral imperfection in Georgiana, we as readers shall make no mistake in seeing Hawthorne's "moral" as applying to something larger than mere physical imperfections. If, for example, the inevitably sensual basis of earthly love so offends your sensibilities that you cannot embrace it, you must live barren and celibate,[38] and if you cannot bear to produce anything that is not perfect, which is in itself a confession of monstrous pride, you will never produce anything at all.

Nothing he ever wrote more reflects Hawthorne's mistrust of science than "The Birthmark." He states his belief unmistakably: nature permits human beings "to mar, but seldom to mend, and, like a jealous patentee, on no account to make."[39] The thing we must not forget is that though Aylmer kills his wife, he succeeds in what he set out to do: he does remove the birthmark. If this reminds us of the old farmer who tried to train his horse to live without eating and was just on the point of succeeding when, out of sheer "cussedness," the "durn critter" up and died, it might be more to the point to remember the surgeon who reported that the operation was a success except that the patient died. The authors of the Eden and Babel stories in the Book of Genesis did not know much about science or history, but they did know enough about human beings to be sure that they may not safely be entrusted with too much power.

"Ethan Brand"

Hawthorne's grimmest tale made its first appearance in the *Boston Weekly Museum* on January 5, 1850. In May 1851 it was published again in the *Dollar Magazine,* just seven months before being collected in *The Snow-Image and Other Twice-Told Tales,* where it carried the subtitle "A Chapter from an Abortive Romance." This is echoed in the reference, near the beginning, to "many years, as we have seen" having passed since Ethan Brand conceived the idea of finding the Unpardonable Sin, and again at the entrance of the village doctor, "whom, at an earlier period of his life, we introduced as paying a professional visit to Ethan Brand." At least one scholar, Nelson F. Adkins, takes this literally, seeing the tale as the "last and crowning chapter" of a novel Hawthorne found it impossible to complete,[40] but it seems generally to have been understood as a mere literary device, designed to add weight and body to the tale by causing the reader to see it as part of a more substantial work.

No tale of Hawthorne's has a simpler story line than "Ethan Brand." Having roamed the world for eighteen years in search of the Unpardonable Sin and having finally found it in his own heart, Ethan returns to the lime kiln he used to tend. Here he converses with the present tender Bartram; the villagers whom Bartram summons from the tavern to see this now legendary character; old Humphrey, whose daughter, Esther, Brand had "made the subject of a psychological experiment, and wasted, absorbed, and perhaps annihilated her soul, in the process"; and a German Jewish showman with a "diorama," who has obviously had some contact with Brand in the past. Finally, upon being left alone to guard the fire, and being now convinced that, with his task "done, and well done," there is nothing left for him to seek or to achieve, he destroys himself by casting his body into the furnace: "Come, deadly element of Fire,—Henceforth my familiar friend! Embrace me, as I do thee!"

The Bible and Hawthorne's visit to a lime kiln, as recorded on September 7, 1838, are probably the ultimate sources of "Ethan Brand." The New Testament basis for the idea of an unpardonable sin is considered hereinafter, but these are not the only Bible passages to consider. Ely Stock makes much of the story of Cain and the legendry that grew up around it, as well as of Byron's *Cain: A Mystery.* William M. White invokes Judges 10 and Luke 13 in connection with Hawthorne's use of an eighteen-year cycle, both here and in "Roger Malvin's Burial," and John McElroy finds Ethan's surname significant in connection with Amos 4:11 and Zacharias 3:2, as well as Meleager's brand in the classical story. John E. Klingel finds the tale "richly allusive" to Goethe's *Faust,* and Hawthorne himself notes that the opening of the door of Bartram's kiln "resembled nothing so much as the private entrance to the infernal regions, which the shepherds of the Delectable Mountains were accustomed to show to pilgrims." Glenn Pedersen brought Blake's Urizen into the consideration, but E. K. Brown disposed definitively of Lewis Mumford's notion, curiously echoed by Newton Arvin, that Ethan Brand was suggested by Herman Melville, which is rendered inadmissible by chronology.[41]

In commenting upon Arthur Machen's use of evil in his stories, Vincent Starrett rightly declared that "the sin with which Arthur Machen is concerned is an offense against the nature of things, it has to do with the evil in the soul, and has little or nothing to do with the sins of the statute book," and Machen himself might have been commenting upon "Ethan Brand" when he called evil "an attempt to penetrate into another and higher sphere in a forbidden manner" or "an effort to gain the ecstasy and the knowledge that pertain only to angels, and in making this effort man becomes a demon." This contrast was never better illustrated than by the juxtaposition Hawthorne achieves by setting Brand over against such villagers as the stage agent, the lawyer, and the doctor. All three have turned themselves into mere fragments of what they might have been through fleshly indulgences. The demon rum played a major share in ruining them all. The doctor too "had an everlasting pipe in his mouth, and, as somebody said, in allusion to his habit of swearing, it was always alight with hell-fire." But sinners though they were, these men had not severed their ties with humanity. Still keeping up "the courage and spirit of a man," and asking "nothing in charity," they fought "a stern battle against want and hostile circumstances," and continued to perform useful services for others, who had therefore "no right to scorn" them. Yet this is exactly what Ethan Brand does. From the eminence of his connoisseurship in evil, he looks down upon them as a great singer or poet might look upon a rock crooner or a country-newspaper rimester. Scorning the black bottle they offer him in their degraded camaraderie, he cries, "Leave me, ye brute beasts, that have made yourselves so, shriveling up your souls with fiery liquors!" No, there is no kinship between Brand and the village derelicts, nor with Bartram, the cloddish lime burner, though we do have a comic parody of his quest in the absurd spectacle of the dog who suddenly makes himself the center of attention by furiously taking off after his own stump of a tail. "Never was seen such headlong eagerness in pursuit of an object that could not possibly be attained," and what other implied comparison could be more devastating?[42]

The identity of the Nuremberg Jew with the "diorama"[43] and his relationship to Brand are less immediately clear. Obviously he and Brand have had some contact before, and obviously something is to be seen in his box besides "a series of the most outrageous scratchings and daubings . . . that ever an itinerant showman had the face to impose upon his circle of spectators." But just what that "something" is seems to depend on who is doing the looking; indeed one "curious youth . . . beheld only a vacant space of canvas." But that does not seem to be all Brand sees, for he mutters, "I remember you now," to which the Jew replies, "with a dark smile, 'I find it to be a heavy matter in my showbox,—this Unpardonable Sin! By my faith, Captain, it has wearied my shoulders, this long way, to carry it over the mountains!'" To which Enoch counters, "Peace, or get thee into the furnace yonder!" that same furnace, the reader should remember, out of which he was reputed to have summoned a fiend in days gone by to confer about the Unpardonable Sin,[44] and into which he himself will go before the night is over.

Probably the most common interpretation of this figure is that he is the Wandering Jew, who spurned Christ on the way to Calvary, bidding him "move on" and was himself condemned to "move on" forever, and who is important in Maturin's *Melmoth the Wanderer*, a novel Hawthorne knew well. But some believe that he is the Devil, who played with Ethan Brand the same role that Mephistopheles plays in *Faust* or even the Devil disguised as the Wandering Jew.[45] The pictures he shows Brand, they argue, are those of "historical occurrences in which the Devil obviously had a hand," and Hawthorne speaks of the showman's hand as it appears in the machine as "the Hand of Destiny." It is when what he shows Brand are the "evils in his own heart" that the latter recognizes him.

If the forces of hell in this story are headed by Brand and the Jew, whatever else besides the latter may have been, the heavenly powers seem required to make do with little Joe, the lime burner's son, who may have been derived from Julian Hawthorne. At the beginning he is disturbed by the roar of Brand's laughter, which his father coarsely dismisses as merely an expression of the jollity of some merry, drunken fellow from the tavern, and the child shows both his intelligence and his sensitivity by replying that "he does not laugh like a man that is glad." When Brand appears, Joe finds something in his face "which he was afraid to look at, yet could not look away from," but by the time he and his father retire, there are tears in his eyes because "his tender spirit had an intuition of the bleak and terrible loneliness in which this man had enveloped himself." Fogle has objected that Joe is "too faintly drawn to be fully convincing."[46] Not too faintly, I think, but the boy is certainly too slight to balance the terrible forces opposed to him, and this is probably what Hawthorne intended, for "Ethan Brand,"unlike Dante's masterpiece, is a tragic story, and in tragedy God does not win.

Yet Hawthorne does not leave his readers without hope. It is Fogle again who points out that though the "last act" is "played out against a *décor* of red and black," because Joe is "the embodiment of human love and sympathy," his appearance is "accompanied by moonlight and afterglow." When the child wakes the morning after Brand has destroyed himself, sunshine is "already pouring its gold upon the mountain-tops, and though the valleys were still in shadow, they smiled cheerfully in the presence of the bright day that was hastening onward." At the same time, the sound of the stagecoach "rattling down the mountain road," with the driver sounding his horn "while Echo caught up the notes, and intertwined them into a rich and varied and elaborate harmony" makes it clear that the normal activities of life are being renewed. No doubt this *might* be used to indicate nature's indifference to human misery. But it seems more likely that what Hawthorne wishes to imply is that the evil embodied in Ethan Brand, Unpardonable Sin and all, struck a false note that life could no longer tolerate. As Alfred J. Levy puts it, "The condition of evil is never permanent. It is always conquered by innocence and goodness, and the victory is reflected in nature."[47]

Probably as many people have gone crazy over the Unpardonable Sin as over any subject connected with religion.[48] The basic reference is in Matthew 12: 31–32 (cf. Mark 3: 28–30 and Luke 12: 10):

Wherefore I say unto you, All manner of sin and blasphemy shall be forgiven unto men: but the blasphemy against the Holy Ghost shall not be forgiven unto men. And whosoever speaketh a word against the Son of Man, it shall be forgiven him: but whosoever speaketh against the Holy Ghost, it shall not be forgiven him, neither in this world, neither in the world to come.

This is obviously a perplexing statement, and it may be well at the outset to try to understand what Hawthorne—and Ethan Brand— understood by it. In his notebook Hawthorne wrote in 1844:

The Unpardonable Sin might consist in a want of love and reverence for the Human Soul; in consequence of which, the investigator pried into its dark depths, not with a hope or purpose of making it better, but from a cold philosophical curiosity,—content that it should be wicked in whatever kind or degree, and only desiring to study it out. Would not this, in other words, be the separation of the intellect from the heart?

While Ethan Brand:

"It is a sin that grew within my own breast. A sin that grew nowhere else! The sin of an intellect that triumphed over the sense of brotherhood with man and reverence for God, and sacrificed everything to its own mighty claims! The only sin that deserves a recompense of immortal agony! Freely, were it to do again, would I incur the guilt. Unthinkingly I accept the retribution!"

Since this may not seem to have much to do with the Holy Ghost, it may be well to have before us, before we proceed further, Thomas Stackhouse's comment in his *New History of the Holy Bible* (1752), which Hawthorne drew out of the Salem library in September 1832. Stackhouse concludes that

The Sin against the Holy Ghost is unpardonable, not because there is not a Sufficiency of *Merit in Christ* to atone for it, or of *Mercy* in God the Father to forgive it, but because those, who commit it, are of such refractory and incorrigible Spirit, that they resist the last utmost Means of the Conviction, and, consequently, neither will, nor can repent.[49]

If, at this point, the reader is tempted to feel that he has been left wallowing in confusion worse confounded, let him at least be permitted to derive whatever comfort he can derive from the realization that a good many Hawthorne critics are wallowing there with him. Sheila Dwight sums up the various descriptions of Ethan Brand's sin that have been offered: "pride, selfish monomania, cold philosophical curiosity, violation of the human heart and soul, separation of the intellect from the heart, final impenitence, or a combination of these." Pride and impenitence have probably been most frequently invoked, but everything that can inspire pride in human character or achievement has been brought into consideration at one time or another. Thus the story has been interpreted as a condemnation of human learning, of art,[50] and particularly, since in the New England out of which it came, the transcendentalists were outstandingly committed to the assertion of human dignity, of transcendentalism.[51] We have also been told that in cutting himself off from his race, Ethan Brand has broken the great "Chain of Being,"[52] most notably perhaps in his treatment of Esther, whom he seems to have destroyed, quite without malice, making her merely a tool to be used and cast away in his monstrous quest as soon as she had served his purpose. All this may be in some measure true, but its connection with the sin against the Holy Ghost is not altogether clear, nor yet why this sin alone should stand beyond the range of God's forgiveness.

The situation begins to clarify itself however once we have realized that the human heart is the dwelling place of the Holy Ghost; if God is to be known by human beings while they are in this life, He must be encountered there.[53] Hence the blasphemy against the Holy Ghost is the banishment of God from the human heart and consequently from this world. No sin can be forgiven and no sinner freed from his sin without repentance, and he who hardens his heart against the Holy Ghost simply makes himself incapable of repentance and consequently inaccessible to God's Mercy. He is unforgiven therefore not because God has made up His mind that there is some particular sin that He *will not forgive* but rather because the sinner has encased himself in the terrible loneliness where, as little Joe perceives, Ethan Brand stands. The key line of *The Divine Comedy* is "His Will is our peace," but Ethan Brand sets this upon its head and all creation with it. As Ely Stock puts it, his life-style "denies the validity of the concept that God's spirit is at work in the world." By making himself his god and his will the only will, he cuts himself off from God and all God's creation. If he goes to hell instead of heaven, it will be because he prefers it. In a very real sense, he has damned himself.

Hawthorne's story is anti-intellectual however only insofar as intellectualism rules out love, inspires arrogance, and isolates its possessor from mankind. Today we are most conscious of that danger in the field of the sciences, but this is only because man's moral and spiritual development has somehow failed to keep pace with his technological development. Nevertheless, no honest worker in the humanities can honestly affirm that there is no danger of arrogance and blinding pride here, and though this vanity is in no danger of blowing up the world, it can still be destructive of insight and values. Charles-Augustin Sainte-Beuve wrote of himself, "I analyze, I botanize, I am a naturalist of souls." And again, "Let us not be afraid to surprise the human heart naked . . . even in the saints." Whether or not such an enterprise runs the danger of making an Ethan Brand of a man must depend upon the spirit in which it is undertaken. It may be done with all the malevolence of a smut hound on assignment for a scandal sheet or it may be undertaken in the disinterested spirit of one who knows that there is no branch of human knowledge more useful or necessary than a knowledge of the human nature we all share. When Sainte-Beuve's American disciple, Gamaliel Bradford, was asked by a magazine editor to do a group of "iconoclastic portraits" of overrated Americans, he replied that "though nothing would amuse me more than to take empty simulacara down from pedestals where they have enjoyed the secure adoration of ages," nevertheless "such a work of destruction . . . was likely to do more injury to the critic than to the character criticized" and that "in every character I have portrayed so far it has been my endeavor to find the good rather than the evil, to set the figure firmly on its common human basis, but at the same time to insist that if the human heart were not worth loving, my work would not be worth doing."[54] But the same differences of character and approach may appear in the way a novelist handles his created characters: Scott and Dickens have been loved now well into their second century not merely because they were great writers but also because they were greathearted men. Whether or not Christopher Brown, the critic who has emphasized this aspect most strongly, was right or wrong in his view that "Ethan

Brand" may "well constitute Hawthorne's treatment of certain tendencies within himself he had come to fear,"[55] Hawthorne was certainly far too honest a man to be aware of the temptations that beset the scientist and the historian while remaining blind to those of the artist.

It is a serious mistake to assume that Ethan Brand's interest in the Unpardonable Sin was from the beginning a desire to commit it. Had this been the case, he would certainly not have thought it necessary to search the world for it. Hawthorne states specifically that Ethan began his search as "a simple and loving man," contemplating his fellows with "pity for human guilt and woe" and the human heart "as a temple originally divine, and however desecrated, still to be held sacred by a brother." It was only when his own heart "had withered,—had contracted,—had hardened,—had perished" that he ceased to be "a brother-man" and became instead "a cold observer, looking at mankind as the subject of his experiment," and finally "a fiend." Yet I think Carl Pedersen goes too far when he writes that at the end Brand "falls into a satanic state, realizes his error, annihilates it, and in effect redeems his sinful life" and that when he kills himself, he destroys "the Self that had become satanic in its dominion over other selves." Ethan's suicide is not an act of atonement but an act of defiance.

I do not mean that Pedersen is the only writer who has tried to show Brand charity. Alfred J. Levy argues that "no act of man . . . constituted the Unpardonable Sin" and that only "the protagonist's reaction to his act" is fatal, and Sheldon W. Liebman thinks Brand may merely be crazy and that when Hawthorne seems to be saying that he committed the Unpardonable Sin, he is actually expressing Brand's own point of view. I must confess however that I am more inclined to agree with John E. Klingel, when he sees Hawthorne echoing but also inverting *Faust* by depicting Brand as "a man who is damned by his own will rather than saved by prevenient grace." Whether he is sane or crazy and whether or not he committed the Unpardonable Sin, it seems to me he still tried his best to commit it. In writing thus I must explain that I am only trying to interpret *what the story says and where it leaves Brand*. As to what his fate may be in another world, or would be if he were a real-life character and not a character of fiction, to dogmatize about that would be for the critic to make Brand's own mistake by putting himself in the place of God.

"Rappaccini's Daughter"

"Rappaccini's Daughter" was first published in the *United States Magazine and Democratic Review* in December 1844 and reprinted in *Mosses from an Old Manse*. As the title indicates, Beatrice is the central character. Hawthorne never created a more enchanting girl, and I do not believe many other writers have either. All three of the male characters are, comparatively speaking, in their various ways, repellent, and between them they manage to destroy her. Yet it is worth noting that the title is not "Beatrice Rappaccini" but "Rappaccini's Daughter,"[56] for, as we see her, Beatrice is, in a sense, her father's creation. Moreover, though the story revolves around her, she is acted upon more than acting; without the others she would have had a character but no story. The whole first part is told from Giovanni's point of view; then, toward the end, as if to guarantee that the reader shall accept her at her true worth, Hawthorne (or the narrator) casts aside ambiguity and puts himself unmistakably on the line for her.[57]

Few tales can boast such a bewildering array of suggested sources as "Rappaccini's Daughter." One critic has remarked that Hawthorne "mingles borrowings from Dante, Ovid, Indian literature, and Renaissance iconography, as well as arcane ontological and toxicological lore,"[58] and the variety of material thus derived goes far to explain the difficulties of readers who have tried to interpret the story as a consistent allegory.[59] The basic idea was recorded in Hawthorne's notebooks from Sir Thomas Browne's *Vulgar Errors:* "A story there passeth of an Indian king that sent unto Alexander a fair woman, fed with aconite and other poisons, with this intent complexionally to destroy him!" This is essentially the story Baglioni tells Giovanni to warn him against contact with Beatrice. But nobody has been able to read the tale without thinking of the Eden story or of the many folktales in which the hero is tested for his ability to deliver the captive princess by solving a puzzle or guessing a riddle, sometimes—even as late as Puccini's opera *Turandot*—with the forfeiture of his life as the penalty for failure.[60]

By putting a statue of Verrumnus in Rappaccini's garden, Hawthorne calls attention to Ovid's *Metamorphoses*,[61] but, aside from the Bible, the most important literary influences stem from Dante, Spenser, Bunyan, and Milton. If the garden is Eden, it is also Spenser's Bower of Bliss. Giovanni lodges in a house perhaps once occupied by a man destined to be immortalized in the "Inferno" section of *The Divine Comedy*, and, in one of her aspects, Beatrice is surely the Beatrice Portinari whom Dante loved and who finally leads him to the Ultimate Beatitude. But Shakespeare is involved also. Beatrice, as isolated in the garden as Miranda on Prospero's island, responds as innocently to Giovanni as Miranda did to Ferdinand, and, though nobody seems to have noticed it, Giovanni's cruel treatment of Beatrice at the end, coupled with his difficulty in shaking off "recollections of the delicate and benign power of her feminine nature," seems to echo Othello's abuse of Desdemona. But Hawthorne handles all this material with easy mastery, recharactering the Eden story, as it appears in both Genesis and *Paradise Lost*, and even reassigning the roles and functions of the characters, when his needs require.[62]

Literary influences have not all been confined to our earlier literatures however. Among the Gothic novels, *Frankenstein, St. Leon*, and *Melmoth the Wanderer* have all had careful consideration.[63] Among the Romantic poets, Shelley has been brought in in connection with *The Cenci* by those who feel that Beatrice derives from Beatrice Cenci as well as Beatrice Portinari, and Keats in connection with his poem about a serpent-woman, "Lamia." One writer has suggested that Beatrice's "sister" plant may have been suggested by the deadly upas tree of Java in Erasmus Darwin's poem, *The Botanic Garden* (1781), while another travels to Germany to examine E. T. A. Hoffmann's story, "The Sandman." Moreover, modern life may have contributed along with modern literature. Though there is no proof that Hawthorne knew about Father Rapp's commune, there are still interesting resemblances between it and the story, and he did know Madame Calderon de la Barca's *Life in Mexico*, in which she describes how people were inoculated with rattlesnake venom to make them invulnerable to snakebite.[64]

"Rappaccini's Daughter" has always been regarded as one of Hawthorne's best tales, and until recent years Dr. Rappaccini himself was more or less simply taken for granted as a heartless researcher, interested only in science and willing, if necessary, to sacrifice his own daughter, to his zeal for knowledge. It was easier to do this because he is kept in the background until the very end of the story, and we hear his voice only when Beatrice is dying. It was always fairly clear that he enticed Giovanni into the garden, probably with the aid of Lisabetta, and that he intended him as his daughter's mate, after his physical being should have been similarly corrupted. What Rappaccini says at the end however does not altogether support the traditional interpretation of his character and motives. Until now he has been an overprotective father, shielding his daughter from all outside forces in his own perverted paradise, yet now it is obviously his intention that she and Giovanni should "pass on . . . through the world, most dear to one another and dreadful to all besides." But what is to be the end of this? Are they to poison "everything and everyone they come in contact with," as Eberhard Alsen has argued, making Rappaccini himself "the father and god of a new, poisonous world"? If it were also a dead world, of what use would it be to Rappaccini or anybody else? M. Thomas Inge replied to Alsen therefore with a more generous reading of the doctor's motives. He was not trying to destroy humanity, but, like Aylmer in "The Birthmark," to improve it, creating a superior race, who will "eventually populate a world where death by disease and poison will have become things of the past." Obviously there are problems of interpretation here, and if Hawthorne, who speaks of Rappaccini's "perverted wisdom," had thought them all through, it is clear that the doctor himself had not. How little he understood his own daughter's nature is proved by her dying words, "I would fain have been loved, not feared." If, therefore, her father now seems less the villain than the nineteenth century considered him, he is only that much more the fool.[65]

Rappaccini's reputation of course cannot be rehabilitated except at the expense of Baglioni's. The latter may well be sincere in his disbelief in Rappaccini's theories and even in his desire to save Giovanni from him, but he also uses Giovanni as a weapon with which to fight a rival of whom he is desperately jealous and of whose intellectual superiority to himself he is well aware: "Perhaps, most learned Rappaccini, I may fool you where you little dream of it!" The thought so delights him that he "chuckles" to himself over it. He admits grudgingly that his rival "has as much science as any member of the faculty—with perhaps one single exception." Obviously he fears Rappaccini professionally. Indeed, he even fears poor Beatrice, for though we are obviously intended to take her disclaimer of scientific knowledge seriously, he suspects her father, or says he does, of grooming her to occupy a professorial chair. Finally, though he grants that Rappaccini has effected wonderful cures, he attributes these to accident, though holding him fully responsible for his failures.

The most serious question of course is that of the antidote. When Baglioni gave it to Giovanni to administer to Beatrice, was he trying to kill her, which is what he does, or to cure? The question cannot be answered definitely, but at the very least he must have known that its use involved a grave risk to which he, of all people, had no right to subject her, and his gloating at the end, "in a tone of triumph mixed with horror," is not reassuring: "Rappaccini! Rappaccini! and is *this* the upshot of your experiment!" Not quite, at least not without Baglioni's meddling.[66]

Though her lover, Giovanni Guasconti,[67] fails Beatrice quite as disastrously as the other two men in her life, there is no question of deliberate villainy here: he is simply a vain, shallow young man, who, because he lacks insight, high fidelity, and faith, necessarily fails to rise to the level of a true spiritual love.[68] In one of the most thoughtful articles that have been written about this tale,[69] Robert Daly argues that Hawthorne set his scene in Padua because the university there was the center of fideist thought in Europe from the fourteenth to the sixteenth century, and the problems debated there were still providing controversy between the transcendentalists and their "common sense" opponents in Hawthorne's New England, particularly at Harvard. "The basic assumption of fideism is that truth is dual, that truths about matter are within the purview of philosophy and can be arrived at through reason but that truths about spirit are within the purview of theology and can be arrived at only through faith." Even without fideism or Daly, however, it is clear that Giovanni is only the "natural man," devoid of spiritual insight.

He is "the man from Missouri," and he "believes what he sees."
Therefore he fails the hero's test to which he is subjected and loses
the girl he thinks he loves because he misses everything of real
significance about her. Friar Lawrence says in *Romeo and Juliet:*

> Young men's love then lies
> Not truly in their hearts, but in their eyes.

To the Elizabethans love of the eyes was shallow, sensual, imperma-
nent love, based on the fleeting attractions of the body, while love of
the heart was true, spiritual, permanent love. One wonders whether
Beatrice was using "word" in the religious sense when she told
Giovanni to forget what he might have "fancied" about her, "but the
words of Beatrice Rappaccini's lips are true from the depths of the
heart outward. Those you may believe." But the beautiful young
man is so vain that, even when he is deeply troubled, he cannot pass
a mirror without stopping to admire himself, and his love for Beatrice wanes when physical contact with her is denied and turns to
cruel bitterness at last. Surely she is right when she tells him at the
end that there was always more poison in his nature than in hers.[70]

Hawthorne as narrator goes beyond committing himself that Beatrice is good; he insists that she is "a heavenly angel," and even in
these days, when literary criticism can hardly claim to have kept
itself free of perversity, there have been few or none to say him nay.[71]
Certainly it is far from my intention to do this, but there is no
denying that she does present certain problems. She forbids Giovanni to touch the shrub she calls "sister" or to touch her, but since
she knew her father could not endure her kind of contact with the
plants in the garden, why did she not realize that she and they must
contaminate Giovanni when he invaded it? How, for that matter,
could Dr. Rappaccini live in the same house with her and not be
poisoned by her breath? And what would have happened at the end
if she had not died? (What, for that matter, *did* happen to Giovanni,
about which nobody seems to care?) It may be well at this point to
remember Walsh's warning not to push the symbolism too far, and
in any event, such questions are not very important. The great difficulty is to accept as a saintly heroine a girl who, though physically
a freak, nourished by the poisons that kill other people, still comes
before us "radiant with life, health, and energy; all of which attributes were bound down and compressed, as it were, and girdled

tensely, in their luxuriance by her virgin zone." One cannot but think, by way of contrast of Arthur Machen's terrifying story, "The Inmost Light" (in *The House of Souls*), in which another monster of a scientist has experimentally drawn his wife's soul out of her body, after which a demon takes up his abode within it. This of course is the kind of thing Austin Warren had in mind when, in one of the few derogatory comments that have been made about "Rappaccini's Daughter" as a work of art, he objected that "the tale falls below the author's highest art by virtue of its false symbolism. The physical and the psychic do not correspond."[72] This, however, would seem to be precisely the objection Hawthorne was trying to meet in his symbol of the pure water of the spring, gushing and sparkling like "an immortal spirit" in close association with a "woefully shattered" fountain. The point has often been made that though Rappaccini's garden inevitably suggests Eden, it is Eden after the Fall. Beatrice, then, lives, as we all do, in a "fallen" world, but her soul, like the pure water of the fountain, sings its song "unceasingly and without heeding the vicissitudes around it." Roy Male's quotation from Hawthorne himself in "The Intelligence Office" is completely apropos at this point: "Sometimes . . . the spiritual fountain is kept pure by a wisdom within itself that sparkles into the light of heaven without a stain from the earthly strata through which it had gushed upward."[73]

The fact that the "heavenly" Beatrice inhabits the garden into which, in countless stories before Hawthorne, the enchantress had lured young heroes to their ruin has also sometimes caused problems.[74] As the passage already quoted would alone serve to make clear, she is far from being a sexless creature, and the garden itself is drenched in sexual suggestiveness. As Charles Boewe, who examines the flowers from the point of view of Hawthorne's contemporaries, has made inescapably clear, the nineteenth century regarded the hybridization of plants as something almost as indecent as what they called the "amalgamation" of races,[75] and what we have in Rappaccini's garden suggests not only copulation but incest. Several of the plants, we are told,

would have shocked a delicate instinct by an appearance of artificialness indicating that there had been such commixture, and, as it were, adultery, of various vegetable species, that the production was no longer of God's making, but the monstrous offspring of man's depraved fancy, glowing with only an evil mockery of beauty. They were probably the result of experiment, which in one or two cases, had succeeded in mingling plants individually lovely into a compound possessing the questionable and ominous character that distinguished the whole growth of the garden.

Above all else, there is the magnificent shrub with gemlike purple poisonous flowers that Rappaccini created by his art the day his daughter was born and which she embraces passionately: "Give me, thy breath, my sister, for I am faint with common air. And give me this flower of thine, which I separate with gentlest fingers from the stem and place it close beside my heart." "Sister" she calls it, but she approaches it more like a lover, and it is at least suggestive that her dependence upon it lessens as she becomes more involved with Giovanni: "For the first time in my life, I had forgotten thee."

There is, to be sure, Julian Hawthorne's report that when his father read the unfinished tale to Sophia, and she asked, "But how is it to end? Is Beatrice to be a demon or an angel?" he answered, "with some emotion," that he had no idea. If this is correctly reported, it means that Hawthorne began writing without having made up his mind about Beatrice, which might explain some of the problems the critics have faced. I have already suggested that the girl's name may have been intended to recall Beatrice Cenci as well as Beatrice Portinari, and, as we shall see, when we come to *The Marble Faun*, Beatrice Cenci, or, more accurately, what was then supposed to be Guido Reni's portrait of her enthralled the whole nineteenth century and nobody more than Hawthorne. Nineteenth-century readers believed, as modern scholars do not, that Beatrice Cenci had been raped by her father, and they accepted her role in his murder, terrible though it was, as a testimonial to a pure girl's reaction to intolerable outrage. Mrs. Hawthorne did not know what she thought about Beatrice Rappaccini upon her first contact with her, but she was in no doubt about Beatrice Cenci or, rather, about the portrait that for her was Beatrice Cenci: she was "a spotless lily of Eden, trailed over by a serpent, and unable to understand the desecration, yet struck with a fatal blight." The incest was there (or they thought it was), however innocent she had been, and the murder was there, however extenuating the circumstances, and who can deny that these things contributed to the fascination our ancestors found in her?

All these considerations are relevant to Hawthorne's presentation of Beatrice Rappaccini, but it would be a mistake to overemphasize them or permit them to cause us to forget that Hawthorne was not an anchorite, nor was he writing a story about a cloistered nun. For him chastity and continence were not synonymous terms, and the remedy for lust was love.

"Young Goodman Brown"

"Young Goodman Brown" made its first appearance in the *New-England Magazine* for April 1835 and was collected in *Mosses from an Old Manse*. Herman Melville thought that though the title suggested "Goody Two-Shoes," the tale was "as deep as Dante," and in 1951 Mrs. Leavis gave it about as high praise as a modern critic of fiction can be expected to command by comparing it to the Walpurgisnacht scene in James Joyce's *Ulysses* to the latter's disadvantage. Today it is probably the most admired of all Hawthorne's tales (more than a decade ago, Robert Stanton counted more than 400 studies); not satisfied with this, some have insisted upon calling it the finest short story in American literature. When the ending was criticized in two college anthologies, both Richard Abcarian and Edward J. Gallagher entered briefs for the defense, and John B. Humma, who believes that "those elders Brown encounters in the forest are present in the flesh" and that "there is no good reason to believe that [he] dreamed or hallucinated anything," seems to stand alone in finding Hawthorne's art in this piece "contrived and finally dishonest."[76]

Yet it took Hawthorne's readers many years to wake up to the story's quality.[77] Julian Hawthorne ignores it; as late as 1902, Woodberry gave it part of a not imperceptive page; and even Henry James, though recognizing its quality, was far from approaching it with the seriousness it now seems to demand. It is a comparatively brief tale, and the story line is simple enough for a child to follow with ease, but the contrast between what Fogle calls its "ambiguity of meaning and clarity of technique" is very sharp. Nor is this by any means wholly due to Hawthorne's asking the reader on the last page, "Had Goodman Brown fallen asleep in the forest and only dreamed a wild dream of a witch-meeting?" nor yet to his replying, "Be it so if you will." Almost as simple in form as (to cite Melville) "Goody Two-Shoes" itself, the tale is deeply multilevel in meaning. To cite but two examples, though the whole atmosphere is dreamlike, the story is set firmly against a background of Salem witchcraft, drawn from bona fide historical sources; again, though I believe firmly in Faith's innocence (her allegorical significance vanishes, and her whole role in her husband's life after his return from the forest makes no sense upon any other hypothesis), I must still ask, why, then, did Hawthorne make her say at the very beginning that "a lone woman is troubled with such dreams and such thoughts that she is afraid of herself sometimes. Pray tarry with me this night, dear husband, of all nights in the year"? How did she know that there was any special peril connected with *this* night? And why should she have any doubt that "you will find all well when you come back"? What I am trying to say is that "Young Goodman Brown" resembles *Hamlet* in that whatever explanation of the problems involved one may adopt, he will have no trouble in finding some passage or passages that may seem to contradict what he believes. But before attempting to explore these or any other angles, it may be well to remind ourselves of what is recorded as happening in the tale, with as little interpretation as is humanly possible.

Three months married, young Goodman Brown leaves his wife at dusk, in their home at Salem village, to undertake an undefined journey that "must needs be done between now and sunrise." He sets out into the forest, bent on "his present evil purpose," but promising himself that "after this one night," he will cling to his wife's skirts and "follow her to heaven." By appointment he meets a man, apparently about fifty years of age, who bears a considerable resemblance to himself and who carries a staff "which bore the likeness of a great black snake, so curiously wrought that it might almost be seen to twist and wriggle itself like a living serpent." That this figure is a supernatural being is made clear when he rebukes Brown for his tardiness and remarks that the clock in the Old South was striking the hour when he came through Boston "full fifteen minutes agone." When Brown voices scruples about continuing on his way with the stranger, the latter lightly brushes his objections aside. To Brown's statement that he comes "of a race of honest men and good Christians," he replies that he was well acquainted with his forebears, and Brown's reference to "that good old man, our minister" sends him into gales of laughter. The travelers soon overtake Goody Cloyse, "a very pious and exemplary dame," who had taught Brown his catechism, with whom the stranger's conversation soon makes it clear not only that she is a witch, footing her way to the coven, where "they tell me there is a nice young man to be taken into communion to-night," because "that unhanged witch, Goody Corey" had stolen her broomstick, but that the stranger himself is the Devil. Inexpressibly shocked, Brown announces that he has made up his mind to proceed no farther. "What if a wretched old woman do choose to go to the devil when I thought she was going to heaven; is that any reason why I should quit my dear Faith and go after her?" Unperturbed, the Devil leaves him to rest a while and use his staff to help him on his way when he decides to proceed.

While he waits, Deacon Gookin and Brown's saintly pastor ride by, obviously also on their way to the coven, the minister, without whom "nothing can be done" until he gets "on the ground," being especially attracted by "the goodly young woman [who is] to be taken into communion." "With heaven above and Faith below," cries Brown, "I will yet stand firm against the devil," but even as he tries to pray, "a wonderful and doubtful sound of voices" comes from the "black mass of cloud" above him. The voices of those who frequent the communion table are mingled with the voices of those who haunt the tavern, but there is also the "voice of a young woman, uttering lamentations, yet with an uncertain sorrow, and entreating for some favor, which perhaps it would grieve her to obtain." When, in "agony and desperation," Brown shouts his wife's name, "something fluttered lightly down through the air"; seizing it, he beholds one of her pink ribbons, and cries, "My Faith is gone! There is no good on earth; and sin is but a name. Come, devil; for to thee is this world given."

Maddened with despair, he pushes on to the coven, a brilliant scene, as elaborately orchestrated as a tone poem by Richard Strauss. Here "are all whom [he has] revered from youth," men and women distinguished in church and in state, saints "famous for their especial sanctity," "ancient maidens, all of excellent repute, and fair young girls, who trembled lest their mothers should espy them."

A dark figure who "bore no slight similitude, both in garb and manner, to some grave divine of the New England churches" now calls for the converts to step forth, among them Goodman Brown, who felt "a loathful brotherhood [with the others] by the sympathy of all that was wicked in his heart." In an eloquent speech, filled with a dark, evil splendor never surpassed by any of the decadents, this figure welcomes the converts to "the communion of your race" upon an earth that is "one stain of guilt, one mighty blood spot." "Evil is the nature of mankind. Evil must be your only happiness." But just in time to prevent Faith and himself from receiving the diabolical baptism, Brown cries, "Faith! Faith! look up to heaven, and resist the wicked one!" whereupon the scene vanishes, and Brown finds himself "amid calm night and solitude, listening to the roar of the winds which died heavily away through the forest."

The next morning Brown returns sadly to his home in Salem village. The minister, Deacon Gookin, and Goody Cloyse are all going about their regular business, and all the other activities of village life seem normal. Faith, "with the pink ribbons," is watching for her husband and is so eager to welcome him home that she skips into the street and, indecorously by Puritan standards, almost kisses him in public. Brown looks sternly and sadly into her face and passes on inside without a greeting. Thereafter he lives for many years, "a stern, a sad, a darkly introspective, a distrustful, if not a desperate man." He shrinks from his wife, and "when the family knelt down at prayer, he scowled and muttered to himself, and gazed sternly at his wife, and turned away." When he dies, he is "borne to his grave," followed by wife, children, and grandchildren, but "they carved no hopeful verse upon his tombstone, for his dying hour was gloom."

Since three Salem women mentioned in the story, of whom two were hanged, were accused in 1692, the scene must be set somewhere before that date. But when the Devil speaks of his intimacy with Brown's ancestors and of their cruelty toward Quakers and Indians, Hawthorne is clearly thinking of his own forebears. More important for the understanding of the tale however than any other single fact is the statement issued in June 1692 by a group of important Boston clergymen, that it was "an undoubted and notorious thing, that a demon may, by God's permission, appear, even to ill purposes, in the shape of an innocent, yea, and a virtuous man." ("It were better," said Cotton Mather, "that ten suspected witches should escape than that one innocent person should be condemned.") This broke the back of the prosecution by ruling out the validity of "spectral evidence," thus making it no longer necessary to choose between believing that either accused persons were necessarily guilty of witchcraft or else that their opponents were malignant liars; from now on, the latter could be perfectly honest in reporting what they had seen yet completely mistaken in their interpretation of it. In other words, Goody Cloyse's victim might, to the best of her belief have "seen" Goody Cloyse, whereas what she had actually seen might have been an evil spirit who had taken on the aspect of Goody Cloyse while that harmless old woman was sleeping peacefully in her bed.[78]

Hawthorne had a wide acquaintance with the standard histories of New England and of Salem witchcraft, including not only Cotton Mather's *Magnalia Americani* but also his *Wonders of the Invisible World* and *Memorable Providences Relating to Witchcraft and Possession;*[79] Robert Calef's skeptical *More Wonders of the Invisible World;* and, as B. Bernard Cohen has shown,[80] Deodat Lawson's *Christ's Fidelity.* But there were more literary sources too: *The Faerie Queene;*[81] *Paradise Lost;*[82] Goethe's *Faust;*[83] and, most interestingly, a story by Cervantes, "The Conversation of Dogs." ("El Coloquiode de los Perros").[84]

Of Faith's pink ribbons Mark Van Doren remarks that "few things in fiction are more startling or more important,"[85] and commentary upon them, their color, and its significance have practically used up all the attention critics have had to give to color and color symbolism in this story. Matthiessen had trouble with whatever it is that seems to come fluttering down in the forest, seeing it as a flaw in an otherwise compelling scene: "Only the literal insistence on that damaging pink ribbon obtrudes the labels of a confining allegory and short-circuits the range of association."[86] It is a little difficult however to see why this objection should apply more to the ribbon than to anything else Brown "sees" in the forest. If either the Devil or Brown's imagination could conjure up his wife and his fellow Salemites, certainly it could not be expected to be balked by the ribbon.

When we attempt to pin down just what the ribbons signify and particularly why they are pink however, unanimity disappears. Paul J. Hurley seems safe enough when he finds a certain unpuritan suggestion of the "frivolous and ornamental" about them, but one might be more inclined to follow both him and James W. Mathews to associate this with superficiality of religious faith and conviction in Brown if he were wearing the ribbons instead of his wife. Mathews finds the pastel of infancy in pink, but since pink is a color intermediate between red and white, William V. Davis prefers to take it as suggesting "neither total depravity nor innocence" but "the tainted innocence, the spiritual imperfection of mankind," a view shared, up to a point, by Robinson, who compares the pink ribbons to Georgiana's birthmark and Beatrice Rappaccini's poisoned body. In his interesting comparison of the resemblances and differences between "Young Goodman Brown" and "My Kinsman, Major Molineux," Richard C. Carpenter is impressed by the use of pink ribbons to indicate femininity in "Brown" compared to a harlot's red petticoat in the other story. Darrel Abel, on the other hand, compares the ribbons to Mr. Hooper's black veil.[87]

In any event, femininity means sex so far as men are concerned, and though Daniel Hoffman has declared that "it is not his implication in sexual sin which damns [Brown], but his Puritan misanthropy, his unforgiving lovelessness, his lack of faith in Faith," a number of other writers, notably M. M. Shriver, have tended to overstress the importance of sex in the tale. If we are to agree with Roy R. Male that "the dark night in the forest is essentially a sexual experience, though it is also much more," we must put heavier stress on the "also much more" than on the "essentially." The meeting of a coven necessarily involved a sexual orgy, but it was neither modesty nor a love for ambiguity that kept Hawthorne from specifying that, in leaving his wife for what, in a different environment, might have been called "a night on the town," Brown was bent upon satisfying the lust of his body, but rather because if the author had tied his hero down to *any* one particular sin, he must have undercut his universal allegorical significance. Shriver, however, exaggerates not only the sexual emphasis in the tale but also the Puritan fear of sex. Where sexual behavior was concerned, the Puritans were legalists, but they were ascetics neither in theory nor in practice, as, on the second score, both the size of their families (including Brown's) and the capacity of their men for wearing out a succession of wives abundantly proves.[88]

But what, then, is the answer to the question Hawthorne flings at his reader at the end: "Had Goodman Brown fallen asleep in the forest and only dreamed a wild dream of a witch-meeting?" In a sense, the answer does not matter, for, like *The Scarlet Letter,* "Young Goodman Brown" is not a story about a sin but about the consequences of a sin. The effect upon Brown is quite the same whether he "really" went to the coven or not. Nevertheless I think it important that Hawthorne's question should be answered and answered correctly.

As Sheldon W. Liebman has ably pointed out, Hawthorne backs his reader into a position where, having been given exactly the same materials that were available to Brown, he must make up his mind by deciding what happened, and (I would add) judge himself, by the decision he makes, just as Brown himself must do. Moreover, I believe that this is true of Hawthorne's ambiguities (or ambivalences, as Walter J. Paulits thinks we should, at least in this instance, call them) in general.[89]

The difficulties involved in accepting the dream hypothesis have been unerringly noted by Robert Morsberger. Did young Goodman Brown "simply walk into the forest and fall asleep like Rip Van Winkle? . . . If so, would he not realize upon waking that he had been asleep? On the level of motivation, why should he go into the forest to spend a night sleeping out, if he were not on his way to a rendezvous?" The only point at which he could possibly fall asleep within the story would be where the Devil leaves him to rest and make up his mind about going on or turning back. But this will not do, for the supernatural element had already entered the tale with the advent of the Devil. As Morsberger says, "The only way in which the dream version can be seen logically is for the entire story to be a dream, and such a reading still does not provide for a transition out of the dream at the end."[90]

Yet it is quite impossible that the author can have expected his tale to be taken literally, so that, even through what Coleridge called that "willing suspension of disbelief for a moment that constitutes poetic faith," the reader should suppose that Brown made an actual nighttime journey into the forest to join a coven and there lost his faith in God, in religion, in humanity, and in life itself through discovering that all the persons he revered and trusted, even the wife whom he regarded as an angel (though it is not clear that he had been entirely faithful to her), were already Satanists or about to become so. The narrator of "Young Goodman Brown" vouches for *nothing* that Brown sees or thinks he sees. Taylor Stoehr has counted thirty such expressions as "as if," "as though," "it appeared that," "it seemed that," "it must have," "doubtless," "perhaps," "were such a thing possible," "he fancies that," "as it was," and "some affirm that."[91] The members of the coven are "figures" or "forms"; only Brown, not the narrator, gives any of them names. Even the Devil is never called that, and the famous pink ribbon itself is only "something" that "fluttered lightly through the air"; it was only after "the young man seized it" that he "beheld a pink ribbon."[92]

Hawthorne does not leave us without guidance in interpreting the meaning of his story. If Brown's night's adventure has been objectively reported, then *all* the worthies of Salem village—men and women, young and old, and (by implication) all men and women everywhere—are totally evil, thoroughly corrupt. In other words, Hawthorne himself must have believed what Brown believes at the end of the tale, and we know positively, from his own writings, from his positive testimony, and from the tenor of his life, that he believed nothing of the kind.[93] When Brown gets home, Faith greets him affectionately, *wearing her pink ribbons*. Neither she nor any of the villagers give any sign of having seen Brown or been seen by him in the forest. If they have all been enlisted in Satan's service, he does not seem to have made a very good bargain. So far as either Brown or the reader can see, they all seem to be going about the Lord's work, with more or less consistency, fidelity, and efficiency, much as they have done it all their lives.

We are told at the beginning of the tale that Brown goes into the forest with an "evil purpose" and that he knows it is evil. He finds what he seeks, as we all do, because he brings it with him, and as he penetrates farther into the gloom, he himself becomes "the chief horror of the scene," projecting upon others the evil he has found in himself. Morsberger uses a simple but effective comparison when he likens him "to the youth who thinks he will just once try drugs, prostitution, or some sort of perversity—just once, to see what it's like, and never again—and who gets hooked into addiction or shocked into fanatical reaction." He does not really intend to go to the devil, but all his good resolutions are for the future; as for now, he will have his fling. And "now" is the only time any of us ever have. Whatever we do must be done "now."

Only, young Goodman Brown is not very good at being a sinner either. At the last minute he draws back. It seems he is no more capable of a commitment in sin than in love (he has been married only three months) or religion; he does not have the character to be either a sinner or a saint. Thus far, but only thus far, those who feel that there might have been more hope for him if he had gone through with the evil baptism are right. As it is, he ends up with nothing. He comes back to Salem without even the memory of pleasure from his night in the forest. Nothing is left but despair.

But if "Young Goodman Brown" is neither the story of an actual night's adventure nor a dream, how then shall it be read? D. M. McKeithan, Thomas P. Walsh, Jr., Frank Davidson, and Robert Emmet Whelan, Jr.,[94] must stand high among those who have worked the problem out. The story is a kind of allegory, describing how sin can destroy both faith and joy. There is no forest journey, but only "an inward journey into the black, despairing depths of [young Goodman Brown's] soul" (Walsh). "When we leave Salem with Goodman Brown, neither he nor we are really doing so except in the sense that we depart from the objective world of Salem into the subjective world of Goodman Brown's heart," nor does he return from the forest "except in terms of the surface story" (Whelan). Brown made no literal journey when he departed from Faith—and faith. What he did "was to indulge in sin . . . under the mistaken notion that he could break off whenever he wanted to" (McKeithan). The whole thing ends with "an evil thought that got out of control" (Davidson). Hawthorne's beloved Spenser himself could not have spelled it out more plainly with his Sansfoy, Sansloy, and Sansjoy. We do not know how long it took, nor what sin seduced Brown; neither do these things matter. They are right who, in this sense, see "Young Goodman Brown" as even more powerful than *The Scarlet Letter*, where we are limited to one particular sin and that committed, by the woman at least, under somewhat extenuating circumstances. For Hester Prynne's sin was the sin of Francesca da Rimini, and though Dante sent Francesca to hell, he put her in the very first circle of the "Inferno" which is the first of positive sin. But the sinner who reads "Young Goodman Brown," whoever he may be, must say to himself what Browning says in "The Statue and the Bust": "De te, fabula!"

"My Kinsman, Major Molineux"

Julian Hawthorne, Henry James, and George Edward Woodberry all completely ignored "My Kinsman, Major Molineux." Even more surprisingly, it does not even appear in the index of Matthiessen's *American Renaissance* (1941), and as late as 1955, H. H. Waggoner could still describe it as "a tale which has received hardly any critical attention." Actually the tide had already begun to turn in 1951 however with Q. D. Leavis's famous *Sewanee Review* article (see note 76), and since then, heaven knows, critics have made up for their former neglect with a vengeance. The learned journals groan under the weight of "Molineux" studies, and neither eccentric interpretations of its meaning nor extravagant estimates of its merits are far to seek. Waggoner himself sees it as "a tale which belongs with the finest Hawthorne produced," but Marius Bewley, as if not satisfied with this, calls it "one of the greatest masterpieces of American literature," and even Neal Frank Doubleday, who finds it "a kind of failure," prefaces his perojative noun with the flattering adjective "fascinating."

What Hawthorne himself thought of it is difficult to determine. It first appeared in the *Token* for 1832, but he passed it over when preparing copy for both *Twice-Told Tales* and *Mosses from an Old Manse,* not taking it up before *The Snow-Image* in 1851. In view of the number of inconsequential sketches he had earlier reprinted, this would hardly seem to indicate that he regarded it very highly, though it is of course possible that he feared it would not be understood.[95] The dedicatory letter to Horatio Bridge prefixed to *The Snow-Image* is on this point noncommittal. On the one hand, the author declares himself "disposed to quarrel" with the early pieces he has reprinted on the ground that "a maturer judgment discerns so many faults," while, on the other, he finds that "the ripened autumnal fruit tastes but little better than the early windfalls."

Though it would be both myopic and disingenuous to pretend that "Molineux" does not represent Hawthorne's narrative power at its very best, its present extraordinary vogue can hardly be wholly explained on the ground of its merits. We are living in an age when many readers find difficulty in distinguishing between stories and crossword puzzles, and since nobody is sure just what the tale "means," it affords a wonderful opportunity for a critic to propound an interpretation that nobody else has ever thought of but which, for that very reason, gives him a chance to demonstrate that he sees his way through what nobody else can. When so sensible a writer as Lea Newman declares that the tale can "be put to good use in history classes, in urban studies, in ethics seminars, in myth surveys, in adolescent-psychology sessions and mob-behavior clinics," one is tempted to reply that though she may understand "Molineux," her ideas concerning the functions and uses of literature must be very curious, and when she goes on to add that "above all, it belongs in all manner of literature classes, from those as general as an introductory survey to those as specialized as a course in the Odyssey theme in the American short story," I for one can only say that, in the first instance, I should be inclined to fear that the poor freshman would be sent away under the impression that literature is something you are not supposed to understand and had therefore better let alone. If art involves communication, then "My Kinsman, Major Molineux"is at best a flawed success.

At the beginning of the story, Robin Molineux, the younger son of a country clergyman, is landed by the ferry one summer evening in Boston. He has come in search of his kinsman, Major Molineux, a minor figure in the colonial government establishment, who has promised to be his patron. He does not know where the Major lives but he supposes both that anyone of whom he inquires his way will be able to point out the dwelling place of so prominent a man and that his kinsman's position will have sufficiently rubbed off on him so that he too will be treated with respect. What he does not know is that a popular revolt is brewing and that this very night Major Molineux is to be tarred and feathered.

All the persons except one of whom he inquires his way treat him rudely, laugh at him, or threaten him with punishment. The solitary exception is a pretty girl in a red petticoat who tries to entice him into her house on the pretext that the Major lives there and that she is his housekeeper. Finally he forces an answer of sorts from a hideous creature, later identified as the leader of the mob, with protruding forehead, hooked nose, fiery eyes, and shaggy eyebrows, and with one side of his face painted "an intense red" and the other "black as midnight," thus constituting him "a fiend of fire and a fiend of darkness," and all he tells Robin is that if he will wait where he is for an hour, he will see the Major pass by. Having no other clue, the boy takes his stand on the steps of a church, where he is joined by "a gentleman in his prime, of open, intelligent, cheerful, and altogether prepossessing countenance," who seems benevolent and who proposes to wait with him until his expectations shall be fulfilled. When at last the Major comes, in a cart surrounded by a howling mob, he turns out to be "an elderly man, of large and majestic person, and strong, square features, betokening a steady soul," but now sitting "in tar-and feathery-dignity," with his face "pale as death," a forehead "contracted in his agony," his eyes "red and wild," and his quivering lips dashed with foam. At first Robin's knees shake and his hair bristles, "with a mixture of pity and terror." Then "a perception of tremendous ridicule in the whole scene affected him with a sort of mental inebriety," and his laughter rings out louder than that of any of the rest. Obviously his kinsman is not going to be able to do anything for him in *this* Boston, and when he comes to himself, he does not at first see any alternative to asking his way not to Major Molineux's house but back to the ferry. His new friend however urges him not to make a hasty decision. Perhaps if he stays in Boston, he may still "rise in the world" without the Major's help.

Hawthorne sets his scene with apparently deliberate imprecision on "a summer night, not far from a hundred years ago," which would place the action during the long period of conflict between the provincial governors and the people that began with the surrender of the colony's charter under James II. What happens has reminded many readers of the rioting of the Sons of Liberty occasioned by the enactment of the Stamp Act in 1765, but Robert Grayson, who sees Caleb Snow's *History of Boston* as an important source (Hawthorne himself refers in passing to Governor Hutchinson's history), and who has shown that the tale is full of topographical color, accurately described, places the action on Midsummer Eve, June 23, 1730.

Multitudinous other literary and historical sources have been nominated. There was an historical William Molineux, who was however not a Tory but a rebel, and there has been learned speculation as to Hawthorne's reasons for using this name. The double-faced leader of the mob may have been taken from Hezekiah Niles's *Principles and Acts of the Revolution,* and one scholar has even invoked Swift's *Drapier's Letters.* The mob action seems to have been colored from Joseph Strutt's *Sports and Pastimes of the People of England,* while Robin's first name could have come either from Robin Hood or from Robin Goodfellow in *A Midsummer Night's Dream,* which Hawthorne mentions. Daniel Hoffman goes back to New England folklore and popular literature to connect the "shrewd" Robin with such country-bumpkin figures as Sam Slick and Brother Jonathan. The classics have also been put to service. Aristotle's pity and terror are obviously involved in Robin's first reaction to his kinsman's humiliation; one scholar discerns a "Theseus motif," while another sees the benevolent stranger playing Virgil's role to Robin's Dante. Arthur J. Broes, who takes a very dim view of both Robin and his prospects, makes not only Dante an important influence but Spenser and Bunyan as well. Nor has modern English and American literature altogether escaped being invoked. Alexander Allison finds the classical allusions employed to create a mock-heroic impression akin to those in Fielding's novels, while others find echoes of Franklin's *Autobiography* and Charles Brockden Brown's *Arthur Mervyn* in Robin's odyssey.[96]

Everything that happens in this story has obviously been designed to carry more than its surface meaning, yet nobody is quite sure what the hidden meaning is. The atmosphere of the whole is dream-like: Robin felt that his mind vibrated "between fancy and reality" and could almost "believe that a spell was upon him." This impression is reinforced by the omnipresent moonlight, with all the superstitions attached to lunar madness and the suggestions of an enchanted summer night that seem to carry over from *A Midsummer Night's Dream.* Is the prostitute, as Fogle suggests, "one of the less reputable moon-goddesses of mythology, a declassée Astarte?" and is the man with the two-colored face the Devil?[97] If he is not, what is the point of surrounding him with so many diabolical suggestions? When, after the procession has passed by, and Robin's companion lays his hand "on the youth's shoulder" and asks, "Well,

Robin, are you dreaming?" what is the answer? how much of the story is dream, and how much is waking? and which, for that matter, is the more "real" of the two? Is there perhaps even a suggestion that life itself may be a dream?[98]

I have complained of Hawthorne's failure unmistakably to communicate his meaning in this tale and, less temperately, of the tendency of some of his interpreters to commit themselves to idiosyncratic, farfetched interpretations of it. Yet, in a sense, there is some truth in nearly all these views, and, desperate as their bewildering variations of emphasis are, there is also an underlying agreement. ("Bring on your creeds," cried the heretic to his judges of the Inquisition. "I will sign them all!") From one point of view, to be sure, there is agreement upon nothing. The story ends without our knowing whether Robin will stay in Boston or go back home, or whether if he does stay, he has made the right decision; neither can we be sure of the motives of the benevolent stranger who has taken him in hand; perhaps he is even as dangerous as the scarlet petticoat. Robin's laughter at the end has become a subject for debate as solemn as that which concerns Hamlet's feigned or real madness. Is it caused by the contagion of mob hysteria? a sudden release from the strain of an intolerable night? a bitterly ironical realization of the joke life has played on him in the cruel disappointment of his great expectations? Certainly discrepancy has been recognized from classical times as one of the important sources of humor, and to some of us these hypotheses would seem pretty adequately to cover Robin's case. Others however think they see here a remnant of the Dionysian rites, or an act of self-preservation, or a surrender to the mob or even to the Devil, or an expression of Robin's latent hostility towards his father and the father's generation, though those who can reconcile this last with the part the father plays in his son's musings at the church door must certainly possess a more brilliant imagination than I can pretend to claim. If it could be shown that the answer to "Well, Robin, are you dreaming?" must be in the affirmative, this would·mean that Robin dreamed the whole tar-and-feathering procession. I do not believe this, if for no other reason than that it would leave the conditions in the town and all Robin's adventures until he reaches the earliest point, before his station at the church, where he could possibly have fallen asleep, unaccounted for. Nor do I believe that he could so quickly and instantaneously have made in his own heart and mind the shift which those who see his laughter actuated by consciously held, cold-blooded, interested motives must require him to have made.[99]

Some things do seem wholly clear however—the quest, the night journey, the initiatory rites. Robin is the young man in the folktales who sets out to seek his fortune, though he is also, to be sure, the young man in search of a father or a father-surrogate, as well as a much more typically nineteenth-century figure, the young man from the provinces in a whole library of fiction of which *Great Expectations* remains the most distinguished representative. We may also be sure that whether his experiences cover a night or a lifetime, he thus comes in contact with and tests and evaluates representatives of manifold social institutions and types of human character, and this regardless of whether he be regarded as having come through his ordeal triumphantly or ignominiously failed. There can be no question then that at the end he has moved notably in the direction of making terms with the community, and Arthur Broes is by no means the only writer who views that as evidence of corruption; neither is it surprising that he should view the friendly stranger, who represents the community and evidently wishes Robin to become a part of it, as a sinister and hypocritical figure, deriving from Archimago of *The Faerie Queene*. The ideal man must learn how to stand on his own feet, but, unless he wishes to accept Hawthorne's Man of Adamant as his ideal, he must also learn how to live in the world, and I suspect that the differences between those readers who see Robin as having supinely acquiesced in all the cruelty and injustice of society and those who think of him as merely beginning to learn how to pay the price for growing up that we must all pay are determined not only by what happens in the story but by what they believe about larger matters. Nevertheless, the need that both parties must recognize is with us always.[100]

In the setting in which Hawthorne has placed it, Robin's odyssey, however it be interpreted, cannot reasonably be detached from the experience of the nation aborning that he inhabits. In studies that focus upon this aspect, he is generally seen as the colonies chafing under British rule, though, since no departure from the main line seems to be barred in reading this story, at least one commentator sees him as representing the six colonial governors to whom Hawthorne refers in his first paragraph.[101] However all this be taken, the theme of maturation or the young man entering upon life, with its mythical overtones and those of the emerging nation superimposed upon it, different as they are, may perhaps still manage with some comfort to keep house together.

3

Romances

This chapter is concerned with the five long stories Hawthorne published during his lifetime, leaving the uncompleted works of his later years for consideration in chapter 4. To the discussion in hand it seems fitting to prefix a brief commentary upon the writer's literary theory and principles.

Nathaniel Hawthorne did not call himself a novelist. He considered himself a romancer. There were times when he thought he liked the novel better than the romance. He greatly admired the work of the great Victorian realist, Anthony Trollope, a passion the latter warmly reciprocated,[1] but he was not quite sure he himself understood some of his own "blasted allegories," which, he feared, might well steal away the "human warmth" of his conceptions. He was never even sure that he was wise to turn back to the past for the story of *The Scarlet Letter.* He knew that there were good stories all about him in the Salem Custom House, and he felt that "the wiser course would have been to diffuse thought and imagination through the opaque substance of today"; if the life that appeared before him seemed "dull and commonplace," the reason surely was that he "had not fathomed its deeper import." For all that however, Hawthorne could never have been a Trollope. Both his temperament and his literary ideals forbade it. Even in deploring his failure to use the contemporary materials around him, he makes it clear that he did not wish to reproduce them but rather to present them as "thought and imagination" had operated upon them, and in the nonfictional *Our Old Home* he informs us that "facts never show their most delicate and divinest colors until we shall have dissolved away their grossest actualities by steeping them long in a powerful menstrum of thought."

His prefaces tell the same story. *The House of the Seven Gables* must not be permitted to "swerve aside from the truth of the human heart," but since it is not a novel but a romance, there can be no objection to its presentation of that truth "under circumstances . . . of the writer's own choosing or creation." Though *The Blithedale Romance* has an actual autobiographical basis, the author's "present concern with the socialist community is merely to establish a theatre, a little removed from the highway of ordinary travel, where the creatures of his brain may play their phantasmagorical antics, without exposing them to too close a comparison with the actual events of real lives." This "Faery Land," this "license with regard to everyday probability," has long been at the disposal of European writers, and "this atmosphere is what the American romancer needs." But the public is not ready for it in "a country where there is no shadow, no antiquity, no mystery, no picturesque or gloomy wrong, nor anything but a commonplace prosperity, in broad and simple daylight." So there is a frank retreat at last to the Italy of *The Marble Faun*, "a fanciful story, evolving a thoughtful moral," which "did not purpose attempting a portraiture of Italian manners and character," but only of giving its author the advantage of utilizing "a sort of poetic or fairy precinct, where actualities would not be so terribly insisted upon as they are, and must be, in America."

Hawthorne's America, to be sure, had a brief past of its own, and he used it freely when it served his purpose, directly in *The Scarlet Letter*, less so in *The House of the Seven Gables*, where he showed it impinging upon the present. But his aesthetic distance was not wholly distance in time and place. Even mirrors and moonlight could "spiritualize" reality, creating "a neutral territory, somewhere between the real world and fairy-land, where the Actual and the Imaginary may meet, and each imbrue itself with the nature of the other."

But is not this then evasion, escapism? Not if you believe with Hawthorne that it is the function of art to "soften and sweeten the lives of its worshippers, in even a more exquisite degree than the contemplation of natural objects" and to illustrate universalities through a "drama truer than history." In his eyes, creation itself was unfinished until "the poet came to interpret and so complete it." As we have seen, he insisted that even in romance, the writer had no license to "swerve aside from the truth of the human heart" (even fanciful settings must be "akin" to the real world), and though he admitted the "marvelous," he insisted upon using it sparingly, like Scott before him, and admitting commonsense explanations of unusual phenomena wherever they explained. It is true that he believed the artist could be at his best only when he worked under the stimulus of a "higher and wiser [power] than himself," but he did not believe that a writer could live apart from his time. "What is called poetic insight is the gift of discerning, in this sphere of strangely mingled elements, the beauty and the majesty which are compelled to assume a garb so sordid." His emphasis upon beauty was matched by his emphasis upon truth. On the other hand, though he was a profoundly moral writer, he was not moralistic, for he believed that "when romances really do teach anything, or produce any effective operation, it is usually through a far more subtle process than the ostensible one." As Jesse Bier has observed, what he aimed for was "a superreality not confined to place or time" that enabled him "to get back into the universal, timeless, real 'territory' to which the essentially poetic vehicle of imagination could transport him."[2]

Fanshawe

Hawthorne published his first long story, *Fanshawe,* anonymously in October 1828, only three years after his graduation from Bowdoin. It was fairly well advertised for the period and in general favorably reviewed. But though he is reported to have paid Marsh and Capen a hundred dollars to print a thousand copies, he was afterwards so ashamed of it that he never acknowledged it and seems to have destroyed every copy he could lay his hands on.[3] It was not republished until 1876, and as late as 1902 the influential critic George Edward Woodberry wrote of it in his study of Hawthorne in the "American Men of Letters" series that "it is as destitute of any brilliant markings of his genius as his undergraduate life itself had been, and is important only as showing the serious care with which he undertook the task of authorship." Of recent years it has been somewhat more favorably viewed however, and today we cannot quite stop with finding Hawthornism only in the sensitive, secluded name character and in the evil Butler, whose melodramatics the author's villains never quite outgrew. If we think Carl Bode too generous in finding "the promising of greatness" in this story, we must at least remember that he was long anticipated by the contemporary reviewer who discerned that "the mind that produced this little, interesting volume, is capable of making great and rich additions to our native literature." Nor can Leo B. Levy's demonstration of *Fanshawe's* anticipation of the "symbolic resonance" of Hawthorne's later work be lightly brushed aside.[4]

The action is centered in the vicinity of a small New England college, obviously modeled upon Bowdoin.[5] Ellen Langton, the temporary ward of the college president, Dr. Melmoth, is loved by both the unworldly Fanshawe, who is supposed to be engaged in studying himself to death, and the more "normal" Edward Walcott, whom she favors. The villainous Butler abducts her under the mistaken impression that she is an heiress, whereupon Fanshawe is sufficiently drawn out of his seclusion by "the exulting tide of hope and joy" he has experienced through his love for her to rescue her, after which she gratefully offers herself to him. Realizing that, being what he is, he could not possibly make either her or himself happy, Fanshawe declines. Four years after his death, Ellen marries Edward Walcott.

Ellen is merely the stock pretty girl of nineteenth-century fiction, with all the virtues but little individuality. There is more shading in the men, even Butler being given a conditioning background. Though Edward Walcott is clearly an extrovert, he is also the class poet, who has gone in mildly for dissipation during his college years. Before his union with Ellen, he has put both his aspirations and his vagaries behind him, clearly with his creator's approval, to settle for a sensible middle-class domesticity and normal, satisfying human love, mildly anticipative of the union of Phoebe and Holgrave in *The House of the Seven Gables*. As for Fanshawe, for all his passion for learning, he is well aware that invincible ignorance is the inevitable lot of scholars as well as clods; he even realizes the futility of his "dream of enduring fame," without however forgetting that "dream as it is," this is, for him, "more powerful than a thousand realities."

But though both these young men have been clearly understood by their creator, they can hardly be said to have been vividly, much less powerfully, delineated. Many readers therefore find themselves more interested in Dr. Melmoth, who had "borne the matrimonial yoke (and in his case it was no light burden) nearly twenty years," and in the landlord Hugh Crombie, the ex-pirate turned innkeeper and amateur poet and singer, than they are in the principals. For them the humorous, Irving-like side of the book, suggestive of many of Hawthorne's early sketches, has worn considerably better than its sensational, Gothic, or sentimental aspects.

Fanshawe had sources in both literature and life. Harley College, as has been observed, is Bowdoin College, where Gorham Deane, one of Hawthorne's classmates, famous for his devotion to study, went to his grave only a few weeks before the commencement in which he would have stood second in his class. The author had also seen the tombstone of another young enthusiast of the same kidney—Cotton Mather's younger brother Nathaniel, who died "an aged man of nineteen years"—and it can hardly be denied that there was something of Fanshawe's love of solitude in Hawthorne himself during the years before his marriage.

The author of *Fanshawe* was obviously familiar with the Gothic tradition in fiction. Jesse Sidney Goldstein was the first to point out his indebtedness to the greatest of the "Gothicks," Charles Robert Maturin's *Melmoth the Wanderer* (1820), from whom Dr. Melmoth borrowed his name. William Bysshe Stein has reminded us that the suggestion that some of Fanshawe's studies skirted occultism may have come from the Faust legend. More recently Robert Sattelmeyer has demonstrated the resemblances between the novel and the views of the Scottish "commonsense" philosophers who were very influential at Bowdoin and whom Hawthorne is known to have read.[6]

More important than all these together however was Sir Walter Scott, whom Hawthorne loved all his life and from whose work he may even have derived the idea of trying to do for New England what Scott had done for Scotland. It is true that he soon came to feel that for himself he needed a "more earnest purpose," "a deeper moral," and a "closer and homelier truth" than Scott could supply and that for these he must turn to Spenser and Bunyan.[7] The real difficulty however was not that Scott lacked any of these qualities but that his wide-ranging vitality, his variety, and his mastery of vigorous action did not supply the right models for Hawthorne's brooding, introspective, and contemplative mood and method.

In *Fanshawe* nevertheless, every aspect of Scott's method is duti-
fully imitated. The setting was studied from life, but Hawthorne
thrusts the action back "about eighty years since," thus recalling not
only one of Scott's own devices but the very title *Waverley: or 'Tis
Sixty Years Since*. As in Scott, the untitled chapters are headed by
epigraphs, mostly from Shakespeare but one (chapter 8) from Maturin. The action shifts from one group of characters to another.
Both "refined" and lower-class persons appear, and the dialogue
moves from high, almost high-flown, eighteenth-century diction to
easy colloquialism. Mysteries are posed and later cleared up. There
is at least a faint touch of the supernatural in the background, which
is always realistically regarded.[8]

The Scarlet Letter

Hawthorne began work on *The Scarlet Letter* in September 1849
and finished it on February 3, 1850, while one end was in the press
in Boston and the other still in his head in Salem. During its production he had been enough absorbed in it to remain at his desk
sometimes for nine hours a day, but though he realized that some
portions were "powerfully written," he was sufficiently convinced
that it was too dismal in tone to be successful on its own so that for
a time he planned to publish it in a collection of "Old-Time Legends" in which it should occupy only half the total space. Even after
it had succeeded, he sometimes tried to persuade himself that it owed
its popularity to the long introductory sketch of "The Custom
House," so hopelessly out of tune with the story itself. This introduction does relate (nonfactually) how the narrator found the scarlet
letter and reference to Hester Prynne in the Custom House ("there
seemed to be here the groundwork of a tale"), and it is true that
Hawthorne's own recent dismissal from the customs service and
what he wrote about his former associates there did for a time give
the book a topical, even slightly scandalous, interest it would not
otherwise have had. Indeed Daniel Hoffman has argued that, in his
search for the "neutral territory" he considered necessary for a romance, Hawthorne felt he must "lead the reader backwards in time,
away from the dull commonplace of the present toward the past in

which the imagination can illuminate reality with a glow like moonlight or firelight." But it is difficult to see why *The Scarlet Letter* should need sixty pages to achieve this any more than any other story set in the past.[9]

James T. Fields published the book on March 15, 1850, bravely venturing a first printing of 2,500 copies, and though some professional viewers with alarm wondered audibly whether the "French era" had arrived in our literature, he was more than justified by a sale of six thousand copies during six months. When the child Henry James saw a copy in his parents' house, he wondered what kind of a letter it might be that was written on red paper. Grown up, he judged the novel to possess "that charm, very hard to express, which we find in an artist's work, the first time he has touched his highest mark—a sort of straightness and naturalness of execution, an unconsciousness of his public, and freshness of interest in his theme." Hawthorne received a royalty of fifteen percent, but since the list price was only seventy-five cents, *The Scarlet Letter* earned him only $1,500 during his lifetime.[10]

It may seem odd, on first consideration, that such gigantic critical commentary should have been inspired by a story of such classical, straightforward simplicity. To all intents and purposes, there are only four characters: the Reverend Arthur Dimmesdale; Hester Prynne, who has committed adultery with him before the book begins; their daughter Pearl; and the husband, Roger Prynne, alias Chillingworth, who, upon his arrival, dedicates his life to ferreting out the minister's secret. The time scheme embraces seven years, beginning in 1642, but there is very little action, and what there is is presented mainly in a series of tableaux, with the three scaffold scenes standing at the beginning, the middle, and the end. In the first, Hester stands alone, exposed before the multitude, with her baby in her arms. In the second, Dimmesdale, tormented by his conscience, mounts the scaffold under the cloak of night, in a kind of histrionic anticipation of his genuine confession and self-exposure at the end. In the last, he finally solves his problem by his repentance and death. "I should think it might possibly succeed as an opera," Hawthorne himself remarked, "though it would certainly fail as a play."[11]

The tableaux are linked by what Edith Wharton would have called "orchestral" passages—that is, chapters of straight narrative, each covering a particular phase or period, some of which run into brief passages of dialogue toward the end. In general the dialogue is formal and dignified, keeping at its best the calm, cool distance of art, but sometimes, especially with Pearl, lapsing into artificiality. The author is always outside his narrative ("it was a circumstance to be noted, on the morning when our story opens"). He frequently reminds us that his action is set in the past ("the new abode of the two friends . . . was in a house covering pretty nearly the site on which the venerable structure of King's Chapel has since been built"). Nor does he ever shrink from authorial comment upon his narrative or attempt to conceal his own value judgments. If the book is compared to such historical novels as *Romola, The Cloister and the Hearth,* and *Kristin Lavransdatter,* its historical coloring must be called slight. For the authenticity he achieves,[12] Hawthorne depends upon his own intimate knowledge and understanding of the Puritan world and mind and not upon either physical furnishings or archaic language. Indeed Willa Cather made *The Scarlet Letter* the prime example in her famous essay "The Novel Démeublé" in *Not Under Forty*: "Whatever is felt upon the page without being specifically named there—that, one might say, is created."

In the opening "scene," the women standing about the pillory serve as a kind of "chorus," expressing the outraged sense of the community and especially the female portion thereof, and Hawthorne digresses into a generalization that, in a measure, anticipates the outrageous remarks about English women he would later include in *Our Old Home:* "The women, who were now standing about the prison-door, stood within less than half a century of the period when the mannish Elizabeth had been the not altogether unsuitable representative of her sex." One young matron and a man are more sympathetic however, and the author skillfully manages the scene so as to cause the reader to agree with them. "There can be no outrage, methinks, against our common nature . . . more flagrant than to forbid the culprit to hide his face for shame." He even dares to suggest that "had there been a Papist among the crowd," he might have seen in Hester and her child a suggestion of "the image of Divine Maternity," but he is careful not to permit the reader to suppose that his sympathy with the culprit implies condoning what she has done. "Here, there was the taint of deepest sin in the most sacred quality of human life, working such effect, that the world was only the darker for this woman's beauty, and the more lost for the infant that she had borne."

Chillingworth makes his first appearance, unidentified, as a spectator of his wife's disgrace; then Dimmesdale appears, as secondary to the older clergyman, John Wilson, who bids him exhort Hester to reveal the name of her partner in sin. Dimmesdale is described before he speaks, and the description, like his exhortation, strikes his keynote. "Take heed how thou deniest to him—who, perchance, hath not the courage to grasp it for himself—the bitter, but wholesome, cup that is now presented to thy lips!" There follows, in chapter 4, the interview between Hester and Chillingworth, when he is called upon to attend her as a physician, and she accedes to his request not to reveal their relationship. The four principals are not brought together again until chapter 8, when Dimmesdale aids Hester by blocking consideration of the plan the magistrates are pondering to remove Pearl from her mother's care.

Hawthorne's denial of the adaptability of *The Scarlet Letter* to the stage has not prevented Malcolm Cowley from analyzing it as "a Racinian drama of dark necessity." Only Hugh W. MacLean seems to prefer an epic structure, organized about three epic quests, but John C. Gerber, Gordon Roper, G. Thomas Tanselle, and Austin Warren all prefer a four-part division, with the emphasis shifting from one character to another. Though these analyses cannot all be equally right, they are much less mutually exclusive than might a priori be assumed.[13]

I must not leave the impression, however, that the classical simplicity of *The Scarlet Letter* is unmodified by other characteristics. Both the characters and the action are soaked in symbolism, and while there is no out-and-out supernaturalism, the superstitions of the characters and of the world they inhabit hover over the narrative and, despite the author's own rationalism, enlarge the stage upon which the action is played out. Hester tells the witch lady, Mistress Hibbins, that she would have gone to the forest and signed her name in the Black Man's book had the authorities taken Pearl away from her, while the townspeople feel that Chillingworth's skill is dependent upon necromancy. In some sense all this is at least figuratively if not literally true. C. C. Walcutt has acutely observed that Hawthorne's symbols sometimes "convey different meanings from those communicated by his statements."[14]

Hawthorne's characteristic ambiguity is omnipresent also. Was the light in the sky during the second scaffold scene really an *A* for *adultery*, as it seemed to Dimmesdale; or did it stand for *Angel* because the saintly John Winthrop had been translated that night; or was there no such manifestation at all? When, at the end, Dimmesdale bares the hidden mark upon his bosom ("Stand any here that question God's judgment on a sinner? Behold! behold a dreadful witness of it!"), we are never told *what* was revealed. Indeed some spectators insisted there was nothing to see. The ultimate extension of this method is achieved when a few scenes are presented as real, only to have the author cast doubt upon their actuality by reducing them to a possible "parable." Thus Mistress Hibbins is only "said to have been passing by" at a crucial moment in Dimmesdale's pilgrimage, and "the tale has surely lapsed into the improbable" in recording that a wolf came to Pearl to be petted in the forest. Such things recall and lend force to F. O. Matthiessen's remark about one particular point of ambiguity, that Hawthorne "does not literally accept his own allegory," but Daniel Cottom cuts deeper when he makes the author's "equivocation" and his detachment from judgment as a narrator a definite characteristic of his style and method.[15]

When all is said and done however, perhaps the basic ambiguity lies in Hawthorne's presentation of his three leading characters. Hester lives—or accepts—a saintly life of service and penitence, but it is rather more than doubtful that she really repents until her return from England to Boston in the last chapter. In the great forest scene she even proposes to return to her sin and would have done so if both Dimmesdale and Chillingworth had not prevented her. The minister inflicts penitential torments upon himself without finding peace—Hawthorne calls him a "subtle but remorseful hypocrite"— yet though the strain under which he lives is clearly killing him, it also increases his effectiveness as preacher and pastor. In the pulpit the "tongue of flame" descends upon him, and his own spiritual agonies vastly increase his ability to understand and to deal with the individual sins and sufferings of his parishioners. Yet even at the end, when he heroically throws off the hypocrisy, pride, and fear that had so long made his life a living lie and mounts the steps of the scaffold at midday, he is also in a sense making a great surrender. Be the consequences what they may, he is dropping a burden he no longer has the strength to carry. But perhaps Chillingworth's position is the most paradoxical of all. As the betrayed husband, the injured party, he claims our sympathy. Yet through dedicating his life to revenge, he becomes the worst sinner of all.[16]

To pass on to the consideration of possible sources, nobody has ever doubted the basic importance of Biblical and theological concepts in *The Scarlet Letter,* but the search for possible classical sources has so far yielded only more speculative results. Thus the attempt of Earl S. Hutchison, Sr., to relegate English and American sources to "secondary importance" by dwelling upon "the relationship between Hawthorne's major characters and the Eastern and Greek Aphrodites, Aphrodite's lame artist-husband Hephaestus, her lover Ares, and their child, Harmonia," to say nothing of comparing Hester's ordeal to the role of Hetaira Phryne in the Eleusinian mysteries, is more fascinating than convincing, while Robert E. Todd's discussion of "the Magna Mater archetype" seems to me to introduce into the discussion considerations that "have nothing to do with the case."[17]

A number of possible English sources have been suggested, mainly in connection with matters of detail. Spenser's Wood of Error seems an obvious candidate for the forest scenes, and Robert Stanton has pointed out allusions to Bunyan. Probably enough has been said about Hawthorne's familiarity with the Gothic novels so that I need only note here that Max L. Autrey has nominated a Victorian "blood," *Varney the Vampire,* in connection with Chillingworth. J. Jeffrey Maybrook has studied Hawthorne's use of heraldic devices, and Donald Darnell would make *The Scarlet Letter* an emblem book. Two different articles have pointed to Andrew Marvell's poem "The Unfortunate Lover" as the source of the epitaph in King's Chapel burying ground.[18]

Hawthorne himself throws out suggestions in connection with both Chillingworth and Mistress Hibbins that he may have had in mind the murder of Sir Thomas Overbury, which involved both the Countess of Essex and her paramour who was King James I's

worthless favorite, Robert Carr, Viscount Rochester. Thanks largely
to Alfred S. Reid's book, *The Yellow Ruff and "The Scarlet Letter,"*
this scandal has now become the most famous English "source" of
the novel. In 1965 however, Kenneth Serb pointed out a number of
really striking resemblances between Hawthorne's forest scene and
the now famous fourteenth-century Middle English poem, "Pearl."
Since this had not been published in Hawthorne's time, he could not
possibly have known it at firsthand, a fact carefully noted by Serb,
who concluded that the "Pearl" poet and the author of *The Scarlet
Letter,* "working four centuries apart, struck upon the same theme,
situation, and imagery merely by chance." In 1982 however Dorena
Allen Wright would argue that Hawthorne could have got everything
he used from Sir Frederick Madden's discussion of and quotation
from "Pearl" in the introduction to his 1839 edition of "Sir Gawain
and the Green Knight," now often regarded as the work of the same
writer.

Continental literature and life would not seem to have been very
important in *The Scarlet Letter,* though Ms. Wright reasonably invokes Dante's Paradiso along with "Pearl," and William Bysshe Stein
has a chapter on *The Scarlet Letter* in connection with his discussion
of the Faust legend, already noted in these pages in connection with
Fanshawe. In a suggestive but somewhat overdeveloped article, Larry
J. Reynolds argues that "the structure, characterizations, and
themes" of the novel were all "shaped . . . in Burkean ways" by
Hawthorne's reading of Guizot and Lamartine and his horror over
the revolutions of 1848–49.[19]

Unquestionably however the most important sources are American. Hawthorne's inbred knowledge of New England Puritanism
was more important here than any specific source, but mention may
be made of Cotton Mather, whose fastings may have suggested Dimmesdale's; of Governor Winthrop's *Journal,* not published complete
until 1825; of Caleb Snow's *History of Boston;* and of Joseph Felt's
Annals of Salem. One scholar has suggested Paulding's "The Dumb
Girl" as a conjectural source, and another has invoked Margaret
Fuller as an influence upon Hester, though Ann Hutchinson, of
whom Hawthorne himself speaks, seems a much better guess.[20]

Hawthorne also drew freely upon his own earlier writings. First,
there are a number of interesting journal entries: "insincerity in a

man's own heart makes all his enjoyments, all that concerns him, unreal; so that his whole life must seem like a merely dramatic representation"; "a man who does penance in what might appear to onlookers the most glorious and triumphal circumstance of his life"; "a story of the effects of revenge, diabolizing him who indulges in it"; "the life of a woman, who, by the old colony law, was condemned to wear the letter A, sewed on her garment, in token of having committed adultery."

There are also passages in *The Scarlet Letter* that recall such tales as "Egotism; or The Bosom Serpent," "Ethan Brand," "The Minister's Black Veil," "The Hollow of the Three Hills," "Roger Malvin's Burial," and "Young Goodman Brown," And in "Endicott and the Red Cross" we read:

There was likewise a young woman, with no mean share of beauty, whose doom it was to wear the letter A on the breast of her gown, in the eyes of all the world and her own children. And even her own children knew what the initial signified. Sporting with her infamy, the lost and desperate creature had embroidered the fatal token in scarlet cloth, with golden thread and the nicest art of needlework; so that the capital A might have been thought to mean Admirable, or anything other than Adulteress.

But though this is the most striking passage, it is by no means the earliest source. Probably the real origin of the final scaffold scene lies in Hawthorne's early interest in Dr. Johnson's penance in Uttoxeter marketplace, of which he makes much in his "Biographical Sketches," and if "The Battle Omen" is his, he had conceived the idea of Dimmesdale's celestial terrors as early as 1825.[21]

It is time to turn to the direct consideration of Hawthorne's characters. Hester Prynne, dark, beautiful of form and feature, and unmistakably of genteel background,[22] was the first great female character in American fiction, and though Henry James was right in maintaining that Dimmesdale is the principal character, in the sense that the book if built around him and he precipitates the denouement,[23] few readers have been as much interested in him as in her. Even Chillingworth apprehends her stature: "I pity thee for the good that has been wasted in thy nature."

Because Hawthorne did not believe that law can deal with sin as distinct from crime, he makes a whole paragraph of the sentence:

"The scarlet letter had not done its office." He seems to have felt that in placing it upon Hester's breast, the magistrates had blasphemously usurped the function of God, as Chillingworth later usurps it in his plot against Dimmesdale. Yet it serves her well in freeing her from all danger of trying to live such a lie as consumes her lover. She presents what she is to the world at all times, so that there is nothing left to fester inwardly.[24]

She conducts herself with what "might be pride" but looked much more like humility. Her way of life suggests that she had determined so to bear her earthly punishment without complaint, in the place where she had incurred her guilt, that "the torture of her daily shame would at length purge her soul, and work out another purity than that which she had lost." She gives so freely of her little means in charity and of the "wellspring of human kindness" in her "warm and rich nature" in loving service and counsel that Michael Gilmore is even tempted to associate her with Catholics and Arminians as mistaking "the covenant of law for the covenant of grace" and seeking "to expiate . . . sin through good works." There were "none so self-devoted as Hester, when pestilence stalked through the town." She sensed in herself the power to detect secret sin and felt a sense of fellowship with all sinners, and she refrained from praying for her enemies only because she feared that a blessing from such as she was might turn to a curse, yet she "struggled to believe that no fellow mortal was guilty like herself." But "her breast, with its badge of shame, was but the softer pillow for the head that needed one," and as time passed, "many people refused to interpret the scarlet A by its original signification. They said it meant Able; so strong was Hester Prynne, with a woman's strength." It even came to take on "the effect of the cross on a nun's bosom. It imparted to the wearer a kind of sacredness, which enabled her to walk securely amid all peril."

All in all, Hester Prynne seems at once to share the community's judgment upon her, yet to accept herself with her past and her destiny intact. As time passes, we are told, her life "turned, in a great measure, from passion and feeling, to thought," and "she assumed a freedom of speculation, then common enough on the other side of the Atlantic, but which our forefathers . . . would have held to be a deadlier crime than that stigmatized by the scarlet letter." Had she thought herself worthy, she might have become a prophetess and "come down to us in history, hand in hand with Ann Hutchinson." Her heresies are specified, however, only to the extent that, in the last chapter, we are told that, during her later years, she looked forward to a time when "the whole relation between man and woman" should be established "on a surer ground of mutual happiness."[25]

Except for her thoughts, which she keeps to herself, the only outlet Hester has for her creativity through her seven years' penance is the fantastic embroidery she bestows upon the very badge of her shame, the scarlet letter itself, and only such sympathetic insight as that of the young matron in the opening chapter can perceive that "not a stitch" in that article "but she has felt it in her heart." Through it she "exhibits her guilt," says John E. Hart, "yet relieves it through art and creativity." And Richard H. Brodhead adds that though "she accepts the designation of adulteress," she accepts it "on her own terms," turning it "into a more complex symbol, one that does justice to the inseparable conjunction of something guilty and something vital and fertile in her passionate nature."[26]

We come then at last to the great forest scene, in which she prepares deliberately to break the chain that binds her and commit herself to open rebellion with her lover. It is quite true, as has been pointed out again and again, that the adultery of Hester and Dimmesdale was a sin of passion and impulse and that their decision to renew their guilty relationship and go away together is the much more serious sin of deliberate will and choice.[27] Yet few critics have done full justice to Hester at this point.[28] She does not decide until it has been made clear to her both that if Dimmesdale stays in Boston, tormented by Chillingworth and his own conscience, he will die, and that she alone can save him. "Think for me, Hester! Thou art strong! Resolve for me what to do." Both parties being what they were, this left her no choice but to decide "that he had a right to her utmost aid." It was no longer a questions of what they *ought* to do, much less of what they ought to *have done* but only of what they now *could* do. There are no morals in the grave. The all-important thing now is to save Dimmesdale while there is still something left to be saved. Hester simply enacts woman's historic role of choosing the "best possible" in a very imperfect world and of cleaning up the messes men have made while she disregards all the theoretical formulations that mean to much to them. Taking another child on her hands, she sins in pure charity, but it is only fair to add that she would no more have acted thus if she had not "still so passionately [have] loved" Dimmesdale than Shaw's Candida would have given herself to the weaker of her two lovers, who was her husband. Many readers no doubt feel that Dimmesdale was not worth such devotion, but who is? and what has that to do with the case? "Use every man after his desert," says Hamlet, "and who should scape whipping?" And in *Measure for Measure* Isabella adds,

> Why, all the souls that were were forfeit once;
> And he that might the vantage best have took
> Found out the remedy.

But even yet there is no "genuine and steadfast penitence"; for that we must wait for the last chapter, which is more an epilogue to the story than the story itself.[29]

The difference between Hester and Dimmesdale is not only one of sex or temperament however, nor even merely that she has acknowledged her sin while his is concealed. He knows the Puritan theology as she does not know it and has a far firmer grasp upon the Puritan faith, but she lives much closer to the vital currents of life. Yet the fact that the scarlet letter has given her a "passport" into regions where he cannot follow is very important. He can violate his code under the influence of passion, but spiritually and intellectually he cannot break out of its confines. Without the stamina to be a sinner and go on living with himself, he can endure horrible mental and physical torture, but the best he can achieve by such means is to combine "the agony of heaven-defying guilt and vain repentance."

He is generally called a hypocrite, but though the life he lives is a lie, he is never quite that. Pride and fear combine to keep him from making a clean breast of things, and the best in him conspires with the worst to keep him silent. A self-called "polluted priest," he is still a faithful pastor, and he cannot bring himself to disillusion those who believe in him and to whom his ministry, besides being vastly more humane than that of most of his associates, and even more effective because of the anguish consequent upon his sin, has been— make no mistake about it—nearly ideal.

Generally speaking, Dimmesdale has met with considerably less charity from the critics than Hester. One, Edward H. Davidson, has presumed to speak not only for Hawthorne but for God in damning the minister not only in time but for eternity. Opposing those who, without arguing the case, have assumed that Hester was the seducer, Neil B. Houston argues that Dimmesdale seduced her. William B. Dillingham calls even his final confession ironical, since "he dies believing it to be a completely open and free admission, while it is hardly more specific than his earlier attempts." But it is William B. Nolte who pulls out all the stops, insisting even that Dimmesdale's confession "cost him absolutely nothing," an interpretation that obliges Nolte to conclude that "the final thirty pages ... are certainly the weakest artistically in the novel" and that "the final scene on the scaffold lacks proper motivation." It is astonishing that a character of fiction should be able to inspire such antagonism.[30]

In the forest scene Dimmesdale throws his burden upon Hester, and she courageously picks it up, but as Robert Stanton has observed, she can only offer him "a philosophy modelled after her temperament,"[31] and in so doing she proves that she does not really understand him. Hester is far from being a wanton, but she is no legalist either, and by casting her out the community has made a heretic of her. Had she and her lover fled from Boston, her painfully developed philosophy, however it be judged, might well have supplied an adequate foundation for reasonable happiness, at least in this life, but Dimmesdale could never have escaped, for he would have carried Boston and the whole paraphernalia of Boston Calvinism away with him in his heart, wherever he might have gone.

The immediate result of the interview in the forest however is not only exhilarating but euphoric. Dimmesdale rushes home to write the Election Sermon that is to crown his ministerial career in such a burst of energy as he had not known since he became a sinner. He eats voraciously and writes furiously, expending his mental and physical energies as recklessly as if he were never to need them again, which, as it turns out, he did not. We are handicapped in our complete understanding of what happened by the fact that we do not hear the sermon; all we know is that Dimmesdale forecast a glorious future for his country. Even Hester does not hear it; all that reaches her, as she stands listening in the marketplace, is the "indistinct, but varied, murmur and flow of the minister's very peculiar voice." Neither do we know how it differed from the other sermon, already partly written, that he threw away, nor at what point Dimmesdale's euphoria collapsed, and, quite without knowing that Chillingworth had discovered his plans, he impulsively decided at last to mount the steps of the scaffold and summon Hester and Pearl to join him there. Perhaps it was his own rapturously received sermon that opened up the way for God's grace to reach out and save him at the last, which, as Darrel Abel has convincingly shown,[32] according to Puritan theology, it did.

The one thing we can be sure of is that the energy that had impelled him thus far, even when he felt himself most inspired, was basically sexual in character. He had never been so close to damnation as in the wild temptations that beset him on the way home to whisper blasphemies and obscenities to such members of his congregation as he chanced to encounter. He had always possessed what politicians now call "charisma" and what the flesh merchants denominate "sex appeal." "The virgins of his church grew pale around him," writes Hawthorne, "victims of a passion so imbued with religious sentiment that they imagined it to be all religion, and brought it openly, in their white bosoms, as their most acceptable sacrifice before the altar." But never until now, except upon one occasion, had what he at least regarded as his unredeemed lower nature threatened to break through its controls.

It is the hallmark of the greatness of *The Scarlet Letter* as a work of art that its power no more depends upon the reader's faith in Calvinistic theology than Homer's power stands or falls with faith in the Greek gods. Whether he was the unhappy victim of a delusion or whether his action was prompted by a true insight into what God required of him, it still remains true that, being what he was and believing what he believed, so far as salvation in any sense of the word was still possible for Arthur Dimmesdale, he could have achieved it only by doing exactly what he did in the third and last scaffold scene.

Pearl, Hester's daughter by Dimmesdale, comes closer to being an allegorical figure than anybody else in *The Scarlet Letter,* yet paradoxically she seems to be the only one that was studied from an actual human being—the author's own strange and exquisite daughter, Una.[33] It may be however that, in the state of knowledge concerning prenatal influences that prevailed in his time, Hawthorne may well have thought Pearl more realistic than she is. And even so there are touches in her portrayal that are startlingly real. The book is nowhere richer in symbolism than in the forest scene, yet Pearl's impassioned reactions to the change in her mother's appearance when she unbinds her hair and discards the scarlet letter are equally true literally and symbolically. As John A. Andola remarks, "Without her mother's sin, Pearl could not exist, nor could she exist without her mother's love, both of which are symbolized in the scarlet A and in Pearl herself."[34] But anyone who has had any experience with small children will also understand how they can react to unexpected changes in persons and things that are dear to them.

Hester named her daughter after the "pearl of great price" in the New Testament, "purchased with all she had,—her mother's only treasure." Because she dressed her, in sharp contrast to her own drab attire, in "the richest tissues that could be procured," arranged with "a fantastic ingenuity" that underlined the little girl's "fairy charm," she was in one aspect the scarlet letter come to life, and when the Reverend Mr. Wilson saw her, he thought she might better have been named "Coral" or "Ruby." She is a natural child not only because she is a bastard but because she is out of tune with society but in harmony with the forest and all the wild things in it, as they with her. "There was fire in her and throughout her; she seemed the unpremeditated offshoot of a passionate action." There seemed to be both depth and variety in her nature, but she "could not be made amenable to rules. In giving her existence, a great law had been broken, and the result was a being whose elements were perhaps beautiful and brilliant, but all in disorder." The "warfare of Hester's spirit" at the time of her conception lived again in her child. "She is my happiness," her mother says of her. "She is my torture."

It is no wonder then that she has become the most variously interpreted child in American literature. Barbara Garlitz, whose study of her constitutes a summary of what had been written up to the time of its publication and constitutes the best introduction to her, notes that she has been seen as demonic, angelic, amoral, "an example of Rousseauistic natural goodness," and "the hypostatization . . . of the Puritan concept of nature."[35] Nor does this exhaust the varieties of interpretation that have been offered. Replying to D. H. Lawrence's queer notion that Pearl was an essentially "modern" child, Charles E. Eisinger argued that she had been portrayed in complete harmony with Puritan conceptions of child nature; to Frederick Newberry she represented art, so that when she and her mother left New England, they took with them "the aesthetic continuity between England and America which they [had] represented"; to Larry J. Reynolds she was the revolutionary "who anticipates what Hester will become"; and as late as 1972 Charles L. May saw her an an Antichrist![36]

Pearl seems to lend support to this last interpretation when Mr. Wilson asks her who made her, and she replies that her mother plucked her off the wild rosebush beside the prison door. But she is only teasing him, for Hawthorne carefully assures us that she knew her catechism, and it is clear that, for all her vagaries, the author had no intention of giving up on her. He lingers over the curious paradox that though "man had marked this woman's sin by a scarlet letter . . . God, as a direct consequence of the sin which man thus punished, had given her a lovely child, . . . to connect her parent forever with the race and descent of mortals, and to be finally a blessed saint in heaven." Even when she is at her worst, Pearl's "unflinching courage," "sturdy pride," and "bitter scorn" of falsehood give promise of rich development to those who have eyes to see. In the last chapter we are given summarily to understand that her later life was prosperous, happy, and worthy, so that Harry Levin can remark wittily that "when we read . . . that she grew up an heiress and traveled abroad, we realize that we can pursue her further adventures through the novels of Henry James."[37]

More seriously one must say that those who see Pearl as a holy child can make a very strong case at least so far as her relations with her parents are concerned. We have Hester's own specific though figurative word that it was Pearl alone who saved her from going to the forest and writing her name in the Black Man's book. As for Dimmesdale, when he defends her mother in chapter 8, Pearl astonishes Hester by stealing "softly towards him, and taking his hand in the grasp of both her own [and laying] her cheek against it," but she is displeased with him in the second scaffold scene because he will not promise to stand there together with her and her mother tomorrow noontide, and she refuses to kiss him in the forest scene because he is not "true." It is only in the third and final scaffold scene that she achieves full humanity, "and as her tears fell openly upon her father's cheek, they were the pledge that she would grow up amid human joy and sorrow, nor forever do battle with the world but be a woman in it." She had at last succeeded in her search for a father and thus established herself in a normal relationship to society, and here at least she justifies Anne Marie Macnamara's claim that "she is grace, the instrument of [Dimmesdale's] redemption."[38]

But if Pearl is a holy child, she is also, whether quite consistently or not, something besides, and the hypothetical inconsistency is part of her charm, for it saves her from fading away altogether into an allegory. There is "a circle of radiance" about her, and in the forest scene it is she alone whom the sunshine always follows. It is true, as Malcolm Cowley says, that "the forest is the meeting place of those who follow their passions and revolt against the community," but it is more than that, for the beasts who dwell there are without sin, and Pearl says rightly, "I wear nothing on my bosom yet." If she is inconsistent, so is nature, or at least man sees her thus. Nature stands juxtaposed to grace, but the Christian God is immanent as well as transcendent, and good Christians have discerned Him in nature as well as above it. Generally speaking, the creeds of the church have been more consistent and systematic than the Scriptures they profess to interpret, and if literary scholars anywhere resemble the theologians, it is when they close their eyes to everything in a work of art that does not fit in comfortably with their own interpretation of it.

The wronged husband, who calls himself Roger Chillingworth, has drawn considerably less comment than the others, and this is not surprising, for, as has already been noted, Hawthorne's villains rarely awaken his deepest powers.[39] Chillingworth's is certainly a much better characterization than Butler's in *Fanshawe*, but essentially he is humanized only by his own free admission that he wronged Hester before she wronged him by knowingly marrying a young woman who did not love him and, more doubtfully, by his not quite convincing bequest of his property to Pearl, whose becoming "the richest heiress of her day in the New World" is the one point where *The Scarlet Letter* skirts the sensational story papers.

Originally "kindly, though not of warm affections, but ever, and in all his relations with the world, a pure and upright man," Chillingworth becomes guilty of what Hawthorne saw as the unpardonable sin by probing Dimmesdale's heart without sympathy, under the guise of ministering to him as a physician, until he has come close to murdering him, both physically and spiritually. Even that champion self-tormentor is able to realize at last that "that old man's revenge has been blacker than my sin. He has violated, in cold blood, the sanctity of a human heart."

Chillingworth's realization of his own large and initial share in the tragedy that has overtaken all three persons is weakened and robbed of its cleansing power by his conviction that everything that has occurred is the result of a "dark necessity." "My old faith, long forgotten," he says, "comes back to me, and explains all that we do, and all we suffer." He is indeed a perverted Calvinist, and as both Darrel Abel and Dan Vogel have shown, his story is developed in the full light of Christian and Puritan theological beliefs. It was in connection with *The Scarlet Letter* that Theodore T. Munger made his pregnant statement that "whatever a man does, he does to himself," and it is therefore not surprising that as time passes, Chillingworth should grow "duskier" and "more misshapen" until at last he has become virtually a fiend (at this point surely he is as much an allegorical figure as Pearl ever becomes). Though William H. Nolte, whose charity failed him with Dimmesdale, managed to say a good word for him, only Allan Lefcowitz defends him wholeheartedly; most commentators have been contented, for once, to leave a character where Hawthorne placed him. The author's insight was sound however when he killed him off within a year of Dimmesdale's death. What was there left for him to live for? And what could have been more suitable than that he should have "almost vanished from mortal sight like an uprooted weed that lies wilting in the sun"? It may be that evil is negative, not positive, being only the absence of good, but falling in hate can be as overwhelming an experience as falling in love; it is fortunate that it occurs much more rarely.[40]

"What we did had a consecration of its own," Hester tells Dimmesdale in the forest, but it is clear enough that though Hawthorne viewed what had happened with complete sympathy and understanding, he did not agree with her. Surely Dante himself might have been satisfied with Hawthorne's considered pronouncement in chapter 18: "And be the stern and sad truth spoken, that the breach which guilt has made into the human soul is never, in this mortal state, repaired." Even in her final phase, living a virtually saintly life, Hester "had long since recognized the impossibility that any mission of divine and mysterious truth should be confided to a woman stained with sin, bowed down with shame, or even burdened with a lifelong sorrow."

Yet while this is what *The Scarlet Letter* "means," it also means more than this or any other formulation; otherwise it would not be a work of art but a sermon; we could stop with the formulation and dispense with the art altogether. As Edward Stone observes, the novel, like life itself, has "many morals." The adultery is over and done with before the book begins, what Herbert Gorman long ago called "a triangle after the event," and, as Woodberry had even earlier remarked, "the love problem is never solved."[41]

Interpretations of works of art are necessary, but no critic can formulate more than he has been able to perceive, and *The Scarlet Letter* is greater than any interpretation of it. That is why it has outlived so many and may be trusted to outlive so many more.[42]

The House of the Seven Gables

The House of the Seven Gables was written at Lenox, Massachusetts, while Herman Melville was writing *Moby-Dick* nearby. By August 1850 Fields was pressing Hawthorne for copy. By November the author thought he was in sight of the end, but he did not actually finish until January 26, 1851. Publication, at first contemplated for March 20, was not achieved until April 9, 1851, and by September nearly seven thousand copies had been printed, the initial sale being larger than that of *The Scarlet Letter*. The only unpleasantness, tactfully handled by Hawthorne, came from a member of a real-life Pycheon family, of whose existence the author had been unaware, who accused him of having libeled the clan.[43]

Hawthorne had pondered various possible titles for his new romance. At one point he tended to favor "The Seven Gables," since "it would puzzle the devil to tell what it means." "Maule's Well" was another possibility, with "The House of the Seven Gables" as a subtitle. Both then and later he tended to prefer the new book to *The Scarlet Letter* as less gloomy, "a work more characteristic of my mind, and more proper and natural for me to write." But he also found that it required "more care and thought" and that he had "to wait oftener for a mood. *The Scarlet Letter* being all in one tone, I had only to set my pitch, and could then go on interminably." Now he was trying

to diffuse thought and imagination through the opaque substance of today, and thus to make it a bright transparency; to spiritualize the burden that began to weigh so heavily; to seek, resolutely, the true and indestructible value that lay hidden in the petty and wearisome incidents, and ordinary characters, with which I was now conversant.

Inevitably, "romantic improbabilities become more glaring" when "brought so close to the present time," and there were times when his whole enterprise seemed to Hawthorne an absurdity. Then he had to comfort himself by trying to remember that

in writing a romance, a man is always, or ought to be, careering on the utmost verge of a precipitous absurdity, and the skill lies in coming as close as possible without actually tumbling over.

But though the main action of *The House of the Seven Gables* is set in Hawthorne's present, this is a present brooded over not only by the past but by the wrongs of the past. "God," cried old Maule upon the scaffold, just before he was hanged for witchcraft, pointing his finger at Colonel Pyncheon, whose greed for his land had brought Maule to his doom, "God will give him blood to drink!"—and the story is essentially an attempt "to connect a bygone time with the very present that is flitting away from us."

The piece is played with muted strings throughout, in a minor key. It makes no attempt to reach the depths of pity and terror at which *The Scarlet Letter* had been aimed, and there is a delightful strain of humor running through it. Nothing much happens for a long time; then, toward the close, events rush rapidly by, with some admixture of melodrama, and neither the deus ex machina nor the conventional happy ending is scorned. Henry James found *The House of Seven Gables* "a rich, delightful, imaginative work, larger and more various than its companions," rich in "tone and density of detail," conveying the impression of a summer afternoon in a New England town, yet "full of all sorts of deep intentions" and "interwoven threads of suggestion." But he also thought it "more like a prologue to a great novel than a great novel itself," and it left on his mind the impression of "a magnificent fragment."

Yet in the last analysis one is less impressed by the variety of its materials and variations of tone than by the way its seemingly slight frame somehow manages to accommodate them. Hawthorne himself told Fields while he was still writing that many passages in the book "ought to be finished with the minuteness of a Dutch picture," and in the story itself he apologizes to the reader for regaling him with "details so minute, and incidents apparently so trifling." It is true that many pages are filled with minute notations of everyday life in Salem. Good examples are the scenes in the Pyncheon henyard, the description of the organ-grinder and his monkey, the interior of the cent shop that Hepzibah opens in the House of the Seven Gables, and, perhaps best of all, the elegant breakfast she serves her brother when he has been restored to her after his long, cruel, unjust incarceration. But none of this is permitted to get in the way of a generous use of Gothic properties, well summed up by Philip Young:

a portrait with magic reactions, a secret spring behind it, a hidden document, a secret drawer, the rumor of a buried fortune in English guineas, ghostly music presaging death, a "strange Grimalkin" that haunts the garden, the sorcery of the Maules, a mysterious crime, a dark wrong, somewhere in the past, an hereditary curse—"blood to drink."[44]

In the eerie chapter 18, so different in tone from the rest of the book, the author almost gloats over the corpse of the evil Judge Pyncheon, who has choked on his own blood, in the same manner and in the very chair where his ancestor the Colonel had died on the day of his housewarming; indeed Hawthorne so revels in the denunciatory, essaylike style he adopts here that the reader is almost constrained to adopt the view that the Judge's original was the Reverend Charles W. Upham, who had been influential in effecting his removal from the Custom House.

Early readers of *The House of the Seven Gables* saw it as an episodic or meandering book; more recent critics have discerned, or fancied that they discerned, a tighter structure. Thus Darrel Abel and Arthur E. Waterman favor a kind of five-part symphonic structure, while William B. Dillingham prefers a tripartite division.[45] The general narrative method is that of the omniscient author. There is less "scene" and less dialogue than in *The Scarlet Letter,* and there is much direct analysis, sometimes running off into generalization. The author is never rigidly consistent in matters of technique, nor does he hesitate to limit the narrator's knowledge where such limitation serves his convenience. He presents himself frankly as the author of a story, yet he analyzes Judge Pyncheon as if he were a creature of flesh and blood, and when Hepzibah gazes lovingly at Malbone's miniature of her brother Clifford, he remarks casually, "It was once our good fortune to see this picture." He gives us our first view of Clifford through Phoebe's eyes, and when Hepzibah leaves the Judge after her final impassioned interview with him, he holds her up for pages to describe her emotions while she negotiates the few steps she needs to reach Clifford's room. Once at least his commentary is painfully and embarrassingly coy: "Far from us be the indecorum," he exclaims while Hepzibah attires herself for the ordeal of opening her cent shop, "of assisting, even in imagination, at a maiden lady's toilet!"

In his preface Hawthorne "provide[s] himself with a moral,—the truth, namely, that the wrong-doing of one generation lives into the successive ones, and, divesting itself of every temporary advantage, becomes a pure and uncontrollable mischief." Hubert H. Hoeltje surely erred in seeing the author here as "only enjoying an impish fun in thus ironically disarming" those who had found *The Scarlet Letter* immoral,[46] for the tendency of the narrative does support Hawthorne's claim. But the story certainly does not underline this "truth" alone, nor quite as a preacher would do it. Colonel Pyncheon robbed Matthew Maule of both his land and his life and, by building his great house "over an unquiet grave," gave the Maules the power to haunt both his house and his descendants, for Hawthorne believed firmly that "all slavery is reciprocal." It was the victim's son, Thomas Maule, who, as architect, designed the house and hid the deed supporting the extensive Pyncheon land claims in Waldo County, Maine, behind the Colonel's portrait, where it was never found until Holgrave released the secret spring at the end of the story, by which time it had become quite worthless. In Holgrave's story of "Alice Pyncheon" in chapter 13, we learn how the son of Thomas, a second Matthew, revenged his family upon the eighteenth-century Pyncheon, Gervayse, by using the man's own greed to get his daughter Alice into Maule's power and at last, only half intentionally, causing her death. The villain in the main action of our tale, Judge Pyncheon, is "the old Pyncheon," that is, the Colonel, "come alive." When his uncle died, he managed to fasten suspicion of murder upon his cousin Clifford, who would otherwise have inherited, and to get him shut up in the prison from which he has only been released at the time of our story. Even now, mistakenly believing Clifford to know where the lost deed is, he was planning when death stayed his hand to pry the secret out of him and have him shut up in an asylum if he fails to cooperate. In the very last chapter Hawthorne virtually repeats the very sternest moralizing of *The Scarlet Letter:* "it is a truth . . . that no great mistake, whether acted or endured, in our mortal sphere, is ever really set right." This is quite true for Clifford and Hepzibah, for though the happy ending of the book leaves them alive and prosperous, nothing can restore to them the years of privation and suffering they have endured; for them Emerson's famous law of compensation has failed to operate.

The difficulty with Hawthorne's "moral," then, is not that it is wrong or ironical but that it inadequately covers a book in which the importance of engaging in "the united struggle of mankind" is quite as heavily stressed as the irrevocability of wrongdoing. Hepzibah suffers agony when poverty causes her to violate her traditional and conventional gentility by engaging in trade, but the immediate result is a temporary "invigorating breath of a fresh outward atmosphere, after the long torpor and monotonous seclusion of her life" and "the healthiest glow" she had known in years. Poor Clifford is further gone than she is; he will never be good for much now beyond blowing bubbles. The attempt he and Hepzibah make to go to church proves abortive; if he had really flung himself through the arched window in his attempt to plunge into the stream of life, he would only have been killed; his half-mad eloquence during the aimless train ride from which he and his sister so aimlessly return is mere nervous hysteria. But Hawthorne's point remains valid; he knew the meaning of "reverence for life" long before Albert Schweitzer framed the phrase.

Life is made up of marble and mud, and without the deeper trust in a comprehensive sympathy above us, we might hence be led to suspect the insult of a sneer, as well as an immitigable frown, on the iron countenance of fate. What is called poetic insight is the gift of discerning, in this sphere of strangely mingled elements, the beauty and majesty which are compelled to assume a garb so sordid.

Donald Swanson has remarked that "a full study of the sources of the characters and incidents of *The House of the Seven Gables* would comprise a volume at least as extensive as the romance itself."[47] The guilt of his ancestors in persecuting Quakers and alleged witches haunted Hawthorne, and a Quaker who suffered in 1669 was named Thomas Maule. Sarah Good's dying curse—"You are a liar . . . . I am no more a witch than you are a wizard—and if you take away my life, God will give you blood to drink"—was actually addressed to the Reverend Nicholas Noyes, but tradition had confused him with Judge Hathorne. The family had extensive land claims in and about what is now Raymond, Maine, but the title deeds were lost and not found again until time had made them worthless. A feud between the Hathornes and the Englishes, going back to colonial times, was ended, like the Maule-Pyncheon feud, by the marriage of two descendants. Clifford Pyncheon's supposed murder of his uncle may have been suggested by the murder of Captain John White, of Salem, in 1830, in which Clifford Crowninshield, a connection of the Hawthornes, was involved.

Great-uncle Ebenezer Hathorne anticipated some of Holgrave's more radical notions. Hawthorne's cousin, Susan Ingersoll, who lived in the house on Turner Street now known as "The House of the Seven Gables," which thousands of Americans visit every year under the mistaken notion, not locally discouraged, that they are viewing the actual scene of Hawthorne's story, may have contributed something to Hepzibah (it is interesting that Colonel John Hathorne once tried to take the house away from her). Uncle Venner may derive from one Uncle Trench, who sold root beer and gingerbread to the Bowdoin College boys, and even little Ned Higgins, the mighty devourer of gingerbread dromedaries, locomotives, and whatnot in

Hepzibah's cent shop, whose periodic appearances contribute both humor and charm and perhaps even contribute to structure, may have originated with a four-year-old whom Hawthorne observed at North Adams. The resemblances between the estate of General Henry Knox in Waldo County, which Hawthorne visited in 1837, and the Pyncheon estate seem to me less close than some have found them, but the station at which Clifford and Hepzibah disembark after their wild train journey is unmistakably the Newcastle station on the Boston and Maine.[48]

The oldest literary source that has been suggested is the *Oresteia* of Aeschylus, with which James W. Mathews found a rather surprising number of resemblances. Hazel T. Emry drew six parallels between the *Seven Gables* and *The Faerie Queene,* finding in Spenser not only "exact imaginative details" but "what is more important a pattern of meaning" that served Hawthorne well. The germ of Hepzibah's shop seems to lie in Irving's "Dolph Heylinger," and it is hard to see how Hawthorne could have suggested that "the ghostly portrait" in Holgrave's story of "Alice Pyncheon" was "averred . . . to have shown itself on the point of descending bodily from its frame" without thinking of *The Castle of Otranto.* William Charvat has reminded us that Hawthorne was reading Dickens aloud to his wife while writing *Seven Gables* without drawing any conclusion, but Jonathan Arac has found resemblances between Hawthorne's romance and *Dombey and Son* as "social fables." (It seems a pity that *Bleak House* is just a little too late to make it possible for us to see Mr. Tulkinghorn's death scene as an influence upon Judge Pyncheon's!) Maurice Beebe has invoked "The Fall of the House of Usher," noting that Poe first elaborated his theory of totality in his two reviews of *Twice-Told Tales,* and (to pass from literature to art), David Jaffe has suggested that Malbone's miniature of Clifford may be the same artist's miniature of William Magee Seton, which Hawthorne may have seen.[49]

The supernatural is used most freely in *The House of the Seven Gables* in the story of Alice Pyncheon, where, since the narrative is presented as a work of fiction by Holgrave, Hawthorne had a free hand. But we are given cause to believe that the change in the water of Maule's well was more probably caused by the digging of a cellar nearby than by witchcraft, and though legend speaks of "the marks of fingers" on Colonel's Pyncheon's throat and "the print of a bloody hand on his plaited ruff," the way is still left open for the reader to ascribe the bloody death the Pyncheons die to no less mundane a cause than a "predisposition" to apoplexy. Yet even though tradition is generally no more than "wild babble," Hawthorne grants that it "sometimes brings down truth that history has let slip" and that "superstitions, after being steeped in human breath, and passing from lip to lip in manifold operations, through a series of generations, become imbrued with an effect of homely truth." Hepzibah suspects her lodger Holgrave of necromancy "up there in his lonesome chamber," but the closest he ever comes to this is to skirt mesmerism through his art. For all that, Hawthorne clearly thought of mesmerism as a kind of modern equivalent of witchcraft, not without dangers of its own, and for him the artist too was a kind of enchanter.

He shows much less restraint, as all his readers know, in his use of symbolism, which, though not supernatural, still constantly suggests that, as Walter de la Mare expresses it, the senses "can only tell us what they are capable of being sensible of" and that "what we see and hear is only the smallest fraction of what is," and here, I believe, Hawthorne goes far beyond Scott, whom he otherwise so much resembles in his handling of the supernatural. When life blooms anew with the removal of the Pyncheon menace in the death of the evil judge and the reconciliation of the rival houses in the marriage of Holgrave and Phoebe, even the garden shares in the renascence, and the nearly sterile Pyncheon chickens regain their old power to lay eggs. Even Ned Higgins, the mighty devourer of gingerbread, must become a symbol, "the very emblem of old Father Time, both in respect of his all-devouring appetite for men and things, and because he, as well as Time, after ingulfing thus much of creation, looked almost as youthful as if he had been just that moment made."[50]

In the generation with which the reader of *Seven Gables* is primarily concerned there are five important characters: Hepzibah Pyncheon; her brother Clifford; Phoebe, the country cousin who comes to stay with Hepzibah; the jack-of-all-trades (presently daguerreotypist), Holgrave, who is really a Maule and who finally weds Phoebe; and the menace, Judge Pyncheon, whose evil doings could be arrested only by death. Uncle Venner, the hungry urchin Ned Higgins, and the two workingmen, Dixey and his unnamed companion, who pass by the house and comment upon its doings, are essentially chorus characters.

Hepzibah's is probably the finest characterization, offering the most infallible test of Hawthorne's humanity, which he passes triumphantly. She is a gaunt, ugly old maid, with a ridiculous turban and a hideous, nearsighted scowl that belies the kindness of her heart. Her creator was too wise to let her go without touching off her vagaries. She "had fed herself from childhood with the shadowy food of aristocratic reminiscences," and it was a part of her religion "that a lady's hand soils itself irremediably by doing aught for bread." Opening her shop, she refuses money from her first two customers, unable not to continue being a lady for a few minutes longer. In a desperate attempt to entertain her brother, she reads to him with the croaking voice he can hardly bear to hear, from old-fashioned authors in whom he has no interest. At one point she even has "solemn thoughts of thrumming" on the ancient, long-unused harpsichord that looks like a coffin "and accompanying the performance with her voice." It is hard to decide whether this or the moment in which she upsets a tumbler full of child's marbles in her shop and goes down on her old hands and knees to retrieve them is the more humorously observed, but in both instances Hawthorne smiles at her in love. And when she rises in wrath to denounce Judge Pyncheon in defense of her brother, it is no exaggeration to say that she recalls the passages in which Edie Ochiltree and others among Scott's humble and comic characters rise to grandeur. "You are but doing over again," she tells him, "in another shape, what your ancestor before you did, and sending down to your posterity the curse inherited from him!" If the judge were not incapable of shame, and thus irredeemable, her scorn would wither him:

"Give over, I beseech you, this loathsome pretence of affection for your victim! You hate him! Say so like a man! You cherish, at this moment, some black purpose against him in your heart! Speak it out, at once!—or if you hope so to promote it better, hide it till you can triumph in its success! But never speak again of your love for my poor brother! I cannot bear it! It will drive me beyond a woman's decency! It will drive me mad! Forbear! Not another word! It will make me spurn you!"[51]

Hawthorne's portrait of Clifford, though no less carefully painted, is somewhat less sympathetic, even when allowances have been made for our seeing him only when he has become but the wreck of a man, "partly crazy and partly imbecile, a ruin, a failure, as almost everybody is,—though some in less degree, or less perceptibly than their fellows." Clifford was born with what is called "the artistic temperament" by people who do not understand that to nurture and sustain a significant career in any of the arts demands a stamina that few others among the sons of men ever possess. Clifford's own aestheticism never gets beyond a relish for pretty things and a recoil from ugliness. The sight of the organ-grinder's ugly monkey makes him weep, but he is almost equally repelled by the plain face and croaking voice of the devoted sister who would lay down her life for him. "Such a man," says Hawthorne, "should have nothing to do with sorrow; nothing with strife; nothing with the martyrdom which, in an infinite variety of shapes, awaits those who have the heart, and will, and conscience, to fight a battle with the world." Actually there was no need why he should ever have been born, but since he had drawn breath, "it ought always to have been the balmiest of summer air." Instead Providence had placed him "at cross-purposes with the world" and cast him into prison, through no fault of his own, leaving him, upon his emergence, only the wreck of the little he might otherwise have been.

Insofar as he is capable of any vital response to life now, he finds it in Phoebe, who brings light and life and sunshine into the House of the Seven Gables. "He took unfailing note of every charm that appertained to her sex, and saw the ripeness of her lips, and the virginal development of her bosom." But his sentiment for her, "without being paternal, was not less chaste than if she had been his daughter." Except for the febrile, nearly hysterical paean in praise of progress with which he bursts out in the train, the only passion of which he is capable now is a voracious appetite for food. I have said that for his sufferings there was no compensation, but there is one exception to this. If he "had enjoyed the means of cultivating his taste to its utmost perfectibility," the sybaritic side of his nature might well have taken full possession of him and "completely eaten out of filed away his affections."

The Pyncheons have become nearly sterile through inbreeding, motivated by the fear of mating with their inferiors, and neither Clifford nor Hepzibah knows "what love technically means." Even their hens have of late years managed to produce only one chick. Nevertheless sexual rapacity hovers in the background. Colonel Pyncheon wore out three wives, and the Judge finished off his in three or four years, after she had produced one son, who will die conveniently in the last chapter, just in time to enable Phoebe and Holgrave to inherit, leaving the symbolic "Pyncheon bull" the family's only living symbol of fertility. The Judge is a model civil servant and civic leader, an aspirant for the governorship at the time of his death, but his zeal for the public welfare is all facade, and his hypocritical fixed smile (Austin Warren noted that we never see him except from the outside)[52] belies him as clearly as the kindhearted Hepzibah is belied by her frown. There are subtle political and sociological implications in his portrait also. It was not for nothing that Hawthorne, the Jacksonian Democrat, made him a Whig, and Henry Nash Smith has even dared to find in him "a few traits suggesting Daniel Webster."[53] But what Hawthorne thought of him as a sexual being is best conveyed to the reader by the way he makes the ignorant-innocent Phoebe recoil from him when he tries to claim the privilege of an elderly relative for a kiss.[54]

Holgrave, who is actually the only surviving Maule in *The House of the Seven Gables,* is the most complicated character and also the one who experiences the most significant change in the course of the narrative. At the outset the reader hardly knows how better to account for him than does his poor landlady, who not only half suspects him of necromancy but is repelled by his companions,

men with long beards, and dressed in linen blouses, and other such new-fangled and ill-fitting garments; reformers, temperance lecturers, and all manner of cross-looking philanthropists; community-men, and come-outers, . . . who acknowledged no law, and ate no solid food, but lived on the scent of other people's cookery, and turned up their noses at the fare.

Though only twenty-two, he had already been schoolteacher, salesman, editor, peddler, dentist, lecturer, and mesmerist, and was presently a daguerreotypist.[55] He had traveled through Italy, France, and Germany and had lived in a Fourieristic commune. He makes Phoebe uneasy by seeming "to unsettle everything" around her and by his "lack of reverence for what was fixed," and he delivers a long diatribe against the tyranny of the past, opposing not only the inheritance of property but even the building of houses substantial enough to outlast their builders.[56] More seriously still, from Phoebe's point of view and from Hawthorne's, "he was too calm and cool an observer to be a sympathetic human being:

"You talk as if this house were a theatre [she tells him], and you seem to look at Hepzibah's and Clifford's misfortunes, and those of generations before them, as a tragedy, such as I have seen acted in the hall of a country hotel, only the present one appears to be played exclusively for your amusement. I do not like this. The play costs the performers too much, and the audience is too cold-hearted."

The great change, by which he saves himself and at last enriches her, comes at the beginning of chapter 14. Having read Phoebe his story of Alice Pyncheon, Holgrave perceives that he has put her into a state in which he could control her mind and spirit, much as Matthew Maule controlled that of Alice. "To a disposition like Holgrave's, at once speculative and active, there is no temptation so great as the opportunity of acquiring empire over the human spirit; nor any idea more seductive to a young man than to become the arbiter of a young girl's destiny." But Holgrave resolutely turns away from this temptation; Michael T. Gilmore goes so far as to call this a conversion experience, in which he "senses as never before his potentiality for evil" and "resists the impulse to become a slaveholder."[57] He joins the human race and thus takes a long step toward achieving the reconciliation with which the story ends.

If Holgrave is the most complicated character, Phoebe is by far the simplest. She is also the moral and spiritual center of the novel (her name in Greek means "shining"), "the only 'complete' character," Maurice Beebe calls her, and she is the one against whom the others are measured. She is health, love, light, and sunshine and flowers are always associated with her. She is "like a prayer," says Hawthorne, and "a religion in herself." But she is too close to being an allegorical figure to be the most successful characterization, and clever people have often managed to misunderstand her.[58]

Only, since she is not purely an allegorical character, she has her limitations. She is no intellectual (after all, intellectuality is *not* the norm), nor does she have much imagination. She inhabits the "Actual," not the "Imaginary," and Hawthorne acknowledges the commonplace side of her nature when he writes that "the path which would best have suited her was the well-worn track of ordinary life; the companions in whom she would most have delighted were such as one encounters at every turn." She was the country cousin of the main Pyncheon line, and her father had married "beneath" him. Like the girl Wordsworth apostrophizes in "It Is a Beauteous Evening, Calm and Free," she is far too modest to be aware of either her own goodness or her spirituality. But when Hepzibah, impressed by "what a nice little body she is," only wishes that she "could be a lady, too," she shows us far more about herself than about the girl. Nor, though Hawthorne does not stress it nor develop it, we must not take our leave of her without noting that her development is not complete until, in the penultimate chapter, "The Flower of Eden," she is introduced to what Joel Porte calls both "active awareness of death" and "knowledge of human evil."[59] Not until then can she accept Holgrave and the larger life into which he can lead her. She has saved him, as Hawthorne believed Sophia Peabody had saved him. It will now be for him to attempt to repay this service.

The change in Holgrave is bound up with the much-discussed happy ending of *The House of the Seven Gables*. He and Phoebe enter into married bliss; the death of the Judge (with that of his only son thrown in for good measure) brings comfort and prosperity to Clifford and Hepzibah; even nature blooms again in the Pyncheon garden. There is no denying that the ending is hurried and summary (once more suggesting Scott), but Joseph Battaglia demonstrated clearly both that the love of Phoebe and Holgrave *had* been prepared for and that Austin Warren was mistaken in his contention that the characters in this novel are static, not interacting with each other nor affecting the progress of the story.[60]

Holgrave's abandonment of his earlier almost revolutionary commitment to progress and his coming into prosperity as a happily married man at the end has also occasioned trouble, but this change too had been clearly foreshadowed as early as chapter 12, where Hawthorne had also taken pains to make his own attitude clear: "As to the main point,—may we never live to doubt it!—as to the better centuries that are coming, the artist was surely right." He was wrong only in supposing that sudden change and emancipation could be forced by the efforts of a brash young man who regarded himself as his own savior and failed to realize that God's patience and providence must be taken into account. Hepzibah had warned the Judge that "God will not let you do the thing you meditate," and Hawthorne himself tells us that "God is the sole worker of realities." "When Holgrave comes . . . to modify his earlier radical position," writes Alfred J. Levy, "it is the result of a well-pointed consistent development. He moves toward a mature awareness of individual prerogative balanced by social and moral responsibility," and Phoebe is "the agent of his maturation."

William B. Dillingham quotes one of Hawthorne's own notebook entries—"To inherit a great fortune. To inherit a great misfortune"—and even finds Hepzibah now destined to "step back upon her pedestal of gentility, there to remain isolated and lost." But perhaps this were to consider too curiously. George Santayana has told us that those who cannot learn from history are condemned to repeat it and absorb its lessons at firsthand, but even this stern dictum seems to leave the door of escape open for those who *can* learn, and that is what Holgrave has done. Not even the Judge's crimes were predestined; his reenactment of the sins of his ancestors was voluntary, and when the last surviving Maule and the last surviving Pyncheon turn their backs upon the past, it is robbed of its power. At the end of *The House of the Seven Gables,* the Judge has been frustrated, and the wrong Colonel Pyncheon did the Maules has been righted so far as this can be achieved now. Even the New Testament does not call money the root of all evil, though it is often misquoted to that effect; it is the *love* of money that is so branded. One may no doubt still argue that since so many intelligent readers of *The House of the Seven Gables* have failed to understand these things, Hawthorne himself may not unreasonably be held to blame for not having driven his point home with sufficient emphasis, but at this date there can at least be no excuse for failing to perceive what he is saying.[61]

The Blithedale Romance

On July 24, 1851, Hawthorne wrote a friend that he had decided to "take the community" as the subject for his next book. The "community" was of course Brook Farm in West Roxbury, Massachusetts, where, as we have seen in chapter 1, he lived from April to November in 1841.[62] On November 23, 1851 he reported that he was about ready to start work. *The Blithedale Romance* was written in the home of Hawthorne's brother-in-law, the educator Horace Mann, in West Newton, Massachusetts, where the Hawthornes were domiciled temporarily, but they moved into The Wayside, in Concord, while it was in press. Hawthorne thought he had finished it on April 30, 1852, writing the preface the next day, but later altered his conclusion and lengthened his manuscript to 201 pages.[63] Titles considered were "Blithedale," "Hollingsworth," "Zenobia," "Priscilla," "Miles Coverdale's Three Friends," "The Veiled Lady," and "The Arcadian Summer." If none of these were used, he thought *The Blithedale Romance* might do. Fields published on July 14, 1852, in an edition of 5,090 copies and sold an English edition to Chapman and Hall. On August 13 a second printing of 2,350 copies followed, but a third small printing did not appear until 1855, and only about 1,000 more copies were produced during the author's lifetime.[64]

Despite the special interest of both Howells and James,[65] to say nothing of Browning and, hypothetically, George Eliot,[66] *The Blithedale Romance* has never been a favorite among Hawthorne's books, though few have been prepared to go the absurd length of the usually sensitive Mark Van Doren, who cavalierly dismisses it with the observation that Coverdale is an "ass," Zenobia's tragedy "trash," and the book without "outstanding virtue of any kind."[67] Howells, the high priest of American realism in his time, speaks of *Blithedale's* "palpitant naturalism" and finds it "nearer a novel than any other fiction of the author," but though one may well agree with James that Zenobia represents "the nearest approach that Hawthorne has made to the complete creation of a person," he is a little hard to follow when he calls a work that contains hardly one completely sympathetic character and ends with the suicide of one of the duo-heroines "delightful," "beautiful," "charming," "the lightest, the brightest, the liveliest" of the author's works, one "told from a more joyous point of view" than the others, and a book whose effect is "to make one think more agreeably of life." Even the title might seem to have been framed in bitter irony unless one goes along with John White's interpretation of "romance" as indicating "a poetic and impractical vision, like a fantastic fairy tale. In this case [he adds], the word functions as a tacit comment by the narrator and perhaps the author on the theme of utopian living."[68]

That *Blithedale* differs notably from Hawthorne's other long fictions is obvious. To misunderstand what happens in *The Scarlet Letter* is possible only for a very gifted critic, but in *Blithedale* almost everything is left to inference; to one reader at least, it is a more difficult novel than anything of James, not excepting *The Sacred Fount*. It has only been during recent years, as obscurity in fiction has come more and more into vogue, that interest in *Blithedale* has notably increased. As far back as 1960, Donald Allen Campbell published, through Yale University Press, a book-length *Critical Analysis of Hawthorne's "Blithedale Romance,"* and since then there have been multitudinous articles, many of which leave the impression that though their author understands the book completely, he is quite sure nobody else does, though in at least two cases he cannot read Hollingsworth's name correctly. It is no wonder that when Frederick C. Crews published *The Sins of the Fathers* through Oxford University Press in 1966, he was no longer able to agree with what he had written in "A New Reading of *The Blithedale Romance*" nine years before.[69]

Blithedale is the only one of Hawthorne's novels that employs a first-person narrator, partially anticipating James's own later preference for seeing and telling his tale "through the opportunity and sensibility of some more or less detached, some not strictly involved, though thoroughly interested and intelligent, witness or reporter." Yet Coverdale is not exactly that either, for in the end he is sufficiently caught up in the action so that some readers have held him partly responsible for the tragic denouement. Serious questions have been raised too about his reliability, both as narrator and observer. Generally speaking, he cues the reader in on his understanding of the others as he evolves it; even his report of the final, fatal encounter between Hollingsworth and Zenobia is incomplete because he does not arrive until a half hour after it has begun. Yet there are places where he almost assumes foreknowledge of what has not yet occurred, and he frankly admits that the important interpolated narratives, "Fauntleroy" and "Zenobia's Legend," are his own, partly imaginative reconstructions of what he has been told.

Everything in *The Blithedale Romance* is shrouded in mystery, so that sometimes Hawthorne seems to have taken almost as much pains to conceal his meaning as he might have taken to make it clear. Sometimes the inferences we need to make are fairly easy to draw, but sometimes too they are difficult or impossible. Priscilla, whose apparently genuine psychic powers have been exploited by the diabolical Westervelt, is, in her public aspect, literally a "Veiled Lady." Her father, the derelict Old Moodie, who was once the criminal spendthrift Fauntleroy, seems to be hiding behind his eye patch, and Westervelt himself finds a disguise in his false teeth and the sinisterly handsome face that looks as if it "might be removed like a mask." Does Coverdale's name refer primarily to his character or to the author's technique? As for Zenobia, we learn who she is, but we never learn her real name, for "Zenobia" is only the pseudonym she employs for her undistinguished writing. What is the nature of Westervelt's hold over her? Has she been his wife or his mistress or neither? and how and to what extent has he contributed to turning the taste of life bitter in her mouth? Since she certainly does not love him now, why does she cooperate with him in regaining his hold over her half sister, Priscilla? Is she malevolent toward the girl or does she merely wish to push her out of the way so that she cannot interfere with Zenobia's own designs upon Hollingsworth? Is Old Moodie responsible for the ruin of her fortune at the end, and if he was responsible, just how did he, in his condition and position, bring it about?

It is remarkable that, in spite of all this mystery mongering, or alongside of it, the book should contain so much more and so much more realistic dialogue than its predecessors; as Brodhead has remarked, the reader gets "an immediacy of involvement" that is new in Hawthorne. This being true, it is not surprising that there should be so much more sexual awareness. Hester Prynne has been branded an adulteress; Zenobia has not. But we are never conscious of Hester's body as Coverdale, from their first encounter, makes us aware not only of Zenobia's womanliness but of her femaleness. Irving Howe calls her "the frankest embodiment of sexuality in Hawthorne's work," "a kind of earth goddess," and "a very intellectual one too."[70] This is not only or primarily because of her own playful statement that she does not plan to assume "the garb of Eden" at Blithedale until after May Day, nor even because Coverdale rejoices in "the glimpse of her white shoulder" that stimulates him to picture her unclothed. Though there is no grossness about her, her whole personality is sexual—her warmth, her freedom, her theatrical ways—and he speculates as to whether she has "lived and loved." He is sure that "there is no folded petal, no latent dewdrop, in this perfectly developed rose!"

One critic has gone so far as to describe *Blithedale* as Coverdale's "interior monologue";[71] however this may be, there can be no doubt that he is telling his story many years after he and his friends have quitted Blithedale (only the final chapter concerns his life at the time of the telling), so that what we get is a double view, his account of his experiences at Blithedale and how they appeared to him afterwards. In chapter 16 he leaves temporarily, and chapters 17–23 take place in Boston. In his last section, the book becomes "another story," and it must be admitted that the long arm of coincidence is stretched pretty far when Coverdale just happens to be able to look from his hotel window into the apartment presently inhabited by Zenobia and Priscilla, and from which they depart with Westervelt. There is one peculiarity of the Blithedale narrative itself, however, upon which I have seen no comment whatever. Though Blithedale is a community, to all intents and purposes there are only four people in this book: Zenobia, Priscilla, Hollingsworth, and the narrator himself. Old Moodie and Westervelt make what might be called "guest appearances," and Silas Foster and his wife live at the farm and perform important services for the communitarians without being of them. The presence of the other enthusiasts is simply assumed; we never see them except at the masquerade in chapter 24, and they are not individualized even there. So far as the story is concerned, the community floats in limbo, and our quartet is almost as much on its own as Robinson Crusoe and Friday on their desert island.

Of this much we may be certain, but if we attempt to proceed further, confusion swallows us up. Sir Herbert Tree used to say that every man has the God he deserves. If it is true that every man also has the book he deserves, no book exists in more editions than *The Blithedale Romance*. Taking his cue from Malcolm Cowley's study of *The Scarlet Letter,* Donald Kay works out a five-act structure for *Blithedale*. Vern B. Lentz and Allen F. Stein not only *diagram* the plot but draw the conclusion that the book is wholly deterministic, with the characters free of responsibility for their actions. To John C. Stubbs, Coverdale is simply "witless," the "comic narrator" of tragic events, unable to achieve anything except an ironic effect. For Douglas Hill, Hawthorne not only failed with first-person narrative but was so unmanned by his failure that he was unable to return to "the solid ground of romance" afterwards. Brodhead finds Coverdale reliable in his facts (when he exaggerates, he is quite aware of his exaggerations) but unable to understand his own motives, and Kelley Griffith, Jr., finds his narrative logical up to chapter 15, after which it takes off into the realm of dreams and becomes "a voyage through chaos—mental chaos," with the anchor up. From the more imaginative of these analyses it is a relief to turn to Louis Auchincloss's study, obviously the fruit of his own skill as a practicing novelist.[72]

The sources of *Blithedale* present no particular problem. First in importance by all means stand Hawthorne's memories of his own stay at Brook Farm, the entries he made in his notebook at the time and the letters he wrote to his fiancée, Sophia Peabody, Most of chapter 27, however, the powerful and terrible description of the finding of Zenobia's body in the river, is taken with only minor changes from a later notebook entry (July 1845), describing what must have been one of the most traumatic experiences of Hawthorne's life, his share, during his residence of the Old Manse, in recovering the body of the estimable and unfortunate Martha Hunt from the Concord River.[73]

Many originals have been suggested in connection with Zenobia, Hollingsworth, and others, but there is nothing definite to go on except that Priscilla seems to have derived something from a little seamstress Hawthorne encountered at Brook Farm. The most controversial figure is Margaret Fuller as a possible original for Zenobia. Hawthorne always denied it, but skeptics have suspected him of having had Priscilla receive a letter from Margaret Fuller and of giving her a trick of squinting up her eyes that resembled Margaret's as devices to throw the reader off the track. Zenobia does resemble Margaret Fuller in her eloquence, her feminism, and her aggressiveness. Like Margaret, she talks better than she writes. Though not a suicide, Margaret died by drowning, and there was some scandal about her life in Italy. She never lived at Brook Farm however, though she did visit there, and because she was decidedly plain, Almira Barlow, who was beautiful and who did, has been brought in to account for Zenobia's glamour and the actress Fanny Kemble for her readings from Shakespeare. Hawthorne decidedly disliked Margaret Fuller however, and this creates some difficulty for those who would identify her with Zenobia.

There are many literary references in *Blithedale*. Virgil, Coleridge, Goldsmith, *As You Like It*, *Robinson Crusoe*, and *Candide* are all referred to, as is Dante's wood of the suicides in the "Inferno," though without being actually named in connection with Coverdale's woodland retreat.[74] One writer finds Biblical echoes. The most interesting study in the Elizabethan field is that of John Shroeder, who finds not only "the controlling seasonal metaphor but also the structure of the romance, several of its episodes, and much of the characterization and history of the narrator" modeled upon Spenser's *Shepheards Calender*. Some of the parallels cited seem very close, and Hawthorne's passion for and intimate familiarity with Spenser lends force to this suggestion.[75] Blithedale means "Happy Valley," and Hyatt H. Waggoner suggests resemblances between the mood of Johnson's *Rasselas* and that of Hawthorne's novel. Balzac's *Père Goriot* has been invoked in connection with the history of Fauntleroy and his daughters, and Charles Swann has plausibly suggested that the name may have been taken from the notorious London banker and forger, Henry Fauntleroy, who was hanged in 1834.[76]

Going farther afield, Peter B. Murray has explored resemblances between *Blithedale* and Greek myth, but we are on firmer ground in John C. Hirsh's article about the third-century Queen of Palmyra, Zenobia, and the literary works inspired by her, especially William Ware's *Zenobia, or the Fall of Palmyra* (1837), whose influence upon *Blithedale* he conjecturally champions. Emerson read it, Margaret Fuller reviewed it, and Hawthorne himself mentions it in a letter. But the most interesting suggestion involving nineteenth-century American literature is to be found in Kathryn Whitford's consideration of Ik Marvel's (Donald G. Mitchell's) *Reveries of a Bachelor,* in which she finds "a technique new in American literature which, in a more sophisticated form, could provide the proper narrative distance for *Blithedale,*" citing many passages and defining characteristics from which Hawthorne might reasonably have taken suggestions or by which he could have been stimulated.[77]

When Coverdale arrives at Blithedale in a spring snowstorm, as Hawthorne himself had arrived at Brook Farm, Zenobia is the first of his three friends-to-be (if that is what they should be called) to greet him. She is also, to my way of thinking, the most thoroughly "done" of the characters in the book, a large "admirable figure of a woman, just on the verge of her richest maturity," radiating "bloom, health, and vigor," who would have made an ideal model for painters and sculptors. Her eyes glow, her gestures are "free," and her whole being is "alive with passionate intensity." If there is any one thing through which above all others her personality is projected, it is the exotic tropical flower she wears in her hair, fresh every morning and always different. To Coverdale it seems like a talisman, so that "if you were to snatch it away, she would vanish or be transformed into something else." It is the most effective symbol in a book that embraces also Westervelt's false teeth and snake-headed cane, Priscilla's silk purses, Old Moodie's eye-patch, and many forms of masks, veils, and disguises. Though fresh flowers would have been comparatively easy to get in Boston and much more difficult if not impossible at Blithedale, when Coverdale encounters Zenobia later in the showy city apartment that is overfurnished enough to suggest a fashionable bordello, the flower has become an exquisite piece of jewelry whose effect is to artificialize the woman too and turn her into a work of art. Before she kills herself, she sends it to Priscilla.

Hawthorne makes it quite clear that Zenobia's appeal to Coverdale is sensual, and when Hollingsworth brings Priscilla through the storm, so frail looking that it almost seems she must melt away like the snow maiden of legend, it becomes evident that the older woman's mind is less lovely than her body. When the girl sinks on her knees before her, praying that "she will shelter me" and "let me be always near her," her reception is decidedly chilly. The best Zenobia can do, even after she has had time to think the matter over, is to resolve that "from this moment I will be reasonably kind to her. There is no pleasure in tormenting a person of one's own sex, even if she do favor one with a little more love than one can conveniently dispose of." At this point, to be sure, Priscilla knows that the two are half sisters, and Zenobia does not. But she can hardly be said to treat the girl much better after she has become aware of their relationship, and when she decorates her with wildflowers she carefully ruins the effect by including a malicious weed "of evil odor and ugly aspect."

It does not take Coverdale long to realize that, fascinating though Zenobia is, her culture is superficial and her mind "full of weeds." She is "passionate, luxurious, lacking simplicity, not deeply refined, incapable of pure and perfect taste." She has grown up without adequate guidance, "passionate, self-willed, and impulsive." Her circumstances being what they were, this was not wholly, nor even largely, her fault, but the effect remains. Even her reformist zeal is superficial. Like Coverdale's own, her commitment to Blithedale is halfhearted, and it seems that she has come there only because she wishes to meet Hollingsworth, who has fascinated her as a lecturer, though she has never met him. As a reformer she could make "no scruple of oversetting all human institutions, and scattering them as with a breeze from her fan." Again and again, her theatricality is emphasized, and we are told that she belongs on the stage. She is capable of "the illusion which a great actress flings around her," but because she fails to distinguish between the stage and the world, she becomes the most important member of her own audience and loses control of the effect she herself has created, as the very greatest actors never do. ("Beware of all artists," said Bernard Shaw, "except very great artists.") It is only at the end that, finally seeing Hollingsworth clearly, she comes closest to seeing herself. Yet her theatricality, like Shakespeare's Cleopatra's, remains, and even now Coverdale can complain that she was not "quite simple in her death."

There has always been difference of opinion as to whether Zenobia's suicide is adequately motivated. In life, suicide generally surprises and shocks us, and in art it is likely to be ineffective unless it has been very carefully prepared for. Look back over *Blithedale* with this idea alone in mind, and you will find a superabundance of passages in which a tragic denouement is forecast. But all this is Coverdale speaking many years after the event, and it still leaves open the question whether the woman's desperate act is successfully grounded in her own character, as Hawthorne has drawn it. Myself, I have never been altogether convinced that it was, and I once wrote, more than half seriously, that probably Zenobia had to kill herself so that Hawthorne could make use of his powerful account of his experience with Martha Hunt. In the penultimare chapter Coverdale sums up the case for her—and for Hawthorne—in a conversation with Westervelt:

"Everything had failed her; prosperity in the world's sense, for her opulence was gone,—the heart's prosperity, in love. And there was a secret burden on her, the nature of which is best known to you. Young as she was, she had tried life fully, had no more to hope, and something perhaps to fear."

Westervelt does not agree, but his opinion on a question involving human sensibility does not seem very important. The question remains open, and every reader must leave it thus or close it as best he can.

I find no evidence to support the suggestion of Lyle H. Justus that Zenobia was crushed by the sudden realization of having wronged Priscilla, and Julian Smith's idea that she was pregnant by Hollingsworth has value only as one more illustration of the now popular indoor sport of ignoring the text in order to read between the lines.[78] There is more to be said however for Terence J. Matheson's argument that Zenobia destroys herself, not, like a betrayed village girl in a ballad, because she has lost Hollingsworth, but because she has lost her self-respect, "the full truth of herself and the extent of her previous self-deception" having at last dawned upon her.[79] We have already seen that she is shallow in her relationship to Blithedale and the Blithedale cause, and Matheson would extend this shallowness to embrace feminism and reformism in general. Except for her complaint against the world's cruelty toward "the woman who swerves one hair's breadth out of the beaten track," and who consequently never sees the world "in its true aspect afterwards," we know nothing for certain about her sexual experience, but we do know that she has surrendered her heart to two very different types of what are colloquially called "he-men," Westervelt and Hollingsworth. When, at Eliot's pulpit, Hollingsworth spouts his classical expression of male chauvinism, Coverdale is shocked by "the intensity of male egotism" he reveals, but Zenobia mildly replies, "Well, be it so. I, at least, have deep cause to think you are right." Clearly she is far from being the strong, independent woman she has fancied herself. Once both Westervelt and Hollingsworth have had their way with her, she might very well have difficulty in going on to live with the woman she now knows herself to be.

James thought the reformer Hollingsworth, with whom both Zenobia and Priscilla fall in love, less successfully characterized than Zenobia herself, and I quite agree. Waggoner finds his name suggesting both "holy" and "worthy," but I find "hollow" quite as reasonable a possibility. It may well be that his characterization was distorted somewhat by Hawthorne's well-known dislike of professional reformers. Some critics indeed have been much more severe than James. Philip Rahv calls him "a mere stick of a character, a travesty as a reformer, and even a worse travesty as a man," and Irving Howe finds him "a dismal failure. He never does anything, he seldom displays any emotional fidelity or complicity, he is rarely given one of those strong human touches which . . . would make more credible his essential inhumanity." This, however, is clearly an overstatement. Hollingsworth has dedicated his life single-mindedly to a benevolent purpose, the reformation of criminals. He begins his day at Blithedale with earnest and sincere prayer. He is revolted by what he considers Fourier's having built his system upon an appeal to the worst elements in human nature. Though he is a strong, shaggy man, an ex-blacksmith whose outer aspect is compared to that of an animal, he nurses Coverdale when he falls sick after his arrival at Blithedale with a tenderness that many women could not match and none surpass. His shortcomings are diametrically opposed to Coverdale's. Coverdale, the uncommitted man, is so capable of seeing both sides of the question that he stands perpetually paralyzed between action and inaction. Hollingsworth, on the other hand, is so devoted to his single cause that he is not only indifferent to everything else but willing to sacrifice everything and

everybody to it. As A. N. Kaul remarks, "his monomaniacal preoccupation with crime is the nineteenth century equivalent of the Puritan preoccupation with sin."[80]

Hollingsworth enters the Blithedale community not because he
believes in it but because he hopes to gain possession of its land for
his own project. He breaks off relations with Coverdale, whom he
professes to love as he has loved few men, because Coverdale will
not enlist heart and soul in his cause, surrendering his own will
absolutely; whoever is not for him, he declares as if he were a god,
is against him. Priscilla obviously attracts him strongly from the
beginning. He "smiled much upon Priscilla," Coverdale tells us—
"more than upon any other person"—and he adds that it often
"amazed me" that he should "show himself so recklessly tender
toward [her], and never once think of the effect which it might have
upon her heart." Though Zenobia did not think so, Priscilla was
obviously the right choice for him, Zenobia herself being much too
strong a woman for him to adjust himself to. What he wanted of a
woman was not that she should share or even understand his motives
but that she should worship him uncritically and serve him. Yet he
would surely have married Zenobia if she had retained control of the
fortune he wished to devote to his work, and it was only after he
learned that this had devolved instead upon Priscilla that, as her sister
rightly perceives and states, he cast her aside like a broken tool. He
would undoubtedly have sacrificed Priscilla quite as decisively as he
sacrifices Zenobia had their positions been reversed.

In our last view of him, as a broken man, he has, in effect,
changed places with his wife, for he is now wholly dependent upon
her care, but he is not yet quite a lost man. In a sense his fall has even
been his rise, for he has given up his hope of reforming criminals to
concentrate upon "one murderer." All this I believe the book makes
quite as clear as anything we learn about Zenobia, and the only
reason I feel James was right in judging hers the more successful
characterization of the two is that Hollingsworth's qualities, though
quite as clearly apprehended intellectually, are less successfully dra-
matized through speech and action.

Priscilla, the little seamstress and psychic, has been generally regarded as what Male calls "the key figure in the story." "Obviously

Hawthorne's redemptive character," says Waggoner; "her love is redemptive so far as the others will let it be." The reader may recall that in an earlier passage I mentioned Phoebe, Hilda, and "perhaps" Priscilla as representing the kind of girl that Hawthorne really liked. That "perhaps" was only meant to indicate that she seems to me to possess rather less force of character than the other two; when, in Boston, Coverdale asks her if she had left Blithedale voluntarily, she replies, "I am blown about like a leaf. I never have any free will." She had been exploited both as a sweatshop worker and, by Westervelt, as a public performer. James, who was not greatly taken by her, remarks that "Hawthorne is rather too fond of Sibylline attributes"; D. H. Lawrence described her as a "little psychic prostitute"; Zenobia regarded her as "the type of womanhood, such as man has spent centuries in making." What is important however is that what all this emphatically does not mean is that we must go along with Barbara F. and Allan B. Lefcowitz, who, in an article that perfectly illustrates both the values and the dangers of "close reading,"[81] use very elegant language to express the monstrous idea that Priscilla's "strangely cloistered past was spent in the practice of sexual activities of less than a pristine or conventionally wholesome nature." The Lefcowitzes are particularly enthralled by the silk purses she makes, whose "peculiar excellence . . . lay in the almost impossibility that any uninitiated person should discover the aperture." Since this is exactly the kind of thing that readers in a Freud-oriented age tend to swallow avidly, it is rather surprising that so few critics seem to have been convinced by it. It is true that Priscilla comes to Blithedale to escape from "an intolerable bondage, from which she must either free herself or perish," but there is no indication that this has been of a sexual character. Nor, even though Stubbs thinks she feared him, is there any reason to believe that Westervelt, bad as he is, tried to use Priscilla sexually or that her old derelict father would have acquiesced if he had. "There was something about Priscilla," we read in the Fauntleroy story, "that calumny could not meddle with; and thus far was she privileged, either by the preponderance of what was spiritual, or the thin and watery blood that left her cheek so pallid." Not even the old gossips of the neighborhood suspect her when Westervelt visits her to groom her for their "act." Surely if she is anything, she is a virgin; her every action and the role assigned to her in the story forbid any other view. Surely too the purses symbolize what Leo B. Levy calls her "inaccessibility" rather than either "covert sexuality" or "concealed guilt"; nor is she ever awakened until she falls in love with Hollingsworth. "Until this point," says Rita K. Gollin, "she has seemed almost disembodied; but her love for Hollingsworth gives her an identity and a hold on reality."

Nevertheless she is not perfect, nor does Hawthorne idealize her out of all semblance of life. It has been rightly remarked that at the end of the book she is the only character who has grown. Who would have supposed that the helpless little girl Hollingsworth brings to the farm at the beginning should end up the protector of a once strong and powerful man? However childish her infatuation for him may have seemed at first, she has accepted responsibility, and her acceptance has paid dividends, as such actions always do. Yet much has passed over her without leaving a trace. That she grieved for her sister's death is disposed of in a sentence: "And deeply grieved, in truth, she was." We do not experience her grief not see any effects of it, and Coverdale tells us why. We had already been told that Priscilla's heart was deep, but of small compass; it had "room for but a very few dearest ones," and now Coverdale recapitulates: "But a character so simply constituted as hers has room only for a single predominant affection." Hollingsworth has simply absorbed all there is of her and everything she has to give. She has nothing left over to react with intensity to anything or anybody else.

Our last character, Miles Coverdale, has drawn an astonishing amount of commentary during recent years, and much of it has been unfavorable. Yet Daniel Hoffman has called him "one of the most interesting and fully revealed characters in American fiction," and so distinguished a Hawthorne scholar as the late Arlin Turner chose him as "the chief character" in the novel and "the one of greatest interest to the author." Since Coverdale is more observer than actor, this would seem to mean that the reflector is more important than the reflected or life itself of value only as raw material for art, which is perhaps what we might expect in a day when novelists seem so introverted as today.[82]

It is interesting that Henry James, who, as already noted, himself made such extensive and impressive use of the semi-attached narrator, and who, in a sense, fathered some of the now dominant tendencies in fiction, little as he would have sympathized with their later developments, found no serious fault in Coverdale, seeing him as "a picture of the contemplative, observant, analytic nature, nursing its fancies, and yet, thanks to an element of strong good sense, not bringing them up to be spoiled children; having little at stake in life, at any given moment, and yet indulging, in imagination, in a good many adventures," and, all in all, "an excellent fellow, to whom one might look, not for any personal performance on a great scale, but for a good deal of generosity of detail." Among later critics, Buford Jones is in virtual agreement with this judgment when he calls Coverdale the one major figure in the book "who is neither consciously malignant nor naively misguided," and Terence J. Matheson is not far from this in his observation that Coverdale is the right narrator for our story because "though sufficiently sensitive to appreciate idealism," he is not the man to have "his head turned by the ideals themselves." Zenobia perceives at the end that he has a heart, as far, she adds, as it goes, and, as has already been noted, he sees through the monstrous egotism of Hollingsworth's chauvinism even when she is infatuated enough to swallow it. It is quite clear that Coverdale is not a bad man; neither is Hollingsworth; nor is Zenobia a bad woman. The only really evil character in the story is Westervelt. The narrator's own retrospective view is that if he erred in his attitude toward his friends, "it was through too much sympathy rather than too little," and though he is an adept at finding noble motives for doing what it merely gives him satisfaction to do, there is something in this, fatuous as he becomes when be berates Zenobia in his thoughts for failing "to appreciate that quality of the intellect and the heart that impelled me . . . to live in other lives, and to endeavor—by generous sympathies, by delicate intuitions, by taking note of things too slight for regard, and by bringing my human spirit into manifold accordance with the companions whom God assigned me—to learn the secret which was hidden even from themselves." A human being does not often get a chance to damn himself more completely than that.

Many readers of *Blithedale* have been puzzled by the uncharacteristic frequency of Hawthorne's references in the opening pages to Coverdale's fondness for alcohol and cigars. This however has not been done idly. Though Coverdale is in no danger of becoming a drunkard, it is clearly intended to indicate the self-indulgent, syba ritic side of his nature. When, after his exposure to the snowstorm, he takes to his bed upon arriving at Blithedale, the weakness thus indicated is more than physical. Having recovered from his temporary enforced isolation from the community, he finds a "hermitage" in the treetops to achieve a similar occasional withdrawal, which is followed, after a time, by a complete relief from the austerities of the farm through retirement temporarily to the comforts and conventionalities of the metropolis. Without this, he is sure, he would lose "the better part of my individuality." Roy R. Male may well be right when he notes that our narrator bears the name of a sixteenth-century translator of the Bible who was not distinguished by his courage or an eagerness to pay a price for his convictions.[83]

That Coverdale realizes his prying is not pretty is shown by the effort he finds it necessary to make in order to justify it to himself! "Thus, as my conscience has often whispered me, I did Hollingsworth a great wrong by prying into his character." Such whispers did not greatly disturb him however. It is from his "hermitage" that he eavesdrops upon Zenobia's conversation with Westervelt, and he is the perfect voyeur when he peers into her Boston apartment from his hotel window. Nor can he be completely cleared of malice in all these activities. He baits Priscilla about Hollingsworth in chapter 14, and his probing of Zenobia in chapter 19 is sufficiently bad mannered so that it richly deserves the rebuke it earns from her who has already dropped her window shade before his eyes like the curtain of a theater. No gossipy old woman in the slums was ever more "catty" in the slang sense of that term than Coverdale is in these scenes.

Coverdale's theatricality is altogether different from Zenobia's, but it is quite as dangerous, for both succeed in deceiving themselves. Not only does he fancy himself the chorus in a play, but he so casts his friends in the drama he is producing under his skull that he actually comes to substitute his idea of them for what they are and at one point begins "to long for a catastrophe." His inability to commit himself is partly, as Robert Stanton says, because "he is afraid both that his faith is foolish and that his skepticism is inhuman," but it is also true that he is just not willing to be inconvenienced. When, in chapter 1, Old Moodie asks him to do him a favor, he replies in effect that he will do it if it is not too much trouble, and the old man promptly withdraws his unspecified request. Later, when Coverdale encounters Westervelt in the woods, he takes up exactly the same attitude, and the fact that Westervelt quite deserves to be repulsed does not make the action less characteristic. Hawthorne takes no chances on the reader's missing this point, for he has Coverdale return to it in the very last chapter and take pains to explain just what kind of man he is:

Yet, were there any cause, in this whole chaos of human struggle, worth a sane man's dying for, and which my death would benefit, then—provided, however, the effort did not involve an unreasonable amount of trouble— methinks I might be bold to offer up my life. If Kossuth, for example, would pitch the battlefield of Hungarian rights within an easy ride of my abode, and choose a mild, sunny morning, after breakfast, for the conflict, Miles Coverdale would gladly be his man, for one brave rush upon the levelled bayonets. Further than that, I should be loath to commit myself.

Coverdale does not mind taking the trouble to ply Old Moodie with liquor however when he wishes to pry some information of interest to himself out of him. "What else could possibly be done for him? How else could he be imbued with energy enough to hope for a happier state hereafter? How else be inspired to say his prayers?"

Though Coverdale is certainly jealous of Hollingsworth's having won the love of both Zenobia and Priscilla, who are indifferent to him, Julian Smith is the only critic who seems to think he should have embraced Hollingsworth's cause, even upon the latter's peremptory terms; most of us must surely find him culpable rather for not informing the community of this borer in their midst. It is Kent Bales however who stands toward him like William B. Nolte to Dimmesdale. Taking off from James's approval, Bales finds that the only reason Coverdale is not universally condemned is that "most readers of Blithedale have been Miles Coverdales, James included"! Mingling "the masochism of self-mockery with sadism," the narrator is "the most deviously, the most decadently selfish" member of the community.[84]

The last sentence and paragraph of Blithedale reads:

I—I myself—was in love—with—PRISCILLA!

This hits the reader with the force and—so far as most readers are concerned—considerably less than the effectiveness of many an

O. Henry surprise ending, and many critics have rejected it out of hand. The principal argument of the skeptics is that what we have been led to believe all along is that Coverdale is in love with Zenobia. He keeps the shoe she lost when going down to the river, and he calls the old women who come to lay her out "tire-women," as if she were a queen. In their last conversation, Zenobia herself tells him it is a pity she did not set herself to win his heart instead of Hollingsworth's: "I think I should have succeeded," The most effective statements of this point of view were both made in 1971, by Ellen E. Morgan and Donald Ross respectively, and both have value, even if we do not share Ross's belief that "the major conflict of the book" is Coverdale's effort "to suppress and to understand two uncontrollable psychological phenomena—sexual desire and dreams."[85]

Though I myself consider the last statement in *Blithedale* ineffective, this is not for the reasons usually given, for I could point out quite as careful preparation for it as for Zenobia's death itself. It is rather because I do not think it necessary to call out the National Guard because a hoodlum has broken into a candy store. Coverdale loves Priscilla *as he is capable of loving,* and he loves Zenobia the same way, each for different qualities. His tragedy in love is simply the old fatal lack of commitment that plagues him everywhere else. Pascal said that while the human must be known in order to be loved, the divine must be loved in order to be known, but this is a false distinction. Love, no less than religion, demands a blind leap into the dark, and the highest compliment that can be paid to a scholar is to say that while he knows the facts of his subject thoroughly, he also knows the secrets that reveal themselves to love alone. Coverdale is Theodore in "Zenobia's Legend"; he will not kiss the lady until he has first raised the veil to look upon her face, and therefore he loses her altogether. More artist than man, and for that very reason inevitably a second-rate artist also, as he himself learns in the end, he cares more for his idea of Priscilla than for the girl herself: "if any mortal cares for her, it is my self, and not even I, for her realities . . . but for the fancy-work with which I have decked her out!" He begins losing her in chapter 1, when he shies away from Old Moodie's veiled request that he take her to Blithedale, though at this point neither he nor the reader knows what he is missing. There is good sense in Louis Auchincloss's observation that had he done this, he might conceivably have won the girl and married her, leaving Zenobia and Hollingsworth to work out their own problem. "The final twist of the ending is that the detached observer helped to cause the tragedy that he thought he was only observing."

The Blithedale Romance in some aspects seems like an almost willfully exasperating book. It never achieves quite the power of *The Scarlet Letter* or the charm of *The House of the Seven Gables*. An odd, minor classic, it seeks out and firmly possesses itself of its own niche. For those who are capable of responding to it, its peculiar fascination never palls, and every time one reads it, one finds something fresh in it.

The Marble Faun

Hawthorne recorded the basic idea for what became *The Marble Faun* in his notebook on July 21, 1858, but did not really get down to producing his first draft until after he had returned to Rome from Florence in October; this was finished in January 1859. In England the author and his family first stopped in London, then moved to Redcar on the Yorkshire coast and thence to Leamington, where the third and final draft of 508 manuscript pages was completed on November 8. The "Conclusion," added by popular demand to clear up some of the mysteries, appeared in the second printing of the English edition and presumably the fourth American printing. The former, under the title *Transformation*, which Hawthorne thought absurd and called Smith and Elder "pigheaded" for using, appeared in three volumes on February 28, 1860, and the latter in Boston on March 7. Actually, as Henry James pointed out, Hawthorne's own final choice of title was no improvement on Smith and Elder's choice, for the book deals with "the living faun, the faun of flesh and blood, the unfortunate Donatello. His marble counterpart is mentioned only in the opening chapter." The English edition went through three printings in two months, and there were 14,500 sets of the two-volume American edition by the end of the year. On the continent of Europe, Baron Tauchnitz also brought out his edition in 1860, and for many years English and American tourists in Italy used it as a standard guidebook. It was no wonder that, in his biography of his father, Julian Hawthorne should describe the *Faun* as "perhaps the most widely read of all Hawthorne's works."

The last novel Hawthorne would ever publish during his lifetime, *The Marble Faun* was not only by all means his longest fiction but also the most complex, elaborate, and ambitious. For the first time he balanced and contrasted two civilizations—old, culturally rich, and, as Hawthorne saw it, corrupt Catholic Europe and young, aspiring, comparatively unspoiled Puritan America. His preoccupation with artists and aesthetic considerations brought the book closer to what cultivated readers in his time considered the proper subject matter of serious fiction than anything else he had written, and the American critic he respected most, Edwin Percy Whipple, called it "the greatest of his works." He himself, as usual, blew hot and cold. He "admired it exceedingly at intervals," but there were times when he thought it all "the most infernal nonsense." Since eight years had passed since he had published a novel, he confided in his publisher Ticknor that he would be reappearing "with all the uncertainties of a new author." Once he told Sophia that the book was based on a foolish idea that nobody would accept, and when readers clamored for the explanation of matters he had never intended to explain, he declared bluntly that "the thing is a failure." This was merely the expression of a temporary mood of discouragement however, and his later considered judgment seems to have been that "if I have written anything well, it should be this Romance; for I have never thought or felt more deeply, or taken more pains."

Into his rich and extensive tapestry, composed of many strands and variegated colors, Hawthorne weaves the story of four lives— Kenyon, Hilda, Miriam, and Donatello—in the artist colony in Rome. Kenyon is a sculptor, and both Hilda and Miriam are painters. The first two of these persons are Americans. Miriam's derivation, though long in doubt, is finally revealed as English, Italian, and Jewish. Donatello, the Count of Monte Beni, is Italian, but he bears an astonishing resemblance to the Faun of Praxiteles and is sufficiently faunlike in character to lend credence to the legend that at some remote time his family had acquired a strain of not strictly human blood. Kenyon loves Hilda and Donatello loves Miriam, both until late in the book, apparently quite in vain.

Miriam is pursued and persecuted by a mysterious and sinister figure from her unexplained past, who has nearly driven her mad before Donatello, out of his devotion to her, flings him off the Tarpeian Rock, where the Romans disposed of traitors. This is the end of the innocence of the Faun, who is forthwith plunged into an agony comparable to that of Dimmesdale after his adultery with Hester Prynne. Hilda, who has accidentally witnessed the murder, commits no sin herself, but the revelation of evil thus vouchsafed her destroys her joy in life. The rest of the story concerns the recovery and maturation of both persons, aided notably by their respective lovers. At the end Hilda and Kenyon plan to return to America and marry, but Donatello is in prison, and we never learn whether or not he and the now-devoted Miriam are finally united.

For all its mystery mongering, *The Marble Faun* introduces its four main characters in chapter 1, quite as directly though not quite so formally, as the principals are introduced in *The Scarlet Letter.* The focus is far from being kept steadily upon all four however. Though Kenyon appears with the others in chapter 1, we see little more of him until chapter 12, and after chapter 23, both Miriam and Hilda disappear while we go with Kenyon to Donatello's tower. At chapter 31 Miriam reappears only to disappear again until chapter 35, and we do not rejoin Hilda, now alone in her tower, until chapter 36. Yet though critics have done their best to find problems in the structure,[86] it moves plausibly enough despite all its fits and starts; the real problems are with the method.

Generally speaking, the story is told by the omniscient author, whose intrusions frequently approach naïveté. Hawthorne begins by introducing the characters "in whose fortunes we should be glad to interest the reader." Donatello's resemblance to the Faun of Praxiteles "forms the keynote of our narrative." As we read on we encounter such asides as "we forebore to speak descriptively of Miriam's beauty earlier in our narrative"; "continuing the conversation which was begun many pages back"; "as all my readers know"; "to make an end of our description"; "thither we must now accompany him"; "what we have been endeavoring to convey"; "but we have already used this simile"; and much more to the same effect. There is also some editorializing that has little or nothing to do with the story, like the dissertation on the differences between the Italian and the American spring in chapter 12.

If this were all, there would be nothing to do save accept it as a convention of story telling more acceptable to the nineteenth century than it is to us. But Hawthorne is not consistent in his omniscience. As John T. Flanagan has remarked, he fails to impose "method, plan, order on his subject" or make the style "consonant with the material," and though his point of view is "ostensibly omniscient, ... it alters from the traditionally objective, third person approach to the editorial first person plural, and, in the conclusion, to the first person singular."[87]

Moreover, though Kenyon never actually becomes the narrator of the *Faun*, as Coverdale is of *The Blithedale Romance*, there are times when he moves at least halfway toward this position. During the long Monte Beni sequence, we see Donatello through his eyes, and towards the end of the story Hawthorne openly cites him as his authority and pretends to have derived his information from him, even though it is perfectly clear that he has told us much that Kenyon could not have known. The truth seems to be that he assumes omniscience when it suits his convenience and arbitrarily limits his knowledge when he wishes to keep his readers in the dark; thus his method in chapter 11, "Fragmentary Sentences," is much like having Coverdale arrive too late at Eliot's Pulpit to hear the whole conversation between Zenobia and Hollingsworth. When he chooses, he is even capable of pretending, à la Defoe and Mrs. Behn, that he is writing history, not fiction, as when he tells us in chapter 36 that engravings of the picture of Hilda as "Innocence, dying of a Bloodstain!" are still extant in the shops. The cat-and-mouse game that Miriam and Donatello play with Kenyon at the end before telling him what they know of Hilda's whereabouts suggests all the fifth-act artificialities of Elizabethan comedy; on the other hand, the hurried, rather indirect account of the murder at the end of chapter 18 seems to me entirely effective.

T. S. Eliot once complained of "all [the] Walter Scott-Mysteries of Udolpho upholstery" of *The Marble Faun*, but there are more serious objections than this. There has never been any really satisfactory reply to the point raised by the London *Saturday Review*, that a "mystery is set before us to unriddle, and at the end the author turns about and asks us what is the good of solving it." No sensible person wants Hawthorne to tell us whether Donatello had furry ears or not, but Miriam's antecedent mystery is another matter. We never learn her true name, nor her exact relationship to her persecutor, nor the nature of the hold he had over her, nor what was the famous scandal in which they were both involved. We are told unequivocally several times that she was innocent, but it is at least a question whether everything else Hawthorne tells us about her, and the aura he casts over her, are entirely in harmony with this. He seems to handle the matter much as he habitually treated the supernatural or as the Romantics in general treated Beatrice Cenci: he could not bear to accuse her, yet he could not quite bring himself to give up the delightful shudder that connected itself with her. What was in the packet that Hilda delivered for her to the evil-omened Palazzo Cenci? and why was she detained by the authorities when she delivered it? Was the priest to whom she had "confessed" in St. Peter's responsible for this? (He appears on the balcony with her when she and Kenyon are finally reunited, but he had previously assured her that there was no need to report the murder to the authorities since they already knew about it.) Why was she released at this point? The best guess is that Miriam and Donatello struck a bargain by giving themselves up in return for her freedom,[88] but this is only a guess. We know that Donatello went to prison and that Miriam did not, but what finally became of them?

There is no overt supernaturalism in *The Marble Faun*, but the suggestion thereof hovers over the book. Miriam strikes the keynote in her description of Donatello at the outset as "not supernatural but just on the verge of nature, and yet within it." It is his almost nonhuman innocence and his startling resemblance to the Faun of Praxiteles that starts off the speculations as to whether furry ears are hidden under his curls and whether or not he may possess a vestigial caudal appendage. Much later a whole chapter is devoted to the legends that have been handed down in his family about the possible union of one of their women with "a sylvan creature, native among the woods," whose characteristics reappear from time to time among their descendants, and even the tower in which he lives is reputed to be haunted. As if Miriam's nemesis were not already sufficiently complicated as a model, a monk, and the curse of her youth, he must rediscover her in the catacombs, where he suggests the "pagan of old Rome, who hid himself in order to spy out and betray the blessed saints who then dwelt and worshipped in these dismal places" and who was condemned to remain there for centuries. After he has been murdered, his body bleeds when the killer approaches it. Hilda, delivering Miriam's packet to the Palazzo Cenci, wonders if she may encounter the ghost of Beatrice there, and at the end Kenyon sets out to search for Hilda in Rome after he has felt her hand "pulling at the silken cord that was connected with his heart-strings" from far away.

But if *The Marble Faun* is sparing of out-and-out supernaturalism, no reader of Hawthorne should need to be told that it is rich in symbolism. Hilda in her tower, tending the Virgin's shrine and attended by her doves, is the most obvious example, but there are many more. When Hawthorne speaks of "an old grapevine . . . clinging fast around a supporting tree" and then adds, "you might twist it to more than one grave purpose," he seems a deliberate symbol-hunter, nor is he much less than that in what he writes of the Laocoön in chapter 43. There have been critics, early and late, who have been unable to resist the temptation to interpret the romance as a sustained allegory, but most readers nowadays tend to agree with Peter A. Obuchowski that though he presents different types of character and experience, Hawthorne, both here and elsewhere, generally keeps his people "from being figures in a morality drama with little signs hanging from their necks announcing The Sensual, The Religious, The Aesthetic, The Moral."[89]

In writing *The Marble Faun* Hawthorne used his European notebooks as freely as he had used his Brook Farm notebooks in writing *The Blithedale Romance*. Nothing seems to have been lost on him, and nothing went to waste; even the bleeding of the dead monk was suggested by what Hawthorne himself had witnessed in the Church of the Capuchins. The basic idea of the Fall comes of course from the Book of Genesis, from Milton, and from the use Christian theology had made of it, and the Faun from classical mythology and specifically from the Praxiteles statue in the Capitol. Miriam borrowed her beauty from the beautiful Jewess Hawthorne saw at the banquet given in his honor on April 7, 1856, by the first Jewish Lord Mayor of London, David (later Sir David) Salomons, and has now been identified as his sister-in-law, Emma Abigail Salomons, daughter of Jacob Montefiore, who was married to Philip Salomons in 1850, when she was seventeen and he fifty-four. She was twenty-three years old when Hawthorne saw her, and she died three years later, eight years before her husband. One scholar has examined the emblem tradition in connection with what he considers "Hawthorne's adoption of its techniques to create the crucial scenes in *The Marble Faun*," and another finds Dantean parallels in chapters 24–35. But except for Hawthorne's use of Beatrice Cenci and possible reference to the Praslin murder case in connection with Miriam's antecedent mystery, the search for sources in this novel has been rewarding mainly in connection with matters of detail.[90]

Thus Hilda's name came from St. Hilda's Abbey at Whitby, which impressed Hawthorne so much that at one time he wished to call his book "Saint Hilda's Shrine," and her "almost perfect independence" in "going fearlessly" about the "mysterious streets" of Rome, "by night or by day," may well have been suggested by the behavior of Mary Louisa Lander, who modeled the author's bust. R. H. Fogle finds "affinities with Coleridge" not only "in Hawthorne's conception of romance" and "the ideas that the book presents," but especially in Hilda, both as artist and as woman." Sacvan Bercovitch finds "An Echo from Cotton Mather" in Miriam's puzzling wedding present to Hilda and, less plausibly, "An Echo from Shakespeare" in Miriam herself. The author acknowledges an obligation to George Sand's *Corinne* in his Fountain of Trevi scene, and if he read Charlotte Brontë's *Villette*, he must certainly have remembered it while writing his "World's Cathedral" chapter. As he himself notes in his preface, he borrowed Paul Akers's statue of the Pearl Diver and Story's Cleopatra to assign them both to Kenyon, and his use of a number of famous European works of art is familiar to all his readers.[91]

What is really interesting in connection with the sources of *The Marble Faun* however is the use Hawthorne made in it of the Cenci tragedy at the end of the sixteenth century and the possible influence of the contemporary Praslin murder case upon him.

In August 1847, in Paris, the Duc de Choiseul-Praslin killed his wife, who seems to have been a jealous and neurotic woman, after

Henriette Deluzy-Desportes had been dismissed as the governess of their children, and shortly thereafter poisoned himself. The case awakened extraordinary interest and indignation in France (as a peer of the realm the murderer had not been arrested), and although Henriette's complicity was never proved, her reputation was ruined. After emigrating to America, she was married to the Reverend Henry Field, brother of Cyrus Field, who laid the Atlantic cable. Until her death in 1875, at the age of sixty-three, she moved in the highest social and intellectual circles, and Hawthorne may very well have met her. When she died, she was lauded by Harriet Beecher Stowe and other notables. Peter Cooper and William Cullen Bryant were among her pallbearers when her funeral services were held in the Madison Square Presbyterian Church, and she was buried in Stockbridge, Massachusetts.

That Miriam's antecedent mystery was derived from Henriette's suspected involvement in the Praslin murder might never have become a part of the *Faun* legend but for Julian Hawthorne's recording that Henry Bright once suggested her to his father as Miriam's original, to which he was supposed to have replied, "Well, I dare say she was. I knew I had some dim recollection of some crime, but I didn't know what." In 1905 Andrew Lang wrote tantalizingly in his *Adventures Among Books,* "I know, now, who Miriam was and who was the haunter of the Catacombs. But perhaps the people are as well without the knowledge of an 'ower true tale' that shook a throne." This could not refer to the Cenci tragedy, but it might to the Praslin case, the agitation over which has been credited with contributing to the Revolution of 1848. Lang's statement, however, seems overdefinite. There is no reason why Hawthorne might not have had both the Praslin and the Cenci murders in mind, and there is nothing in his novel that could have necessitated his thinking about Henriette in any more definite way than his son reported.[92]

Beatrice Cenci, a Roman gentlewoman, was executed in Rome on September 12, 1599, at the age of twenty-two, for having conspired with her stepmother and her brothers to have her father murdered. Thanks largely to the famous portrait by Guido Reni, which "haunted" not only Dickens but the whole nineteenth century, and with which it is hardly an exaggeration to say that Hawthorne fell in love, she became one of the favorite heroines of the Romantic peod. Shelley produced a neo-Elizabethan tragedy about her (*The Cenci*, 1819); Stendhal wrote about her; F. D. Guerrazzi produced a famous novel (*Beatrice Cenci*, 1878); she was an influence upon Melville's *Pierre* (1872) as well as *The Marble Faun*.[93]

Hawthorne's description of the Guido portrait, both in his notes and in the novel is nearly ecstatic. The following passage is from chapter 7 ("Beatrice"):

The picture represented simply a female head; a very youthful, girlish, profoundly beautiful face, enveloped in white drapery, from beneath which strayed a lock or two of what seemed a rich, though hidden luxuriance of auburn hair. The eyes were large and brown, and met those of the spectator, but evidently with a strange, ineffectual effort to escape. There was a little redness about the eyes, very slightly indicated, so that you would question whether or no the girl had been weeping. The whole face was quiet; there was no distortion or disturbance of any single feature; nor was it easy to see why the expression was not cheerful, or why a single touch of the artist's pencil should not brighten it into joyousness. But, in fact, it was the very saddest picture ever painted or conceived; it involved an unfathomable depth of sorrow, the sense of which came to the observer by a sort of intuition. It was a sorrow that removed this beautiful girl out of the sphere of humanity, and set her in a far-off region, the remoteness of which—while yet her face is so close before us—makes us shiver as at a spectre.

A few pages later, in what is perhaps the finest example of Hawthorne's ability to use his objets d'art to reflect and express the character of their viewers, Miriam and Hilda discuss the latter's superlative copy of the picture. Says Hilda in part:

"But while I was painting her, I felt all the time as if she were trying to escape from my gaze. She knows that her sorrow is so strange and so immense, that she ought to be solitary forever, both for the world's sake and her own; and this is the reason we feel such a distance between Beatrice and ourselves, even when our eyes meet hers. It is infinitely heart-breaking to meet her glance, and to feel that nothing can be done to comfort her; neither does she ask help or comfort, knowing the hopelessness of her case better than we do. She is a fallen angel,—fallen, and yet sinless; and it is only this depth of sorrow, with its weight and darkness, that keeps her down upon earth, and brings her within our view even while it sets her beyond our reach."

But Miriam, carrying the burden of her own past misfortune or wrongdoing, cannot quite accept this:

"You deem her sinless?" asked Miriam; "that is not so plain to me. If I can pretend to see at all into that dim region, whence she gazes so strangely and sadly at us, Beatrice's own conscience does not acquit her of something evil, and never to be forgiven!"

To which, after consideration, Hilda replies;

"Ah! . . . I really had quite forgotten Beatrice's history, and was thinking of her only as the picture seems to reveal her character. Yes, yes; it was terrible guilt, an inexpiable crime, and she feels it to be so. Therefore it is that the forlorn creature so longs to elude our eyes, and forever vanish away into nothingness! Her doom is just!"

But later, in chapter 23, after the world has been darkened for Hilda by Donatello's murder, she looks at her picture with new eyes:

Now, opposite the easel hung a looking-glass, in which Beatrice's face and Hilda's were both reflected. In one of her weary, nerveless changes of position, Hilda happened to throw her eyes on the glass, and took in both these images at one unpremeditated glance. She fancied—nor was it without horror—that Beatrice's expression, seen aside and vanishing in a moment, had been depicted in her own face likewise, and flitted from it as timorously. "Am I, too, stained with guilt?" thought the poor girl, hiding her fact in her hands.

A supposed kinship between Miriam and Beatrice Cenci was first suggested by Hawthorne's son-in-law, George P. Lathrop, in 1878 but awaited further development for an article by Louis B. Haselmeyer in 1942, and the fullest and best study of it now available is that of Spencer Hall in 1970. Oddly enough, the generally cautious Randall Stewart chose to go out on a limb on this one:

Her guilt [he wrote of Miriam], is probably incest . . . . The analogy repeatedly implied between the fate of Miriam and that of Beatrice Cenci would suggest that interpretation . . . . Again, in the following passage in which the model addresses Miriam—"Miriam,—for I forbear to speak another name at which these leaves would shiver above our heads . . . "—the name to be supplied would seem to be "daughter" or perhaps "sister."

So far as I know, Frederick C. Crews, in *The Sins of the Fathers*, is the only later writer who has shown any signs of accepting this, and I have no desire to join him. On the other hand, I do agree with Claude M. Simpson, who, in his introduction to *The Marble Faun* in the Centenary Edition, criticizes Hilda's taking Miriam's letter to the Palazzo Cenci as indicating "an awkwardly literal connection" between Miriam and the Cenci. "Even a symbolic parallel between her secret and the incestuous cause of Beatrice's plight would require a harmony of details that Hawthorne does not bother to achieve." On the contrary, in both journal and romance, he writes that the expression of sadness in Guido's picture of Beatrice is the result of "the intimate consciousness of her father's sin that threw its shadow over her."[94]

One of the commonest criticisms made of *The Marble Faun* is that the novel fails to achieve unity because though Hawthorne declared in his preface that "Italy, as the site of his Romance, was chiefly valuable to him as affording a sort of poetic or fairy precinct, where actualities would not be so terribly insisted upon as they are, and must needs be, in America" and that he had tried "merely to write a fanciful story, evolving a thoughtful moral, and did not purpose attempting a portraiture of Italian manners and character," this statement misrepresents his book. Thus Henry James complained that "the action wavers between the streets of Rome, whose literal features the author perpetually sketches, and a vague realm of fancy, in which quite a different verisimilitude prevails," and as late as 1980 Samuel Coale felt not only that Hawthorne was "unable to resolve the clash between Hilda and Rome" but even that "actual Rome overwhelms the fable of the soul's possible growth."[95]

There is some justification for these views. Certainly there is topical material in chapter 15 ("Aesthetic Company"), and chapter 48 ("A Scene in the Corso") is by no means the only one that suggests an Italian travelogue. We may or may not be convinced that Miriam and Donatello would masquerade, as they do toward the close, as peasant and *contadina*, but it is hard to avoid feeling that Hawthorne enjoyed having them do it because it gave him such a perfect excuse to describe the carnival at length.

Yet to stop there is to get it all but the point. If there is anything in the book that is unrealistic, it is the suggestion that Donatello is part faun, but does anybody believe that this might just as well have been presented against a Boston as a Roman background? On the other hand, the book's grappling with the problem of evil is anything but fanciful, and what are Rome's ruins and dirt, her inheritance of ancient crime and present corruption, even her malaria if not symbols of human imperfection and the tragic human condition? The action, says Arnold Goldman, is set "in a complex field of Italian history, past and present. There is not only an evocation of the preclassical and imperial history of Rome and its Christian, Medieval and Renaissance periods; the status of the Papally-dominated, French-governed city is carefully delineated." Along this line, both Goldman and Gary J. Scrimgeour argue reasonably that even some of what are generally seen as the improbabilities of the plot are made believable by a knowledge of the conditions that existed in the police-state Rome of Hawthorne's time, and Sidney P. Moss goes beyond even this in seeing the book as charting "the stages in the moral development of Italy" and perhaps even "the progress of Western man. In this sense . . . the Italian background is a realistic motif of Donatello's spiritual progress."[96]

The importance of Hawthorne's Italian backgrounds is particularly notable in connection with art. It hardly seems necessary to attempt to list here all the painters and sculptors, paintings and statues he mentions in his story. Guido's portrait of Beatrice Cenci and Story's Cleopatra statue have already been noted. "The bronze equestrian statue of Marcus Aurelius" on the Capitoline Hill enters into the narrative, and Miriam and Donatello come together under "the bronze pontiff's benediction" in Perugia marketplace. Sometimes, as in his impassioned description of Sodoma's picture of Christ bound to a pillar in chapter 37 and the connected dissertation on the moral and spiritual limitations of art itself, it is clear that Hawthorne is giving us his own impressions as well as those of his characters. But if there is any one masterpiece with which he fell in love to the same extent that he loved Beatrice, it must be the Venus de Milo, which, unlike the painting, did not torture him with psychological subtleties and moral ambiguities.

I have already referred to Hawthorne's skill in indicating the responses of his characters to works of art as an element in their characterizations. "In conferring an extra dimension upon his characters by associating them with counterparts in the sphere of art," remarks Harry Levin, "Hawthorne resembles Proust." There is nothing but admiration in the innocent Hilda's reaction to Guido's picture of Saint Michael having subdued the demon, but the more sophisticated Miriam finds it unconvincing that he should present so unruffled a front after such a confrontation with evil. After the murder, Fra Angelico is no longer the painter for Donatello, and he sees only Divine Wrath in the stained-glass windows through which for Kenyon shines the Glory of God. For Hilda the galleries in general lose their charm after the sky has been darkened by sin, and even after she has reconciled herself to life, her attitude has changed.

She could not yield herself up to the painter so unreservedly as in times past; her character had developed a sturdier quality, which made her less pliable to the influence of other minds . . . . She had known such a reality, that it taught her to distinguish inevitably the large portion that is unreal, in every work of art. Instructed by sorrow, she felt that there is something beyond almost all which pictorial genius has produced.

Rita K. Gollin has observed that Hawthorne "defines Miriam and Hilda in terms of where they paint, how they paint, and how they respond to paintings." Hawthorne does more than this however. In one of his notebooks he says of a painting that "each man interprets the hieroglyph in his own way," thus recognizing the frankly subjective element in criticism, but he goes beyond this also when he adds that the painter may have "had a meaning" that not only remained unapprehended by any of his critics and even adds that he may have "put forth a riddle without himself knowing the solution." Creation, then, it appears, can sometimes pull itself free of the creator, as when Kenyon, modeling Donatello's bust, catches by accident a character-revealing expression that had eluded all his pains.[97]

Kenyon was called Graydon until Hawthorne had reached chapter 30 in his manuscript. I think Carl Van Doren exaggerates when he describes him as having "only technical duties to perform"[98] (he is far from being merely a utility character), but he certainly calls for much less analysis than the other principals. Though we do sometimes see the others from his point of view, we never enter into his consciousness to the extent that we enter Coverdale's in *Blithedale*. He is more involved in the action than Coverdale; unlike him, he gets his girl. He is more likable also, and there are no problems or important disagreements about him. But for that very reason, nobody has been tempted to find him the most interesting or important character in the book.

Miriam faults him in chapter 14, where she is tempted to confide in him but backs off upon sensing his hesitation to receive her confidence. This seems pardonable under the circumstances however, for he does not really repel her. Her approach has been very sudden, and his immediate, involuntary reaction is quite understandable on the part of a sensitive man. Peter Obuchowski is the critic who has commented upon this most thoughtfully, and though I think he overstates Kenyon's detachment, he rightly accents the importance of his discovery upon unearthing the marble woman in chapter 46 that something else has become more important to him than art. This is the only development he is called upon to undergo in the course of the book, but it is a significant one.

If there are no problems connected with Kenyon, there are plenty in connection with the girl he loves. It may be that our increasing toleration of the gamin and the wanton, in literature and life, indicates an advance in Christian charity, but I must leave to others the interpretation of our increasing impatience with the ideally spotless heroine whose vogue extended from time immemorial well into the nineteenth century and in popular literature considerably beyond it. Hilda gives a handle to her enemies not only by her personal spotlessness but more importantly by her repudiation of Miriam after the murder: "Do not come nearer, Miriam!" Miriam pleads their friendship—"Am I not the same as yesterday?"—and argues that "when a human being has chosen a friend out of all the world, it is only some faithlessness between themselves, rendering intercourse impossible, that can justify either friend in severing the bond." But Hilda will not be moved. Though she prays God to forgive her if she has said "a needlessly cruel word," for her it remains true that when the look of "hatred, triumph, vengeance, and, as it were, joy at some unhoped-for relief" in Miriam's eyes encouraged Donatello to fling the model off the rock, she committed a deed that "darkened the whole sky!"

Clare Goldfarb launches an almost hysterical attack not only upon both Hilda and her lover but even takes in Emerson for good measure, arguing that, in Hilda, Hawthorne "condemns isolationism, and by doing so, he condemns the Emersonian doctrine of self-reliance." (There is nothing like birdshot if you want to bring *something* down.) Peter D. Zivkovic attacks from a different angle. To him it is clear that only the "intellect" of the "orthodox idealistic" Hilda is "isolated and evil" and that "*she* is good," He also perceives clearly that Hawthorne, like Kenyon, is on her side. Hawthorne, in fact, was blinded by her. "She was what the Puritan in him wanted her to be." But by all means the most influential attack upon her has been that of Hyatt H. Waggoner, to whom Hilda is "a lifeless convention lifted bodily from the nineteenth-century romances and the steel engravings of the Christmas gift-books." She is "Mark Twain's conception of Olivia and Hawthorne's of Sophia." She is "completely unbelievable," and "if she can be judged in moral terms at all, she must be considered guilty of a pharisaical form of spiritual pride." "Throughout most of the story she rejects the world because it is sinful while she is perfectly pure."[99]

There is no denying that Hilda fails in friendship toward Miriam in chapter 23, even after we have made all due allowance for the nature of Hawthorne's dialogue, which not only here but elsewhere sometimes tempts us to attribute to priggishness what may be due rather to a somewhat stilted formality. This appears not only in this chapter but again in Hilda's scene with Kenyon in chapter 40, and it involves Kenyon, Miriam, and Donatello, all three, in Perugia marketplace. Unfortunately the gain Hawthorne seemed to have made toward writing lifelike dialogue in *Blithedale* was not carried over into the *Faun*.

For all that, Hilda does fail in chapter 23. When Miriam comes to her, she is no healer of souls. What her critics overlook is that to expect her to function thus at this point is like criticizing somebody who has been almost fatally injured in a traffic accident because she does not rise up forthwith to succor her fellow passengers. At this point in her pilgrimage, Hilda is not the healer. She is the patient. For her, to use an old river term, the bottom has dropped out.

She has been forced to confront life's evil in the most painful possible way for a person of her temperament and inexperience, by finding it in her best friend. I cannot think of any action of which she could be considered capable at this point unless it might be suicide. There was a time when suicides were punished, by arrest and prosecution if they survived and by being buried at the cross-roads with a stake through the heart if they died. But the law has now got beyond this, even if criticism sometimes has not.

Can we be sure that Hilda "rejects the world because it is sinful while she is perfectly pure"? What she says to Miriam is this:

"If I were one of God's angels, with a nature incapable of stain, and gar-ments that could never be spotted, I would keep ever at your side, and try to lead you upward. But I am a poor, lonely girl, whom God has set here in an evil world, and given her a white robe, and bid her wear it back to Him, as white as when she put it on."

The conclusion she draws from this, that she must henceforth avoid Miriam may well be all wrong. For a more sophisticated person or a saint, it certainly would be. But coming from her, in her present condition, it sounds to me much more like humility than arrogance.[100]

Moreover, Hilda does not remain permanently on the level of chapter 23. Though she continues to reject all forms of moral rela-tivism, she is not untroubled by doubt. "Miriam loved me well," she tells herself, "and I failed her at her sorest need." If she learns that sin exists even in sacred art, as well as in Roman history and all human life, she also learns that a picture of the Madonna is not robbed of all value because the painter's mistress sat for it. She comes to recognize *herself* even in the portrait of Beatrice, and when she learns that the doves and the tower and the Virgin's shrine will not alone satisfy her, she turns at last to Kenyon, whose love she has hitherto ignored though not scorned. In a very different manner from Pearl at the end of *The Scarlet Letter,* she gives promise of no longer doing battle with the world but of being a woman in it.

Two minor points must be glanced at before we leave Hilda. The first is her work as a copyist. While still in America, she had painted original pictures, "scenes delicately imagined, lacking, perhaps, the reality which comes only from a close acquaintance with life, but so softly touched with feeling and fancy that you seemed to be looking at humanity with angel eyes." Had she continued along this line, "she might have produced original works worthy to hang in that gallery of native art which, we hope, is destined to extend its rich length through many future centuries." In Europe however she was so overwhelmed by the glory of the great masters all about her that she became a copyist. Generally she did not attempt to reproduce the whole picture. Instead she would select "some high, noble, and delicate portion of it, in which the spirit and essence of the picture culminated." If it had "darkened into an indistinct shadow . . . or had been injured by cleaning or retouched by some profane hand, she seemed to possess the faculty of seeing it in its pristine glory." Sometimes, even, she was "enabled to execute what the great master had conceived in his imagination, but had not perfectly succeeded in putting upon canvas."

Paul Brodtkorb, Jr. remarks that as a copyist Hilda had become a painter of painting, which placed her "at one remove from art, and at a double remove from life," and one cannot deny that this would be suitable enough for her in her then state of development. But it is clear that for Hawthorne this did not quite cover the case. "It strikes us," he writes, "that there is something far higher and nobler in all this . . . than there would have been in . . . the production of works from her own ideas. She chose the better and loftier and more unselfish part, . . . and therefore the world was the richer for this feeble girl." Agree or disagree, it is clear that he conceived her as a copyist of genius. She had the capacity of giving herself to the great masters as the saints give themselves to God, to whom indeed, for her, they built a pathway. Her painting had become less self-expression than a form of devotion. She lent her brush, her hand, her eyes, her intuitions to the masters; through her sensitivity the Spirit of Art extended its sway in the world. It has been said that the finest criticism of a great work of art in any field is another fine creation inspired by it. In this sense, Hilda's copies may be said to have performed the service of a superlatively fine critical interpretation of the pictures she loved.

The other point concerns Hilda's "confession" to the priest in
Saint Peter's Cathedral. It is not a real confession, for she is "a
daughter of the Puritans" as Hawthorne was their son, and she
scorns the idea of receiving absolution from a mortal man. But, as
Nathalia Wright has observed, unlike Hawthorne's other innocents,
she has "vital connections with the past and with the Old World,"
and "it is the confessional which saves her from the greatest peril by
which she is threatened: isolation from her fellows." Her creator
marveled at the wonderful adaptability of the Catholic religion to
human need, but he saw the visible church as riddled with corruption, and there are passages in *The Marble Faun* that must be painful
reading for faithful Catholics.[101] It is only when Hilda has nearly
reached the bottom in her pit of despair that, having nowhere else to
turn, she enters the confessional stall marked PRO ANGLICA LINGUA
in the cathedral. With one exception, the incident seems to me admirably managed. I think the *complete* and *instantaneous* relief she
experiences unconvincing. "For peace had descended upon her like a
dove."

Though Miriam Schaefer is a much more sophisticated and complicated woman than Hilda, much of what must be said about her
has been anticipated under other headings. She is a Dark Lady of
great, somewhat-exotic beauty, whose background and origins are
obscure. Though far from shy, she still has the gift of keeping people
at a distance. An "impossible and impulsive creature" of contradictory and irreconcilable moods, she can be sharp, superior, and ar-
bitrary, as in her treatment of Donatello, whom she considers
"underwitted" and the more fool for his devotion to her. Like the
Byronic hero, she has a cloud on her brow, for she is "burdened with
a doom that she tells to none." She feels that a great evil is hanging
over her. Sometimes she thinks she will go mad over it, and sometimes she fears she will die of it. She says she has been tempted to
fling herself from the Tarpeian Rock, and there is a moment in the
Coliseum scene when she seems utterly beside herself. Yet she thinks
she might still be happy if she could only forget one single day of her
life. Fascinated by the Cenci tragedy and by Guido's picture of
Beatrice, she would like to believe that the girl's sin "may not have
been so great; perhaps it was no sin at all under the circumstances."

If she could but "clasp" the girl's ghost, she would draw it into herself. The pictures she paints are more distinguished by their vivid expression of passion than by technical excellence. She is fond of deriving her subjects from the more sinister characters in Scripture, such as Jael, Judith, and Salome, but when she introduces herself into scenes of domestic life, it is always as a lonely figure, looking on at happiness she cannot share.

The shadow that hangs over her obviously derives from a notorious crime and scandal in which she has been involved. Legally Miriam incurred no guilt, and in chapter 14 she tells Kenyon that her conscience is "still as white as Hilda's." In chapter 47, when she finally tells him the story she had backed off from confiding in him in chapter 14, he clearly agrees with her: "No, you were innocent. I shudder at the fatality that seems to haunt your footsteps, and throws a shadow of crime about your path, you being guiltless." Moreover, the author himself says at one point:

Yes, let us trust, there may have been no crime in Miriam, but only one of those fatalities which are among the most insoluble riddles propounded to mortal comprehension; the fatal decree by which every crime is made to be the agony of many innocent persons, as well as of the single guilty one.

If we are to accept this, then Miriam, sickened by a crime she witnessed but in which she did not share, came closer to Hilda's position after Donatello's murder of the model than has been generally recognized. For all that, we cannot completely rule out the consideration that human beings often "trust" in vain, and if Miriam was wholly innocent, what did Hawthorne mean by writing, when she stands over the model's dead body, that "this form of clay had held the evil spirit which blasted her sweet youth, and compelled her, as it were, to stain her womanhood with crime"?

The one thing we can be quite sure of is that this malign creature, who torments her almost to madness until Donatello relieves her from one form of torture only to replace it with another by killing him, knows something whose revelation could, in one way or another, destroy her. Critics have identified him as her father, her brother, her father's murderer, the depraved kinsman her family wished her to marry, and the killer of this man under circumstances that suggested her complicity. All these suggestions are futile, for Hawthorne has not given us the material we should need to establish or refute any one of them. The various complications he introduces into his treatment of this man are perhaps inconsistent and irreconcilable, but in any case they are impenetrable. The mysterious creature reencounters Miriam and attaches himself to her in the catacombs, where another dimension is added to his portrait by the suggestion that he has been wandering there for fifteen hundred years; later his face appears as the demon in what seems to have been a preliminary sketch, some two hundred years ago, for Guido's picture of Saint Michael. After he comes back into Miriam's life, for all the horror she feels of him, he becomes her model, yet after his death he is found to have been also a Capuchin monk, renowned for his piety. It has been suggested that his motive in haunting Miriam is blackmail, but at one point he tells her that he is not acting of his own free will, that their fates are intertwined, and that nothing either party can do will alter this.

Donatello's destruction of the model was in a sense a sudden impulse, reinforced by what he interpreted as an approving glance from Miriam, but this was not the first time the idea had occurred to him.[102] He had been tempted to drown the man in the Fountain of Trevi, and he had asked Miriam whether the Roman executions at the Tarpeian Rock had been well advised, to which she had replied that they were because they disposed of "men that cumbered the world, . . . whose lives were the bane of their fellow creatures" and who "polluted the air, which is the common breath of all, for their own selfish purposes." But once the scoundrel has been slain, and Donatello's joy in life along with him, she immediately accepts coresponsibility for his death. "Yes, Donatello, you speak the truth! my heart consented to what you did. We two slew yonder wretch." Her honesty here gives us the strongest argument we could ask for to encourage us to believe her when she avers her innocence of the earlier crime of which she had been suspected.

The immediate effect of the murder is a passionate exhilaration that Matthiessen appropriately compared to the "drunkenness . . . of Adam and Eve after the temptation" in *Paradise Lost*. The bond that now binds the two is "closer than a marriage bond," and their new sympathy has "annihilated all other ties." In an instant Donatello has won the love of a woman who had at best tolerated him before. "Surely," she cries, "it is no crime that we have committed. One wretched and worthless life has been sacrificed to cement two other lives for evermore." And Donatello replies, "For evermore, Miriam! cemented with his blood!"

Unfortunately—or perhaps fortunately if their ultimate spiritual condition is to be weighed in the scales—this mood cannot be sustained. Perhaps it might have been if he had been more like her. But he who until now had lived a life limited in scope but perfect within its range had all at once been plunged into the world of moral reality. And even she soon realizes that though they are now bound together, the tie that binds them is like the coils of a serpent. Their "separate sin" has made them "guilty of the whole," and they are both "members of an innumerable confraternity of guilty ones, all shuddering at each other." She faces the issue bravely. "As the case now stands between us, you have bought me dear, and find me of little worth. Fling me away, therefore! May you never need me more! But, if otherwise, a wish—almost an unuttered wish—will bring me back to you!" They part, not to come together again until they receive the bronze pontiff's benediction in Perugia.

For some time she does not repent on her own account. Perhaps she never does. "I put myself out of the question," she tells Kenyon, "and feel neither regret nor penitence on my own account. But what benumbs me, what robs me of power . . . is the certainty that I am, and must ever be, an object of horror in Donatello's sight." Certainly she does *not* feel, as he does, the obligation resting upon him to surrender himself to human justice, for unlike him she is intelligent enough to know that justice exists only with God. Human beings must choose between cruelty and kindness.[103]

Whatever else may be said about her, she is a brave and gallant woman who grows through suffering, and though her development is much less fully traced than Hester Prynne's, she holds the reader's sympathy along with her predecessor. With the exception of one point, the effect of the murder upon her seems to me quite as convincingly drawn as that upon Donatello. But her realization of her overwhelming love for him comes too suddenly to be altogether convincing. I do not say that it could not happen but only that Hawthorne does not quite convince me that it did. Perhaps he felt that a woman *must* love a man who has proved that he loves her enough to kill for her. Perhaps this may even be true. But I do not believe that any *man's* opinion on this point can be worth much—certainly not mine, possibly not even his.

Donatello has inevitably intruded into the foregoing discussion of Miriam; it is time now to move him to stage center. James thought him "rather vague and impalpable" as a character; "he says too little in the book, shows himself too little, and falls short, I think, of being a creation." This seems an overstatement, but I do agree with E. P. Whipple, who, despite his high praise of the *Faun* in general, felt that Hawthorne's failure to make Miriam's persecutor more than "an allegorical representation of evil" made it more difficult for the reader to feel the force of Donatello's sin and consequently of his repentance and redemption. It is hard to realize that he has killed a human being; instead, we are tempted to rejoice "in the hero's victory over the Blatant Beast or Giant Despair." Perhaps this is part of the price a writer must pay for attempting to mingle realistic and allegorical elements in a single work of art.[104]

As we first encounter Donatello, he is "an amiable and sensual creature, easy, mirthful, apt for jollity, yet not incapable of being touched by pathos." Though one would not look to him for "sacrifice or effort for an abstract cause," he might still possess "a capacity for strong and warm attachment, and might act devotedly through its impulse, and even die for it at need." Miriam understands this well enough to warn him that she is dangerous to him. "If you follow my footsteps, they will lead you to no good. You ought to be afraid of me." Even before the murder, he realizes that a change is coming over him. "Methinks there has been a change upon me these many months; and more and more, these last few days . . . . Feel my hand! Is it not very hot? Ah; and my heart burns hotter still!"

His sufferings after the murder, though less powerfully portrayed, are similar in kind to Dimmesdale's in *The Scarlet Letter*. In his agony he almost loses his physical resemblance to the Faun, though as he fights his way back to reconciliation with life, he partially rewins it. "How it was first taught me, I cannot tell; but there was a charm—a voice, a murmur, a kind of chant—by which I called the woodland inhabitants, the furry people, and the feathered people, in a language they seemed to understand." Now only venomous reptiles seem attracted to him. "All nature shrinks from me, and shudders at me! I live in the midst of a curse, that hems me round with a circle of fire!" Had he been less a coward, he might have killed himself; had he been less a hero, he would have perished in the "dark valley," where, as Kenyon warns him, it is dangerous to tarry long. Finally, as Miriam perceives, "he traveled in a circle, as all things heavenly and earthly do, and now comes back to his original self with an inestimable measure of improvement won from an experience of pain." At the end of his tour in Perugia, he "has accepted a place within the community of sinful mortals," and, as Merle Brown says, "is in a state to be saved."

This brings us to the debate over the so-called "fortunate fall," which agitates Miriam, Kenyon, and Hilda, and disturbs the critics even more. Miriam first propounds it to Kenyon at the end of chapter 47: "Was the crime—in which [Donatello] and I were wedded— was it a blessing, in that strange disguise? Was it a means of education, bringing a simple and imperfect nature to a point of feeling and intelligence which it could have reached under no other discipline?" And if the answer be yes, does this mean that the same thing is true of the Fall of Man itself? Was the sin of Adam "the destined means by which, over a long pathway of toil and sorrow, we are to attain a higher, brighter, and profounder happiness, than our lost birthright gave?" To this Kenyon replies that he cannot "follow" her. "It is too dangerous, Miriam! . . . Mortal man has no right to tread on the ground where you now set your feet." Yet he restates the proposition to Hilda: "Sin has educated Donatello, and elevated him. Is sin, then, . . . like sorrow, merely an element of human education, through which we struggle to a higher and purer state than we could otherwise have attained? Did Adam fall, that we might ultimately rise to a far better paradise than his?" Hilda is inexpressibly shocked, as he must have known she would be, and he hastily retreats: "Forgive me, Hilda! . . . I never did believe it . . . . O Hilda, guide me home!"

These are profound, tantalizing, agonizing questions, and Bernard J. Paris conveniently summarizes what the critics have made of them. It has been urged that Hawthorne accepts the view of the fortunate fall, that he rejects it, that he holds it in suspension, and that he accepts it in some respects but not in others.[105]

The one thing we can be sure of in connection with this question is that it is too late in the day to go along with Dorothy Waples's cavalier attempt to settle the question by reading the subject of the *Faun* as "nature softened by a share of guilt," but that Hawthorne "tempers it to the shorn lambs who may read it."[106] The idea of the "fortunate fall" was far from being original with Hawthorne. It occurs in the Exultet for the Holy Saturday Mass: *"O felix culpa quae talem et tantum moruit habere redemptorem."* Milton skirts it in *Paradise Lost,* where Adam muses:

> Full of doubt I stand
> Whether I should repent me now of sin
> By me done and occasioned, or rejoice
> Much more, that much more good thereof shall spring,
> To God more glory, more good will to men
> From God, and over wrath grace shall abound.[107]

But Saint Paul had raised and answered the question long before Milton, in the fifth and sixth chapters of Romans:

Moreover the law entered that the offence might abound. But where sin abounded, grace did much more abound; That as sin hath reigned unto death, even so might grace reign through righteousness unto eternal life by Jesus Christ our Lord. What shall we say then? Shall we continue in sin, that grace may abound? God forbid. How shall we, that are dead to sin, live any longer therein?

For Saint Paul, for the doctors of the church, and even for the great heretic Milton, the fortunate element in the Fall of Man was that it made way for the redemption of mankind through Christ. As Terence Martin has observed, Hawthorne says nothing about this.[108] He was writing a romance, not a theological tract, and as a romancer it was his task not to solve all the moral and theological problems of his readers, but to create his characters and tell us what they made of their experiences and the ideas suggested by them. He could therefore, if he chose, leave the idea of the fortunate fall in suspension and still discharge his full obligations as a romancer. Nevertheless Hawthorne was no iconoclast, and though theology as such did not greatly interest him, he always inclined strongly toward affirmation rather than denial. Obviously the idea of the fortunate fall, whether it concerned Adam and Eve as representatives of mankind or Donatello as an individual, interested him, as it must interest any man who thinks about moral questions at all, and obviously he was interested in having it considered. But it would not be like him to use a romance to propagandize in behalf of a subversive idea. In *The Scarlet Letter* he had refrained from even specifying Hester's heresies. Hawthorne was no primitivist, and it should be remembered that, for all Donatello's charm, his creator had taken pains to make it clear that in the men of Monte Beni, this was likely to pass with youth, being succeeded in later years by "a sensual, surly animality." But Hawthorne was no moral revolutionary either. Much has been made of Kenyon's loverlike subservience to Hilda in withdrawing the idea of a fortunate fall as soon as he has expressed it, but it has gone almost unnoticed that Miriam herself had promptly modified her original proposition. "Ask Hilda what she thinks of it," she tells Kenyon. "At least, she might conclude that sin—which men chose instead of good—has been so beneficently handled by omniscience and omnipotence, that, whereas our dark enemy sought to destroy us by it, it has really become an instrument most effective in the education of intellect and soul." This is a very different proposition from what she had originally suggested. That God can use the wrath of man to praise the Lord is by no means an unorthodox idea, and though God "tempteth no man," no Christian has ever been shocked by what Henry Ward Beecher called God's loving man in his sins for the purpose of helping him out of them.[109]

4

Experiments

The last years of Hawthorne's life, after his return to Concord in 1860, were invested in an agonizing, abortive attempt to write one more romance that he hoped would be his crowning work. Nobody can attempt to write about this period without being deeply indebted to Edward H. Davidson, the unchallenged authority in this field. It was he who dug out the relevant manuscripts from the libraries in which they had been deposited. In 1949 he described them elaborately in *Hawthorne's Last Phase*. In 1954 he published, for the first time, both drafts of *Doctor Grimshawe's Secret,* together with the "studies" the author had made for them, and in 1977 he coedited volumes 12 and 13 of the Centenary Edition of Hawthorne's writings as *The American Claimant Manuscripts* and *The Elixir of Life Manuscripts*. Frederick C. Crews, to be sure, while acknowledging Davidson's scholarship, has labeled his criticism "superficial," but this means only that he is not in line with what the great Elizabethan scholar E. E. Stoll, used to call "the bad news out of Vienna."[1]

Four stories or groups of manuscripts are involved, which will be referred to here, for convenience, by the names by which they are best known. The idea for the first, "The Ancestral Footstep," had come to Hawthorne before he began work on *The Marble Faun,* but he put it on the back burner after his imagination had been fired by seeing the Faun of Praxiteles. What we have was written in April and May 1858, and Rose Hawthorne's husband, George Parsons Lathrop, divided it into three sections and subtitled it "Outlines of an English Romance." It was first published in the *Atlantic Monthly* in 1882–83 and achieved its first book publication in an appendix to volume 11 of the Riverside Edition in 1883.[2] Both drafts of *Grimshawe* were written in Concord, probably in 1861, and

Julian Hawthorne's edition of that story was published in December 1882 and dated ahead to 1883. Julian followed the second draft as far as it carries the story, then turned for his ending to the first (called "Etherege" in the Centenary Edition), shifted the dream vision from the end to the middle, added chapter titles, and did considerable editing. The first complete "generic text" was published in 1954, as already noted, and the Centenary version of 1977 was based, we are told, "on a thorough reexamination of the manuscript" and presented "several hundred new readings." *Septimius Felton,* conjecturally dated 1861–63, also exists in two drafts (the Centenary Edition differentiates between them by calling the second "Septimius Norton"). Continuing the work her late mother had begin, Una Hawthorne, with some counsel from Robert Browning, published the first serially in both the *Atlantic Monthly* and *St. Paul's Magazine* beginning in January 1872, and book publication followed.[3] The much longer "Norton" draft (254 Centenary pages as against 192), which stops shortly after the death of Aunt Nashoba, did not appear in its entirety until it came out in the Centenary Edition in 1977. As for "The Dolliver Romance," Hawthorne's final and, fragmentary though it is, certainly, as far as it goes, the most successful of the efforts he had made to handle his recalcitrant materials, the first part appeared in the *Atlantic* in July 1864 and the second in January 1865, but the third was left to make its first appearance in *The Dolliver Romance and Other Pieces* in 1876. The one encouraging thing about Hawthorne's dreadful struggles during these last years is that he did improve as he went on: *Grimshawe* is better that the "Footstep," *Septimius* is better than *Grimshawe,* and "Dolliver" is better than *Septimius.*[4] Contemporary reviewers compared Hawthorne's unfinished work with that of Dickens (*The Mystery of Edwin Drood*), Thackeray (*Denis Duval*), and the painter Washington Allston (*Belshazzar's Feast*); a little later they might have added Stevenson's *Weir of Hermiston.*[5] Today we are more likely to be reminded of Mark Twain's *The American Claimant* (to say nothing of his many unfinished works) and of both "A Passionate Pilgrim" and *The Sense of the Past* by Henry James.

Hawthorne's methods and technique in story telling are not radically different in these last writings from what they had always been. He can use omniscience when it suits his convenience or limit his knowledge when this serves his purpose better. His narrative had always been mainly "an internal one," as he says in *Septimius Felton,* where the "central object" of the story being merely "to record the dreams, or realities, whichever they might be, of a young man who stakes whatever prospects he had in life upon a strange pursuit," historic events were alluded to "only because it was unavoidable," and, in the "Norton" draft especially, he came pretty close to "not really caring much for anything that took place outside Septimius's brain." Yet he accounts for some of his knowledge by telling the reader that there is "in our possession" some portions of the manuscript of Francis Norton, the young British officer Septimius kills, "as transcribed" by the hero. On the other hand, the circumstances of Felton's enlistment of Sibyl Dacy as his companion in quest of the formula to ensure earthly immortality is "not upon record" nor his ultimate fate within the narrator's knowledge, and in "Dolliver" he has "not ascertained" how the little girl "came by the odd name of Pansie."

The prose, however, is considerably less taut and, at least as Hawthorne left the manuscripts, less clear than it had been in his prime, and if he ever deserves Mark Twain's complaint that he "analyzes the guts out" of his materials, it is in some of what we have here. There are places too where the author's own intrusions into his narrative seem gauche: "We shall attach our story to the consciousness of this person." "As Dr. Dolliver . . . is likely to remain a considerable time longer upon our hands, we deem it expedient to give a brief sketch of his position, in order that the story may get onward with the greater freedom when he rises from the breakfast table." Because he would like to be done with the doctor's antagonist, Colonel Dabney, Hawthorne is glad he "happened to die at so early a period of the narrative." Still more intrusive is the apologetic observation that if Septimius had destroyed the recipe for immortality, the author would "have been spared the pain of relating" such "strange and gloomy passages."

Though there is more Gothic machinery in these final narratives than Hawthorne had used before, his attitude toward the supernatural remains what it had always been. He cherishes it because it stimulates his imagination, but he will not quite commit himself to believing in it. It was the ignorant who saw Doctor Grimshawe's pet spider as his familiar. The path that Septimius wore upon the hill above the Wayside by walking up and down there was only reputed to be due to some "unnaturalness" or unholiness in himself; some whispered that the ghost of the old Sagamore, his ancestor, walked with him there; some believed that he called upon the Devil; and still others "said that by certain exorcisms he had caused the appearance of a battle in the air." Sibyl Dacy too was invested with a certain supernatural coloring, as when she warned Septimius not to touch her, as he might not find her flesh and blood. To the sensible Rose Garfield, Sibyl is only a "poor brain-stricken girl," but Septimius himself was half inclined to see her as "a thing of witchcraft, a sort of fungus-growth out of the grave, an unsubstantiality altogether." As for Septimius's Aunt Keziah (or Nashoba), she is "an awful mixture of the Indian squaw and herb-doctress, with the dry old maid of New England pattern, and a sort of wild witch-aspect running through the whole, and a skin as yellow as gold, being either the hue of her Indian intermixed blood, or else the effect of her herb-drink; and she looked, moreover, as forbidding as if she were a dragon guarding the threshold." She admits that this terrible drink that nobody else can bear to taste lacks the one ingredient it would need to confer immortality, but she sips it all day long, liberally laced with liquor, and smokes the iron pipe inherited from a witchlike ancestor. That she had sold herself to the Black Man she categorically denies, but though she prides herself upon her church membership, she admits at the end that she would have liked to be a witch and that she is inclined to regret the good times she might have had with the coven; in the "Norton" draft, she does not wish to be with "other Christian people" after she dies but with "great-aunt Tituba, and perhaps with Old Bloody Foot himself, if he is there." She seems indeed as complicated a mixture of good and evil as Doctor Grimshawe himself, though I am not quite sure whether her characterization is less successful than his or whether her complications may be due to the confusion of the manuscripts themselves.

There is assuredly no shortage of the Hawthornian image or symbol in these stories, and except that there are too many such for any writer to be able to handle effectively, there is nothing essentially wrong with the symbols as such. The bloody footprint, the elixir, the spider, the key, even the golden ringlets into which a dead woman's body is supposed to have been completely absorbed—any of these and others might, under altered circumstances, have been handled as effectively as the more successful symbols or images in his other books. Unfortunately, however, Hawthorne was never able to make up his mind just what he wished to do with them. There is a half-hearted attempt to make the spider represent Grimshawe's "craft and wickedness," but Grimshawe is far from being consistently an evil character, and when he dies the spider is reduced to an empty shell. In *Dolliver* the Brazen Serpent as an apothecary's sign is introduced as if it were to be a symbol of evil, but nothing comes of this. Even Edward M. Clay, who makes the bravest attempt to find "The Dominating Symbol in Hawthorne's Last Phase,"[6] is forced to admit at last that the "unified symbolic pattern" he has done his best to establish in *Septimius Felton* at least is "only apparent." Hawthorne, he concludes "can no longer maintain confidence in a symbol long enough for it to develop."

Whether or not there is a "dominating symbol" in the romances however, there can be no doubt that the bloody footprint is the one that spawned the largest number of variations. Essentially it belongs to the American claimant group, but it intrudes into the elixir tales also. Hawthorne first heard of it in April 1855, when Mrs. Ainsworth of Smithell's Hall in Lancashire told him of George Marsh, a Protestant martyr of "Bloody Mary's" time, who was burned for heresy in 1555.

Being examined before the then occupant of the Hall and committed to prison, [he] stamped his foot in earnest protest against the injustice with which he was treated. Blood issued from his foot, which slid along the stone pavement of the hall, leaving a long footmark printed in blood; and there it has remained ever since, in spite of the scrubbings of all after generations.

In August Hawthorne saw it, "a dark brown stain in the smooth gray surface of the flagstone." With his customary skepticism, he tried to figure out a rationalistic explanation, and with his customary appetite for wonders, he concluded that "at any rate, the legend is a good one."

A much more elaborate medieval version is related by Sibyl Dacy in the "Norton" draft of *Septimius Felton*. The central figure here is a nobleman who, like Septimius, is engaged in the quest for the elixir of immortality, but since he was "a man of loving and noble nature," for altruistic motives, to do good to the world. Like Bernard Shaw, in his *Back to Methuselah* phase, he thought the normal life span too short to accomplish anything; "continually there have to be new beginnings, and it takes every man half his life, if not the whole of it, to come up to the point where his predecessors left off." His quest succeeds, but a terrible condition is attached: he must pay nature another life, that of "a pure young girl" whom he dearly loves. So good as to be "quite unfit for this world," she gladly agrees to the sacrifice, but he accidentally sets his right foot in her blood and thereafter leaves a bloody track behind him, wherever he goes. Elsewhere we hear of a regicide who stepped in the blood of King Charles I with equally horrible effect and of an Indian sagamore who had drunk so much of the blood of his enemies that it oozed out of him, and much more besides, some of which is only hinted at in Hawthorne's notes and studies.

The basic difficulty with all this seems to have been that Hawthorne's way with symbols had ceased to work for him. When Dickens was asked about the origin of *The Pickwick Papers,* he replied that he "thought of Mr. Pickwick." As I have written elsewhere, in that sense Hawthorne never "thought" of any character. When he set to work on a story, first came the "meaning" or the idea. Next came the symbol or image in which the idea was to be embodied and through which it was to be expressed, and the characters in whom all this must be acted out followed last of all. When it worked, as it did in *The Scarlet Letter, The House of the Seven Gables,* and, to a lesser extent, *The Marble Faun,* to say nothing of a number of distinguished tales, this method was very effective, but when it failed him, it became mere symbol mongering. The symbol floated unattached in general space, without any vital meaning having attached itself to it. And this, unfortunately, was what happened in this final period.

The record of Hawthorne's frustrations, as preserved in the meditative passages that break into the narrative portions of his manuscript, especially in the first *Grimshawe* draft, make heartbreaking reading. Edith Wharton has recorded that her characters always came to her *with their names* and that these she was thereafter powerless to change. At the other extreme, Julian Hawthorne has said of his father that in the *Grimshawe* papers "each personage figures in the course of the narrative under from three to six different names." I have not checked his figures, but the phenomenon is not peculiar to *Grimshawe*. The American claimant is called Middleton, Etherege, and Redclyffe. In the second draft, Septimius is called not Felton but Norton consistently until well toward the end when (heaven knows why) he becomes Hilliard Veren, and when Doctor Grimshawe strays into this narrative, he is first called Ormskirk and then Portsoaken. Similarly, the British officer whom Septimius kills is Francis Norton, except once when he is Francis Veren. Certainly Mrs. Wharton's experience with names is not shared by all novelists, but the contrast between control and lack of control indicated in this comparison is certainly not without significance. Nor are Hawthorne's relationships less fluid than his nomenclature. Rose Garfield is introduced into the narrative as the love of Septimius Felton, but after Sibyl Dacy enters, she gradually preempts this position, and Rose becomes a sister of Septimius, considerately provided for with Robert Hagburn, who seems to have been waiting in the wings since the beginning for just such an exigency.

A multitude of suggestions relating to the progress and motivation of his story are preserved in Hawthorne's manuscripts, most of them only to be rejected forthwith: "What unimaginable nonsense!" "Pshaw." "Bubble and squeak!" "But that is vulgar." "What, what, what! How, how, how!" "That won't do; it is paltry and not new." "This is the right sow; but I cannot catch her either by ear or tail." In his book on Hawthorne, Mark Van Doren fills more than two full pages with such exclamations. Sometimes the tormented writer generalizes and pauses to take inventory: "Some damn'd thing is the matter." "I don't advance a step," "I don't see my way." "At present . . . the stubborn old devil will not move." "The life is not yet breathed into this plot, after all my galvanic efforts. Not a spark of passion as yet. How shall it be attained?" "I have not yet struck the true keynote of this Romance, and until I do, and unless I do, I shall write nothing but tediousness and nonsense." To say nothing of the most heroic and most pathetic exclamation of all: "Try back again."

For some reason, he even chose to do public penance in the dedicatory epistle to Franklin Pierce that opens the only book he managed to complete and publish during this period, *Our Old Home:*

> I once hoped that so slight a volume would not be all that I might write. These and other sketches, with which in a somewhat rougher form than I have given them here, my journal was copiously filled, were intended for the side scenes and backgrounds and exterior adornment of a work of fiction of which the plan had imperfectly developed itself in my mind, and into which I ambitiously proposed to convey more of various modes of truth than I could have grasped by a direct effort. Of course, I should not mention this abortive project, only that it has been utterly thrown aside, and will never now be accomplished. The Present, the Immediate, the Actual, has proved too potent for me. It takes away not only my scanty faculty, but even my desire for imaginary composition, and leaves me sadly content to scatter a thousand peaceful fantasies upon the hurricane that is sweeping us all along with it, possibly, into a Limbo where our nation and its polity may be as literally the fragments of a shattered dream as my unwritten Romance.[7] But I have far better hopes for our dear country; and for my individual share of the catastrophe, I afflict myself little, or not at all, and shall easily find room for the aborted work on a certain ideal shelf, where are reposited many other shadowy volumes of mine, more in number, and very much superior in quality, to those which I have succeeded in rendering actual.

Had Hawthorne been able to follow out all the multitudinous suggestions that jostled each other through the corridors of his brain, he would indeed have emerged not with a book but with a library, though much of it surely must have been on the level of the penny dreadful. It is Hugo McPherson who seems to have made the most determined attempt to study how he reworked his materials or they reworked themselves under his hands, but though this sympathetic critic argues rightly that "the sheer power of the imaginative, myth-making centre of Hawthorne's mind would not die without a titanic struggle," he is still obliged to emerge with the conclusion that his plot remained "chaotic."[8]

The "Outlines of an English Romance" known as "The Ancestral Footstep" may best be regarded as a series of practice exercises, a combination of scenario, scene, and commentary, in which names, events, and characters shift freely, sometimes canceling each other out. Though much interesting material is included, all this is too confused to admit of authoritative interpretation as a unit; the reader can hardly be expected to make it more logical or consistent than the author did.

It opens with the American, Middleton, on the tramp in England, in search of validating his birthright and perhaps establishing his claim to an ancestral estate. He falls in with and becomes the guest of an old man "who interested him more than most of his wayside companions," but Hawthorne has hardly got started before he pauses to give "an abstract of the gist of this story," covering the departure from England of the founder of the American branch of the family and the bloody footprint he left behind him. Middleton experiences a curious sense of identity with "that very personage, returned after all these ages, to see if his foot would fit the impression left of old upon the threshold" and has "a curious sense of being in one dream and recognizing the scenery and events of a former dream."

Exploring the estate in question, Middleton encounters its present possessor, Squire Eldredge, who accosts him rudely as a trespasser, calls him villain, and strikes him with the butt of a pistol, which thereupon goes off and kills the squire himself. At this point, a note by George Lathrop informs the reader that "Eldredge is revived, and the story proceeds in another way." Eldredge is not "revived"; Hawthorne simply moves on in complete disregard of what he has here written.

Middleton now encounters Eldredge, who seems to be "a good, ordinary sort of gentleman" in the usual way of social intercourse, and in another commentary we have a different account of the departure of the American founder and the origin of the bloody footprint. Later there is still a third account of the meeting of Eldredge and Middleton, with the squire now a half-Italian Roman Catholic, who has clearly borrowed color from the "Italianate Englishman" of Elizabethan melodrama. There are also two accounts of Middleton's search for the documents he would need to establish his claim. In the first, he opens a secret drawer in a miniature palace contained in a wonderful cabinet in the ancestral mansion and finds it empty. In the second account, he finds hidden documents but declines to examine them because "he felt that there would be a meanness and wrong in inspecting those family papers, coming to his knowledge of them, as he had, through the opportunities offered by the hospitality of the owner of the estate."

Though one commentator has been reminded of the classical story of Meleager and another of Theseus, generally speaking Hawthorne's own life experiences, as recorded in his notebooks or held in memory, are more important than literature as sources for his aborted romances. William Bysshe Stein, to be sure, has made a case for "The Spectre of Tappington" in *The Ingoldsby Legends* of Richard H. Barham, and Jane Lundblad rightly observes that in these final writings, Hawthorne "heaped more relics from the Gothic storerooms of his mind than perhaps ever before," though without naming specific sources. At one point in "The Ancestral Footstep" the author rather amusingly sighs for access to "the Newgate Calendar, the older volumes, or any other book of murders." As to "The Spectre of Tappington," it is true, and it is interesting, that both the ancestral estate and the bloody footstep are there, but since the story is entirely different, Hawthorne can hardly be said to have incurred any real indebtedness.[9]

Passing from literature to life, it may be noted that as consul at Liverpool Hawthorne had contacts with many Americans, some of them weak in the upper story, who fancied themselves to possess claims to English estates, and that at least as early as the beginning of 1855 he had in mind the idea of an American who had in his possession a secret unknown to the present owner. For that matter, though he himself carried no such claim, he did engage unsuccessfully in an attempt to trace his own English roots. "My ancestors left England in 1635," he once wrote. "I sometimes feel as if I myself had been absent for two hundred and eighteen years." It was in April 1855 that Mrs. Ainsworth stimulated or (if the reader prefers) burdened his imagination by telling him the story of the Marian martyr, George Marsh, but the story of the coffin overflowing with hair came to him from a woman he knew much better, the wife of his friend John O'Sullivan. "After her grandmother had been buried for many years," so Mrs. O'Sullivan related, "the tomb was opened and the coffin was 'found to be filled with beautiful, glossy, living chestnut ringlets, into which her whole substance seems to have been transformed.'"

Since Julian Hawthorne's heavily modified version of *Doctor Grimshawe's Secret* is the only one of the last romances that has ever been offered to the public as if it were a finished work (even Una's edition of *Septimius Felton* contains some slight editorial apparatus), it has probably been more widely read than any of the others. Its most ardent admirer seems to be Jac Tharpe, who judges it "potentially [Hawthorne's] greatest work" and one which, though it uses "a good deal of allegory and myth," might still have become "the most realistic of his novels," It "includes Hawthorne's major themes, intensifying some of them, and to some extent suggests where Hawthorne would have gone in later development."[10] Though I think nobody else would go quite that far, the rum-soaked, tobacco-reeking Grimshawe, whose house is festooned with undisturbed cobwebs because he hopes to distill from them a nostrum to cure most of the ills of mankind, and whose particular joy is an enormous, evil-looking spider, based on Hawthorne's memory of a South American specimen he had seen in the British Museum, may well be his creator's most memorable eccentric. He appears in the manuscripts in different aspects and under different names, but, but for all his conniving, the two little children who live with him, and whom he treats kindly, regard him as a kind of saint. Davidson thinks the suggestion for the boy Ned, whom the doctor took from an almshouse, was derived from the pitiful scurvy-ridden child who attached himself to Hawthorne under the circumstances indicated in my final chapter, and that Grimshawe himself and little Elsie came from Seymour Kirkup, painter, necromancer, and friend of Byron, Shelley, and Leigh Hunt, who later helped Mrs. Browning develop her interest in spritiualism, and Kirkup's daughter Imogene. Certainly there can be no doubt that, as Davidson says, the doctor's portrait is "drawn with amazingly deft lines" and his relationship to the children "exquisitely treated" nor yet that Elsie takes on "those shimmering lights of spirituality and elfishness in which Hawthorne loved to bathe his little girls."

Grimshawe's development and that of the children is more fully traced in the second draft ("Grimshawe" in the Centenary Edition) upon which Julian Hawthorne based his text after he had discovered it. This covers all the American part of the story and is more than four times the length of the corresponding portion of the first draft.

Moreover, more than one-third of the first draft is not narrative, being composed of Hawthorne's communings with himself as to the future development of his story. He is surely not the only writer who has ever faced such problems, but I know of no other instance in which a celebrated author has actually made a record of his frustrations in his manuscript itself.

Doctor Grimshawe dies in both versions, and the tale resumes with Ned, or Edward Etherege, now a successful lawyer and politician, rediscovered in England, from which Hawthorne proceeds along the same general lines mapped out in "The Ancestral Footstep" but culminating in a kind of wild Gothic phantasmagoria. Attacked and left for dead on a lonely path, Etherege is succored and taken to a hospice by Pearson, one of the aged pensioners there. He thinks Pearson's daughter Elsie the girl he was brought up with by the doctor, but for some unknown reason she seems unwilling to recognize him. He receives an invitation to stay at what is now called Brathwaite Hall from its present half-English, half-Italian owner, and despite the warnings of Pearson and Elsie, he accepts. After having drunk heavily drugged wine, he wakes up in a dungeon, from which he is only rescued through the persistent efforts of Elsie and Pearson, aided by the warden of the hospital, with whom he had made friends. The key he had found in the Salem churchyard opens the coffin he finds there, but instead of containing valuable papers, it contains only the ringlets about which Mrs. O'Sullivan had told Hawthorne. Not much has been accomplished by this, and it turns out that the true heir to the estate is not our hero but a fellow prisoner whom he had found in the dungeon with him. Nor does any of this seem very closely connected with the first, or Salem, part of the story, which is, in any event, the part that everybody remembers.

Faith in the Christian doctrine of human immortality was always important to Hawthorne, nor can the unorthodox idea that it might be possible for man to learn how to live forever upon this earth be said to have occurred to him for the first time when he wrote *Septimius Felton*. He had read William Godwin's novel, *St. Leon*, also, but though other possible sources have been mentioned,[11] the immediate inspiration for *Septimius* would seem to have been derived from Thoreau's telling him that the Wayside had once been inhabited by a man who fancied himself immortal.

Another important source of *Septimius Felton* was the Civil War, now beginning to wreak its ravages as Hawthorne wrote. He put his scene back into the days of the Revolution (even if there had been no other arguments against it, his attitude toward the current conflict was too uncertain for him to attempt a contemporary setting), but his excellent picture of the excitement, both pleasurable and harrowing, that war brings, even, or perhaps especially, to those like Septimius who try to hold themselves aloof from it, has plainly been colored by the situation the author himself confronted. Indeed at one point he says specifically, "We know something of that time now." Though the redcoats have "something in their faces, . . . kindly, homely, hearty, honest, obtuse, that made you remember that they had mothers, and homes, Septimius is tempted to pick off one of them from where he lies in ambush as they pass him on the Lexington Road on their retreat after the battle at the North Bridge. Like Tom Sawyer, who, when depressed, would like to "die temporarily," Septimius would like to "kill, and yet commit no murder," and Hawthorne does not attempt to decide whether this feeling comes from Satan, his country's guardian angel, or his own nature. Hawthorne had heard of a country boy who in Revolutionary times, more apparently by way of nervous reaction than out of deliberate malice, had killed a wounded British soldier with the ax he had been using to split wood near the Old Manse. The gay, generous, winning young fool of a British officer Septimius does kill had angered him by snatching a kiss from Rose when stopping near the Wayside for water on his way to the battle, but Hawthorne takes pains to make his hero as nearly guiltless as possible by having the Englishman force their confrontation upon him.

For all that, Hawthorne's handling of this episode is, for him, rather curious. Septimius had "no such strong conviction of our right, as would justify me in shedding blood, or taking life"; indeed such killing would still be murder, even could that right be clearly established. Yet once the deed has been done, he adjusts himself to going on to live with himself with surprising ease when compared to the agonies Hawthorne's other sinners experience over their sins. Moreover, this is true again when his reckless experimentation in adding what he thinks may be the flower of immortality but which is actually a poison fungus to Aunt Nashoba's drink kills the old woman. "Perhaps it was his Indian trait stirring in him again; at any rate, it is not delightful to observe how readily man becomes a blood-shedding animal." In the "Norton" draft, Septimius rebukes Rose harshly when she grieves for the Englishman, and though he disposes of all the officer's other property according to his directions, after having buried him on the hillside where he fell, he keeps out the packet containing the directions for achieving earthly immortality. As the end he even wonders whether remorse ever really exists in any sinner's own breast or whether what seems remorse is only caused by "the condemnation of the world or some influential part of it." It is interesting to note that in the first *Grimshawe* draft, Etherege even questions the utility of conscience itself, which again brings Hawthorne close to Mark Twain, in both *Huckleberry Finn* and *The Mysterious Stranger.*

Something has already been said about Hawthorne's handling of Aunt Nashoba and of Sibyl Dacy. The latter is introduced as a mysterious, probably malevolent, possibly even supernatural creature. She assumes that the hillside where the soldier is buried is her home and belongs to her, and it is even suggested that she has grown up out of his grave. Later we learn that the officer Septimius killed was her lover and that she came to Concord in league with her uncle, Doctor Portsoaken (the *Septimius Felton* variation of Doctor Grimshawe) to avenge herself upon his slayer. It was she who planted the fungus she knew to be poison but which she hoped Septimius would mistake for the flower of immortality, as he does. As Doctor Portsoaken finally explains, the true flower of immortality "had not been seen on earth for many centuries" and the fungus was only "a sort of earthly or devilish counterpart of it." But she is "a weak, weak girl—only a girl, Septimius; only eighteen yet!" and she had not sufficiently allowed for the fact that "a girl's fancy is so shifting." After she falls in love with Septimius, she rises to heroic stature when she saves his life by, as she says, making herself immortal before him, drinking the elixir he had intended they should drink together and then shattering the glass to fall dead at his feet. It was with this highly theatrical scene that Hawthorne chose to end the only draft of *Septimius Felton* he ever completed, and though it is by no means the greatest encounter he ever described, he never matched it in kind. Any great actress of the nineteenth-century theater, like Sarah Bernhardt, could have done wonders with it.

Septimius himself however, especially in the "Norton" draft, is even more complicated than Sibyl. A young Harvard theologue, he is from the beginning considerably more than merely a young man who had conceived the wild dream of earthly immortality. His divided mind shows from the beginning, in his uncertainty about his chosen profession, about the war, and even about Rose, long before Sibyl has entered the picture. I have spoken of the coolness with which he takes Aunt Nashoba's death, but this coexists in a convincingly lifelike way with an upsurge of emotion that surprises even him. Hawthorne insists too that there was a core of realistic common sense in him in spite of all his extravagance. Consider too his long delay in opening the English officer's packet and then his doing it suddenly and impulsively, as if impelled by a force outside of himself, "before he consciously thought of what he was doing."

In the beginning, his reason for desiring earthly immortality seems to be simply that life as we now have it is too short to accomplish anything. Unselfish, positively altruistic motives are not specifically enunciated until comparatively late, and even then his plans for the long future, which at one stage include unlimited indulgence in evil, not for its own sake, but so that he may encompass universal experience, are obviously chuckleheaded. It is true that "grand and heroic qualities" are attributed to him in the scenario Hawthorne wrote before setting to work on the "Norton" draft, in which he was at last to die after he had completed the reformation of the world, destroying "war, intemperance, slavery, all manner of crime," but since the "Norton" draft breaks off shortly after the death of Aunt Nashoba, none of this was ever really actuated.

His quest therefore does not get very far. Already in Study A he felt that he "had taken himself out of the category of the human race," and in Study F he reflected that "were he to marry, his wife would be but a concubine, because she would soon be divorced from him forever by death, his children would be playthings of a moment." Even in the first draft he soon comes to feel "that he was concentrating his efforts and interests entirely upon himself, and that the more he succeeded the more remotely he should be carried away." To a degree, to be sure, such isolation is forced upon the artist also, as well as upon the devotees of causes, but nobody has ever doubted that Hawthorne chafed at the kind of distortion he thought this imposed upon reformers, and there were even times when he felt that neither was the artist's pursuit quite free of guilt. And even if one had brought himself to endure the isolation, could he also embrace the sense of illusion that might easily go along with it?

All unreal!; all illusion! Was Rose Garfield a deception too, with her daily beauty, and daily cheerfulness, and daily worth? In short, it was such a moment as I suppose all men feel (at least I can answer for one), when the real scene and picture of life swims, jars, shakes, seems about to be broken up and dispersed, like the picture in a smooth pond, when we disturb its tranquil mirror by throwing in a stone; and though the scene soon settles itself, and looks as real as before, a haunting doubt keeps close at hand, as long as we live, asking, "Is it stable? Am I sure of it? Am I certainly not dreaming? See; it trembles again, ready to dissolve."[12]

"The Dolliver Romance," Hawthorne's last effort in search of the elixir for his art and for himself, is only a fragment, or more accurately three fragments, for they are not consecutive, and Davidson has conjectured that Mrs. Hawthorne removed something, for unknown reasons, between the second and the third. The aged Doctor Dolliver (the "Doctor" is a courtesy title) dwells, like Doctor Grimshawe, beside the graveyard that adjoined the Peabody house in Salem, but this time he has only one child to care for (and to hold him to life), his three-year-old great-granddaughter, "the one earthly creature that inherited a drop of the Dolliver blood." His beloved wife had been dead half a century, and he had since "deposited a further and further portion of his heart and its affections in each successive one of a long line of kindred graves." Many undeveloped possibilities are suggested in the "studies" Hawthorne made for this story,[13] and in one of these, the child is a little boy, not of his blood, but the descendant of a friend who had lost his life for Dolliver. In what was written, however, the boy has become a little girl, who resembles Elsie in *Grimshawe* but is probably even more like Una at her age. Moreover, she owns one of the most enchanting kittens in literature. When Pansie and her great-grandfather sit down at table, the kitten soon joins them.

First, she showed her mottled head out of Pansie's lap, deliberately sipping milk from the child's basin without rebuke; then she took post on the old gentleman's shoulder, purring like a spinning wheel, trying her claws in the wadding of his dressing gown, and still more impressively reminding him of her presence by putting out a paw to intercept a warmed-over morsel of yesterday's chicken on its way to the Doctor's mouth. After skillfully achieving this feat, she scrambled down upon the breakfast table and began to wash her feet and hands.

Unlike Grimshawe however, Dolliver is as gentle a soul as ever lived and "as pious and upright a Christian, . . . with as little of the serpent in his character, as ever came of Puritan heritage."

Years ago, an unknown customer had left a recipe for a certain medicine with Doctor Dolliver and ordered it compounded but never came back to claim it. But there was "one gap—one torn or obliterated place" in this recipe, which supposedly gave the name of the vital ingredient. It is suggested that Pansie's father discovered this, but since he had been found dead in his laboratory, it seemed that he "had died by incautiously testing" this or some other drug upon himself. There are suggestions also that the mysterious ingredient may now be found in a shrub growing in the doctor's herb garden, which Pansie and her kitten uproot, the child mistaking it for a "big, naughty weed."

At the beginning of our story, Doctor Dolliver, increasingly feeble with the infirmities of age, had laid aside his customary caution to try the mysterious medicine at the rate of a single drop a day. The results are sensational; his stiff joints begin to limber up, his eyesight improves, he gains fresh vitality, and all in all he seems in a fair way if not to achieve immortality at least to resist the aging process and set himself moving in the reverse direction.

In the last of the three fragments, Doctor Dolliver is confronted by a wealthy citizen of the town, one Colonel Dabney, a Judge Pyncheon–like character, and a "grim old wreck . . . moving goutily and gathering wrath anew with every touch of his painful foot to the ground," who is quite as vividly presented as Judge Pyncheon himself. For some unexplained reason, Colonel Dabney regards the elixir as his "hereditary property" and threatens Dolliver with the law if it is not surrendered to him. Finally he seizes the bottle, greedily swallows its entire contents, and falls dead, as Sibyl Dacy dies, self-sacrificingly, under far different circumstances, in *Septimius Felton*. and there "The Dolliver Romance" maddeningly stops. As far as it goes, it is nearly enough first-rate Hawthorne to suggest that it was having the same effect upon Hawthorne's talent that the elixir exercised upon its protagonist. Unfortunately however, it was too late for it to have the same effect upon the author's worn-out body. As early as 1876, George Parsons Lathrop had suggested that "in order to defraud nature of her dues, we must enter into compact with the Devil." If the last romances have any "meaning" or "moral" or establish any conclusion, it would seem to be that it is not wise for Americans to try to establish their titles to English estates or for any human being to break the ties that bind him to the rest of mankind.

5

The Man

Hawthorne was about five feet, ten and one-half inches tall; his hair was dark and the shape of his face oval. Many thought him handsome, though there are dissenters. Emerson, who cared nothing for his books, called him "regal," and to Anthony Trollope he was the handsomest of Yankees. Charles Reade found his eyes the most magnificent he had ever seen in a human head. But some thought the upper half of his face much better than the lower, and Tom Appleton described him as "a boned pirate."

Until his health broke at the beginning of the 1860s, he seems to have been an exceptionally well man, though he was always capable of notions, such as his fixed conviction that he was never well away from the sea. Though he could be lethargic and apathetic, he had plenty of physical energy when he cared to use it, and it is said he could leap as high as his shoulder from a standing position.

His wife and children called him "our sunshine" and "the light of his house." "He was like a boy," says Una. "Never was there such a playmate as he in all the world." George Hillard strikes the same note: "There was nothing morbid in his character or temperament. He was, indeed, much the reverse of morbid." But he was far from being what is called a "clubbable" man. He often avoided contacts when he could and manifested a wonderful gift for silence when they were forced upon him. He himself well knew that his "native propensities were toward Fairy Land," and Emerson, Longfellow, Lowell, and Bronson Alcott all felt that there was a large feminine element in his makeup. Yet, as his son Julian perceived, his "sympathetic and intuitional qualities" were well balanced by his "critical and logical faculties." He was as hardheaded as Solon Shingle, and he was capable of the faith of the child in the Gospels.

He was less well equipped for life materially than spiritually. The Hawthorne family had come down in the world, and in the Salem of Nathaniel's boyhood, only laborers and servants looked up to them. His uncle Robert Manning sent him to college, but he did not live lavishly there. In Old Manse days, after his marriage, it is hard to see how he and Sophia could have kept alive without the garden and the river. He had little or no interest in money for its own sake, but he did not underrate its importance. He never enjoyed the feeling Thoreau gave him that it was disgraceful to have a house to live in or two coats to wear. What he would really have liked was a small regular income that would have allowed him to forget about that side of life altogether. After he became a successful Ticknor and Fields author, he conducted the business side of his literary life like a babe in the woods. He never knew how much his books had earned or were earning. The publishers acted as his bankers, paying his bills for him upon request and honoring all his demands but making no seasonal remittances and never rendering an account. After his death this led to a bitter disagreement between his widow and James T. Fields, in which, though she seems to have been technically in the wrong, they, as experienced business men, were certainly much more at fault than she was.[1] He pulled every string he could to get the Liverpool consulate from Franklin Pierce, and he came out of Europe with thirty thousand dollars, out of which he shortly lost one-third by lending it to John O'Sullivan without security. There might have been more if the Hawthornes had come straight home when his consular service was over instead of traveling in England and on the Continent, and if he had been able to resist the ever-present temptation to give his money away to those who thought they needed it more than he did.

According to Hawthorne himself, he did not like to go to school and avoided it whenever possible. He disliked mathematics, metaphysics, and declamation and refused to apply himself to them, but he was noted for his fine translations from the Latin. He seems to have been reasonably at home with Greek, and he had some familiarity with Spanish and Italian. As a family man, he had some interest in genetics; otherwise science seems to have interested him mainly as it stimulated his imagination. He mistrusted scientists, even physicians, and feared the coming scientific and technological age, and he was quite in character when he chose to do his own dying without the aid of medicine.[2]

From boyhood he was a slave to print, and like most bookish persons he often saw life itself in terms of literature. He read much factual as well as literary material, especially biography and travel, and made considerable use of encyclopedias, anthologies, and compilations. He knew his Bible well, but his classical references are no more nor less than what might have been expected from a man who had been a good Latinist in college.

Chaucer was not much within his range, but he did well with both Shakespeare and Milton. His favorite books were *The Faerie Queene* and *The Pilgrim's Progress*. Scott was of course his British novelist par excellence. He read many of the great eighteenth-and nineteenth-century novelists, but I get the impression that Dickens meant considerably less to him than he did to either Longfellow or Whittier. His favorite English novelist seems to have been Trollope, who wrote "as if some giant had hewn a great lump of the earth and put it under a glass case, with all its inhabitants going about their daily business and not suspecting that they were made a show of." About poetry he gives the impression of having determined to be as crotchety as possible. He thought of the poet as "a seer, a revealer of internal truths, a prophet," and one "above contact with mere mortals," yet he could also claim that he disliked poetry. There is some evidence however that he did more reading even in the minor English poets than he is generally given credit for. His references to foreign literature are scattered enough to suggest considerable breadth of choice. American literature, naturally, was for him mostly contemporary literature, and much of it was the work of personal friends. Among the poets Longfellow was easily the favorite. During his Lenox period his relations with Melville were close, and *Moby-Dick* was dedicated to him. In his later years, he warmly admired the rising Thomas Bailey Aldrich.

Music was the art that meant least to him. He seems to have been nearly tone-deaf, though he was very sensitive to the sound of the speaking voice and to rhythm in prose. Fond of the theater when it came his way, he was deeply moved by Kean's Lear in Boston and greatly disappointed, upon his arrival in Paris in 1858, to learn that Rachel had just died. As early as 1837 he was interested in the portraits at the Essex Institute in Salem, but he thought he would rather look at a basilisk than at the pictures in the Boston Athenaeum! The Great Exhibition of 1857 in Manchester marked a stage in his aesthetic education, which developed even more during his stay in Italy, as my discussion of *The Marble Faun* has already shown. His response to the work of the Old Masters that he could see only in decay did not differ greatly from that of Mark Twain in *The Innocents Abroad*. His admiration for Gothic architecture was passionate, but he was not sure that Gothic buildings were at home in America. Nor did he ever think of himself as having acquired any real knowledge of art in a technical sense.

He was appreciative and responsive toward those who admired his own writings, but he was inclined to be uncertain in his own judgment of them, though he always insisted that both his publishers and his readers must accept what he had to give just as he chose to give it or else leave it alone. He saw his muse as a jealous mistress, who must be served for disinterested motives, but he could never write—or thought he could not—except when conditions were just right. Among other things, this generally meant when he had no other employment. In fact, he swings back and forth between the practical life and the aesthetic life to such an extent that it often seems not as if he were so much balancing one against the other as using the one for a refuge from the other. "Stories grow like vegetables," he once wrote, "and are not manufactured like pine tables."

In the nineteenth century the nature cult was so influential that many turned to nature for what most of us try to get from our fellow men and even in many cases made it a surrogate for religion. Hawthorne had abundant opportunity to learn to love nature during that portion of his boyhood spent in the Maine woods, and we are told that when he lived in the Old Manse he never stayed indoors except during bad weather. He skated; he boated; he bathed. Once he and Thoreau floated down the Concord River on an ice floe, drawing their boat behind them. But though he felt strongly the importance of living in harmony with nature, he loved it best in its association with human life. He liked apple trees for their suggestion of friendliness toward man and preferred Concord's "broad and peaceful meadows" to more spectacular scenery elsewhere. His relations with birds and animals were generally cordial and happy. His favorite animal was the cat, but at one time, as a boy, he had a pet monkey.

Though he was never taken in by any Rousseauistic nonsense about natural goodness, he still inclined toward a kindly view of human beings whenever possible. He liked to be able to think well even of people he had only read about, and when he was shown a piece of embroidery executed by Mary, Queen of Scots, he felt that "there can hardly be many more precious relics than this in the world." He could denounce whole classes of human beings as violently, and apparently as entertainingly, as Mark Twain, but, unlike Mark, he did not generally write his denunciations. He also had considerably more race consciousness and race prejudice than would be considered seemly in a man of his intelligence and sensitivity today. But when it came to individuals, he could generally be counted on for kindness and understanding, whether it took the form of almsgiving or personal attention, and especially when the other party was one of the broken crocks for whom nobody else cared. Once, when asked why he had replied so courteously to the salutation of a toper, he replied, "I would not have a drunken man politer than I." In Custom House days, he was always out on the wharf at the earliest possible hour, in all kinds of weather, simply because he knew that the wages of the wharf laborers depended upon the time they put in, and he did not wish to be responsible for holding them up. It is interesting that from the publication of *The Scarlet Letter* on, strangers used to seek him out to confide their secrets to him, as if he had been a priest.

The legends that have developed around his solitude have been largely of his own making. "I have made a captive of myself and put me in a dungeon," he told Longfellow, "and now I cannot find the key to let myself out." Again he declared: "For the last ten years I have not lived but only dreamed of living"; "If I could only make tables, I should feel myself more of a man"; "I'm a doomed man, and over I must go." It was his own view that Sophia Peabody saved him from this fate: "Indeed, we are but shadows; we are not endowed with real life, all that seems most real is but the thinnest substance of a dream—till the heart be touched."

Nevertheless his boyhood seems to have been "normal" enough, both in his association with his peers and participation in their activities. He was fond of writing about solitaries, but both in his tales and his essays, he is clear that "man is naturally a social being, not formed for himself alone." At the Old Manse, he and Sophia had a reasonable number of calls from neighboring literati, but they were also left a good deal to themselves. In Salem, as an officer of the lyceum, he invited Emerson to stay in his house when the Concord sage came there to lecture, and at Lenox he had considerably more society than he had had at Salem. When he went to England as the representative of his country, he carried off his many duties with apparent ease, even to the extent of developing a certain capacity as a public speaker. "I don't in the least admire my own oratory; but I do admire my pluck in speaking at all." Sometimes he even felt the orator's sense of being en rapport with his audience.

Hawthorne, then, did a man's work in the world and did it well. Nevertheless, he always remained a deeply introspective man, and the world within was more important to him than the world without. People confided in him, but he did not confide in them. At the Saturday Club, Henry James, Sr., thought he behaved like a rogue in a company of detectives, and he always had a gift for avoiding the society of people (like the Alcotts) with whom he did not feel at home. But the Irish immigrants, living in grass-covered shanties and working on the railroad, never understood how he could be called distant or cold, and when Delia Bacon told him about her difficulty in meeting people, he replied, "I can entirely sympathize with you . . . . To tell you the truth, though I see people by scores, every day, I still shrink from any interview of which I am forewarned." The truth seems to be that extreme fastidiousness and sensitiveness, not shyness, lay at the root of his reserve. In human relations he was not a gourmand but an epicure. He enjoyed contacts with humanity upon his own terms, and when they ceased to be rewarding, he dropped them.

The worst handicap a man can have in his relations with others is an excessive regard for himself. Hawthorne was not a self-assertive person; he made almost a religion of his unwillingness to exercise power over other human beings. Yet even as a boy he resisted hectoring and was prepared to fight if necessary rather than submit to it. Both in the family he was born into and in the one he established, he was always regarded with more than respect, and he had no need to assert his authority because it was never questioned.

For many people social life is complicated by their attitude toward currently popular vices and indulgences. Drinking, smoking, and gaming (of which last we hear nothing thereafter) were all part of Hawthorne's life in college days. There are a good many temperance passages in his writings, and despite all his dislike of meddling, there are records of his having tried to save friends from the dangers of excess. How much he himself drank is problematical, but he was noted for having a good head, and I do not see how this could have been established without his having tried it out. In his paper on "English Poverty" in *Our Own Home,* he shows his awareness of the depredations wrought by gin drinking in London's slums, but he also makes it clear that so long as poverty-breeding conditions were allowed to exist there, he did not believe that cutting off gin would in itself solve the problem. Hawthorne's brother-in-law, Horace Mann, once told him that he could never have the same respect for him after having learned that he smoked. Here again testimony varies. Hawthorne's daughter Rose says he smoked one cigar a day, but Julian did not believe he got through more than half a dozen boxes during his lifetime.

Politically Hawthorne was a good Jacksonian Democrat, though he had no interest in the science of politics for its own sake and very little respect for politicians. "Their hearts wither away, and die out of their bodies. Their consciences are turned to india-rubber—or to some substance as black as that, and which will stretch as much." Yet he had sufficient political perspicacity to be able to outline Franklin Pierce's career to him in advance, upon his election to the New Hampshire legislature. As Randall Stewart says, he was "involved in politics, either as an office-seeker or an office-holder, for twenty years." A beneficiary of the spoils system, he was quite willing to have others removed to make way for him, and as consul at Liverpool he even managed to keep the Manchester agency vacant for three years in order that he might pocket the fees that would otherwise have gone to his subordinate. Though he would never have avowed it, he angled for a government appointment under Pierce and wrote the campaign life of his friend with a view to such a reward.

From the great characteristic reform movement of his time, abolition, he stood apart. The Fugitive Slave Law angered him as it did other New Englanders, but he felt much more for white laboring men than for black slaves. To him slavery was an evil that it was vain to try to treat as if it were not part of the warp and woof of a fallen world. Hawthorne was not indifferent to reform. He spoke out against dueling, and he doubted the value of capital punishment, but he had serious doubts that even a great leader might achieve any important reform except as an agent of the spirit of the times.

Because he was the only great New England writer except the Quaker Whittier who did not wholeheartedly support the Civil War, modern pacifists are sometimes tempted to make a hero of Hawthorne, but this view would be difficult to sustain. It was not that military glory had ever appealed to him. He considered a professional soldier a professional ruffian, and in his view no man ought make a career of the army unless he were fit for nothing else, a view shared, surprisingly enough, by another distinguished American, not commonly considered a pacifist, Theodore Roosevelt. Hawthorne saw every army camp as a canker on the landscape, brutalizing the men and debauching the women. Even the Concord battlefield, adjoining his home at the Old Manse, which people came from far and near to see, left him cold. "For my own part," he said, "I have never found my imagination much excited by this or any other scene of historical celebrity, nor would the placid margin of the river have lost any of its charm for me had men never fought and died there."

His attitude toward England however sometimes seems quite out of harmony with all this. Twisting the British lion's tail seemed to attract him, and there are times when he gives the impression of not being quite sure that the War of 1812 was over. In England everything was wrong, from government to trees to women. "After all the slander against Americans, there is no people worthy even to take second place behind us, for liberality of ideas and practice. The more I see of the rest of the world, the better I think of my own country." Certainly what he wrote about English women in *Our Old Home* was not only outrageous but incomprehensible and unbelievable as the utterance of a gentleman. It is amazing to find Fields writing him, after this chapter had come out in the *Atlantic*, that friends had stopped him on the street to laugh about it. Evidently the famous nineteenth-century squeamishness in matters of taste was of a highly selective variety.

But what is more to the point here is that when Anglo-American relations were strained during the 1850s, Hawthorne behaved like a little boy kicking up dust on the playground. Though he would not say he wanted war, he was not willing to "bate an inch of honor" to avoid it. He wanted England to be humiliated, and he seems to have felt it a great pity that if we did not fight her now, we could never fight her at all! Through his association with John O'Sullivan, George N. Sanders, and others, he was, in some measure, caught up in the notorious "Young America" movement, which was supported by German and Italian immigrants and by Tammany Hall. "Young America" favored a vigorous foreign policy and the military and naval forces to back it up. It even inclined to advocate American intervention in behalf of democratic movements abroad, and Hawthorne's connection with it cannot be explained entirely in terms of his support for Pierce or even his stand for social equality. As American consul in London, Sanders placed diplomatic dispatch bags at the service of European revolutionaries, opened his own living quarters to conspirators, and finally himself advocated the assassination of Louis Napoleon. In 1854 he was recalled to America. The great mystery here is how a man who was so afraid as Hawthorne was of the abolitionist danger to peace in America could support such a dangerous policy abroad.

As for the Civil War itself, Hawthorne's attitude toward it was far less logical than that of Pierce. On July 4, 1863, he went to Concord, New Hampshire, with Pierce, and sat on the platform while the latter excoriated Lincoln and the war, and in his essay "Chiefly About War Matters," he declared that he despised the administration "with all my heart." But this was about the only point upon which he and Pierce were agreed. Pierce never wavered in his adherence to "the grand idea of an irrevocable Union." He opposed the war simply because he did not believe "aggression by arms" was "a suitable or possible remedy for existing evils." Throughout the war he stood publicly for an immediate armistice and a return to the status quo antebellum. Hawthorne does have flashes of brilliant insight, as when, in response to the silly statement attributed to Emerson—that when John Brown was hanged, he would make the gallows as holy as the cross—he declared bluntly that no man deserved hanging more. Taken as a whole however, his Civil War utterances are not notable from either a pacifist or a militarist point of view.

The truth is that Hawthorne's American patriotism was essentially a sectional affair. For himself he had "never loved" the South. "We do not belong together, the Union is unnatural, a scheme of man, not an ordinance of God." After it had been broken up, New England would "still have her rocks and ice, and a nobler people than ever heretofore."

He would not fight, then, either to free the slaves or to preserve the Union. But why, in that event, fight at all? Because otherwise Washington would become the capital of the Confederacy, and Maryland, Virginia, Kentucky, and Missouri, all of which were capable of being salvaged as free states, would be lost. As Hawthorne saw it, the best practicable solution of the crisis would be "a separation of the Union giving us the west bank of the Mississippi and a boundary line affording as much Southern soil as we can hope to digest into freedom in another century." Inasmuch then as Hawthorne was consistent at all in his Civil War utterances, he advocated prosecuting the war so that the North might be in a position to dictate peace terms and establish the best conditions possible for the existence of a northern and western free state.

Nothing has been said so far concerning Hawthorne's relationship to the most basic of human drives. Obviously, he was in every sense of the term a highly moral man, but it is also clear that, though there is no record of intimate contacts with women and girls before his marriage,[3] his attitude toward them was completely normal, and he recorded his frank, unembarrassed observation of them in a number of passages. His alleged prudery in what he wrote about nudity in art has been blown up out of all proportion. It is true that he did not like Rubens's fat women, but he did not like fat women when they had their clothes on either. As far as sculpture is concerned, his objection does not go much beyond insisting that it was ridiculous to sculpt modern men like George Washington, who never went naked in life, to stand naked on pedestals. The nudity of such as the Apollo Belvedere and the Venus de Medici he not only accepted but delighted in.

Nor does he seem to have been unduly squeamish about nakedness in life. We are told that he considered it "utterly impossible for the wit or ingenuity of the wisest or most imaginative of men to suggest the slightest improvement" upon the structure, uses, or beauty of the human body. There were nude objects d'art in the Red House at Lenox, and in *A Wonder Book* Mr. Pringle's home contains a reproduction of Horatio Greenough's *Angel and Child*. When, near Cambridge University, Hawthorne saw "troops of naked boys" bathing in the river in full view of all the world, it did not seem shameful to him but rather Arcadia come again, nor was he in the least embarrassed when, in a lower-class London theater, he saw a young woman bare her whole breast unconcernedly to nurse her baby. Evidently the Hawthorne children were not taught to be ashamed of their bodies when they were small, and there is a charming pen picture of Una "preparing for bed, and running about the room in her chemise, which does not come down far enough to serve the purposes of a fig-leaf. Never were seen such contortions and attitudinizing—prostrating herself on all-fours, and thrusting up her little bum as a spectacle to men and angels, being among the least grotesque."

When the Hawthornes were married in 1842, Sophia Peabody was approaching her thirty-third birthday, while her husband had just passed his thirty-eighth. Ada Shepard, who was the governess of the Hawthorne children in Rome, did not think her at all beautiful, and Julian seems to agree in a technical sense, though he adds that in her presence nobody would have thought of raising the question. Though twentieth-century readers sometimes find Mrs. Hawthorne's aestheticism and aspiring idealism a bit hard to take, she was far more realistic and less inclined to extremism than either of her sisters—Mary (Mrs. Horace Mann) or Elizabeth Palmer Peabody, the very high priestess of transcendentalism.[4] From the point of view of the modern scholar, she took unauthorized liberties in somewhat prudishly editing her husband's notebooks, but it is very doubtful either that he would have disapproved of anything she did or that either of them could have got the material published in their time upon any other basis.

Despite their poverty in their early days, the life of the Hawthornes at the Old Manse has often been called idyllic, and so far as their personal relations were concerned, the epithet does not seem misplaced. "I have married the Spring!" he cried. "I am husband to the month of May!" "Oh, I cannot begin to tell thee how I love thee." And her tone with reference to him was just the same. A month after their marriage, he was "the loveliest being who ever breathed life. Yes, with all his strength and spirit and power, he has the most perfect loveliness of nature I ever witnessed or imagined." Nor did either of them ever change their minds.

All this is more, not less, impressive because, after all, they were not living in Eden but in a very imperfect world. Mention has already been made of their poverty. Moreover they both had in-laws, and neither one ever considered the other's family anything like so perfect as they found each other. What can a mother do with a sister-in-law who will offer a child candy, and when the child replies that her mother does not allow her to eat candy, attempt to cut the Gordian knot by telling her that she does not need to tell her mother that she has had it? It was fortunate that, with all their idealism, there was mingled in both the Hawthornes a sure, dependable fund of hardheaded common sense. Nathaniel worshiped Sophia as a goddess, but he also loved her with a man's passion, which, since she returned it, caused no difficulty. She even, somewhat startlingly, wrote her sister that "Mr. Hawthorne" respected her delicacy and that his "passions were under his feet." But if they respected each other's delicacy, they also, which is quite as important in a successful marriage, respected each other's peculiarities, and neither asked from the other more than that other could give. On her part, Sophia soon learned that her husband was a "most unmalleable man." Even during their engagement she could not get him to go to hear the great preacher of the Seaman's Bethel, "Father" Taylor, whom both Dickens and Jenny Lind considered one of the attractions of Boston and whom Melville wrote into *Moby-Dick;* neither did she ever succeed in making a transcendentalist of him. He had dominated his own mother and sisters before he was married, and it cannot be doubted that he was also the dominating partner in his marriage. Julian makes the interesting statement that his father always deferred to his wife when he was in doubt. This may be true, but he was often sure, even about her clothes, and though he did much for her in "loving care," even loving care can be trying when it is "immitigable."

The one curious and amusing peculiarity in the Hawthornes' domestic arrangements was the husband's notion that his wife would somehow be soiled if she should attempt to do any housework. Longfellow, to be sure, felt the same way, but Longfellow had married a rich girl and lived with her in a big house. "I never in my life saw my mother cook anything," wrote Rose. "It was my father's desire that she never should." In those days when both food and "help" were cheap, even the poor could usually find a servant who was poorer than themselves. The Hawthornes always ate off "the finest French china," for it was inconceivable to Sophia that her "*second-best* service" should be used for her "most illustrious guest," her husband. (Who *did* use it? one wonders.) When other domestic service failed, it was he, not she, who took over in the kitchen, so that when she came to breakfast, she needed only to sit down to the table. But the perfect touch to all this is that though Hawthorne could get a meal ready if necessary, he would not rake up leaves. When that had to be done, Sophia must do it. "I wonder what becomes of them, when there is no 'neat-handed Phillis' to sweep them away." What, indeed? Obviously they must not look to Corydon. For if Phillis could rake but not cook, Corydon could cook but not rake.

Besides being a good and loving husband, Hawthorne was a good and loving father, but here again there are curious oddities. From the time he stopped his writing for the day, he was at the disposal of his family, playing with the children and making them wonderful playthings, reading aloud and telling them enchanting stories. They were not supposed to intrude upon him while he was at work, but being children, they did not always do what they were supposed to do, and he does not seem to have resented it.

Yet he claimed to have no "natural partiality" for his children. "I love them according to their deserts—they have to prove their claim to all the affection they get, and I believe that I could love other people's children better than mine, if I felt that they deserved it more." According to his own testimony, he liked girls but never felt that boys were good for anything. It would of course be humorless to take such a statement at face value, but though he seems always to have taken the best care he knew how of Julian, it may be doubted that he ever cared as much for him as he did for the girls. For that matter, there is little or no sentimentality in his references to any of his children in his notebooks. His own family thought him much too starry-eyed when he named Una after the heroine of *The Faerie Queene*, but what he called her was "Onion," and though he was not insensitive to her beauty, he found it "transitory, evanescent, and unaccountable," and there are passages in what he wrote about her in which he seems to be observing a little monster. When she nearly died of malaria in Rome, his sufferings were terrible; indeed Mrs. Hawthorne thought he never did quite get over it. But what are we to make of Maria Mitchell's statement that, upon her sixteenth birthday, which would be less than two years after the onset of her illness, Hawthorne drank his daughter's health in a glass of water and then added, "May you live happily, and be ready to go when you must"? If correctly reported, this seems an incredibly gauche, inconsiderate, and tactless action, which I should have expected from some memento mori type of religious fanatic but not from Hawthorne.

Hawthorne's indifference to the church as an institution has prevented many conventionally minded readers from realizing that he had a religion. As a small child, he hated the bust of John Wesley in his house so dearly that he filled it with water and put it in a cold place in the hope that it would burst; later he hated the portraits of the clerics who had lived in the Old Manse before him with equal zest. And though he seemed distressed by the neglect of religion at Bowdoin during his college days, he did not join the missionary society there, nor did he often attend Sunday services at any time.

Yet, as we have seen already, he knew his Bible well, and *The Pilgrim's Progress* was one of his favorite books. "This morning my wife read to me the Sermon on the Mount most beautifully; so that methinks even the Author of it might be satisfied with such an utterance." There is at least one passage in which he distinguishes between the Bible and "uninspired" literature, and the same distinction seems to be made in "Earth's Holocaust." In one early letter, he refers to Christmas as "the holiest of holy days—the day that brought ransom to all other sinners" (*he* had to work), and once he wondered why Saint Luke did not record what Christ told his disciples when he joined them on their walk to Emmaus after his Resurrection—"whether He was God, or Man, or both, or something between, together with all other essential points of doctrine." In still another passage, he seems to take the story of the Transfiguration on the Mount literally.

Hawthorne's use of the heritage his Puritan ancestors had bequeathed to him was discriminating rather than either credulous or rebellious. Against their Calvinism he did not need to rebel, for it had never been thrust upon him. Hawthornes had married Anglican girls as early as the eighteenth century, and the East Salem Church, which Nathaniel attended as a boy, was described as "then on the verge of Unitarianism." Julian says he never heard his father pronounce the name of God except in reading and that though as a child he supposed they were Unitarians, all he knew about Unitarianism was that it was "good Bostonian." Yet in "Monsieur de Miroir" as it originally appeared in 1837, "Universalist or Unitarian infidelity" was coupled with "Roman Church idolatry." Hawthorne cut the sentence when he reprinted the piece in *Mosses from an Old Manse,* but which communion he was trying to spare is an open question. On the other hand, the fundamentalists knew what they were doing when they reprinted "The Celestial Railroad" as a tract, for no more blazing indictment of those who feel at ease in Zion has ever been penned.

Hawthorne's attitude toward Catholicism has perhaps been sufficiently explored in connection with *The Marble Faun* in chapter 3. Of the other forms of faith alien to his upbringing with which he was brought into contact, the most interesting for the understanding of his personality is spiritualism, a very lively religion indeed in his America. His affection for ghost stories and other forms of supernaturalism might have been expected to foster credulity here. Both temperamentally and by conviction he was strongly antimaterialist, and few men have had a stronger "strangers and pilgrims" feeling in this world. "The grosser life is a dream," he told Sophia, "and the spiritual life a reality." Moreover he had psychic experiences of his own. He himself has described how he repeatedly encountered the ghost of Dr. Harris in the Boston Athenaeum, and two of the houses in which he lived—the Mall Street house in Salem and the Old Manse in Concord—were haunted. In Florence he and Sophia were drawn into the Browning circle, and their own governess, Ada Shepard, herself unwilling and unbelieving, developed a flair for automatic writing. Yet though Mrs. Hawthorne, like Mrs. Browning, was sympathetic, both Hawthorne and Browning were anything but that.

Hawthorne never doubted that spiritistic phenomena occurred, nor did he attempt to refute the testimony of others in their behalf. Intellectually he was open-minded toward spiritualism, but emotionally he was bitterly hostile. All the phenomena of the séance room disgusted him, and he felt a "sluggish . . . repugnance" to have anything to do with them. The puerility of the "messages" that came through, professedly from another world, suggested that the "spirits," if that was what they were, must have become "imbecilic" since having passed over. But his basic objection was that the authentication of spiritual matters by material means seemed monstrous to him; "the view which I take upon this matter is caused by no want of faith in mysteries, but from a deep reverence for the soul and the mysteries which it knows within itself." Consequently, spiritualism and other borderline psychic religious movements seemed to him allied to ancient necromancy. His horror of one human being exercising control over another being what it was, it was inevitable too that he should reject mesmerism. At Brook Farm he may have seen or heard of Anna Q. T. Parsons, a gifted psychometrist in whom some of the persons there were deeply interested. On phrenology he reached no conclusion in print. I have found nothing on numerology except that as a child Una once asked him to write "64" on her hand. He did so, and thereafter adopted "64" as a doodle. "Probably there is some destiny connected with this particular matter," he says. Perhaps there was, for he died in 1864.

Hawthorne once tenderly reassured a little girl who came to him in tears because she had been told he was an infidel. More sophisticated persons have made the same mistake. Despite all Hawthorne's uncertainties, what he believed was large and important. He believed in God. He believed in immortality. He believed in Divine Providence. He believed in the infinite value of every human soul.

About the first of these beliefs he says little, for the simple reason that it never occurred to him there was anything to argue about. He habitually thought of God as the giver of every good and perfect gift and the only refuge of helpless men and women. "Pray GOD for it, my Dove," he tells Sophia, "for you know how to pray better than

I do." And again, about one of her pictures, "Thou couldst not have done it, unless God had helped thee." When Una seemed recovered from her illness, he gave the credit to "God's providence and a good constitution" and not to medicine. Best of all, there is Bliss Perry's beautiful story of how he once sent a sunflower to sorrowing neighbors with the message, "Tell them that the sunflower is a symbol of the sun, and that the sun is a symbol of the glory of God.[5]

About immortality he says more, yet he does not give the impression of being obsessed by it, as Tennyson was. He hopes that Anne Hutchinson's Indian-reared daughter was reunited with her mother in heaven and thinks of Sir Isaac Newton as carrying on his work in the spiritual world. He promised Horatio Bridge that he would regain in Eternity the daughter he had lost here, and he sweetens what would otherwise be the cynical ending of "The Wedding Knell" by presenting the marriage of the elderly couple as "the union of two immortal souls." But he loathed the whole hideous nineteenth-century ritual of funerals and graveyards: "Our thoughts should follow the celestial soul and not the earthly corpse."

As a man with a Calvinistic inheritance, Hawthorne had to do more thinking about Providence than about immortality. The old Calvinistic foreordination and election were not for him; as he saw it, depravity, though universal, was not total. Yet he was not ignorant of the problems involved in reconciling free will with destiny. He recognized the limitations imposed on choice by inheritance and temperament, and, above all, by our own acts, which may, at last, so enmesh us that the area in which we are able to move freely is very narrow.

Yet for him Providence was a loving Providence because God was a loving God. During his early days a young man was drowned in Crooked River. The Freewill Baptist minister who preached his funeral sermon was doubtful as to his salvation, but if the Symmes diary is genuine, Hawthorne did not share this view. "I read one of the Psalms to my mother, and it plainly declares twenty-six times, that 'God's mercy endureth forever.' " He strikes exactly the same note when he rejects the condemnatory Christ in Michelangelo's picture of the Last Judgment, which inspired him to take the side of the damned and ask for "at least a little pity, some few regrets, and not such a stern denunciatory spirit on the part of one who had thought us worth dying for." And he goes on to tell the story of the hideous scrofulous child he encountered in an English workhouse, who took a fancy to him as he was being shown through and begged to be taken up and fondled, and whom he accommodated in expiation of some other's blood guilt. "It was as if God had promised the child this favor in my behalf. I should never have forgiven myself if I had repelled its advances." Only, we must read the English notebooks to learn that Hawthorne was himself the child's victim and the recipient of his affection. When he wrote up the incident in *Our Old Home*, he transformed himself into "one member of our party" and "a person burdened with more than an Englishman's customary reserve."

Like Henry James, Hawthorne had a very clear realization of the presence of evil in the world. But unlike Goodman Brown, Roderick Ellison, and others, he was not obsessed by it. Nor was he ever guilty of oversimplification in his presentation of evil—or of good either. He knew that we live in an imperfect world and must accept it as such, but he never gloried in its imperfections. Any obscurities that may appear in his attitude on this matter, and by which some have been misled, are due to his realism, his understanding of ethical complexities, and his determination to present moral problems on a higher level than that adapted to the primary class. There is no Swinburnian swooning in Shakespeare's "soul of goodness in things evil," and there is none in Hawthorne. There is only a recognition of the fact that nothing that God has made can be utterly corrupted. And to see men redeemed through the suffering and sorrow that follow sin is not to ascribe to sin itself a starry-eyed healing virtue. It is simply to accept thankfully the operations of Divine Grace under the only conditions we can any of us expect to encounter it or benefit by it while we are in this life.

Nathaniel Hawthorne had his limitations as an artist and as a man. His range as a writer was more deep than wide; there were aspects of experience that did not interest him very much; he often said no where other men say yes. We know more about the dark places in the heart of man—and about the tigerish aspects of the world—today than we did in his time, but nothing we have learned seems to make him a less-important writer now than he was then. Even his suspicion of science and technology, once set down to mere obscurantism, now seems to men haunted by the nightmare of destruction by atomic energy considerably less unreasonable than it did then.

He could be stubborn and willful, for he was a human being and not a god. He was sensitive and highly cultivated, with a streak of human coarseness occasionally showing through all his cultivation. He was kind and loving, but he was sometimes cold at the same time. There was a dark side to him, but he faced the light. If there was a potential Ethan Brand in him, he watched and guarded against him and in the end strangled him and beat him down. During his last years darkness laid claim to the weakness of his body and dragged it down, but his soul passed into the light that is of God and illuminates the whole exhilarating, infinitely varied realm of world art.

Appendix

Tales by Nathaniel Hawthorne Not Considered in Chapter 2

The abbreviations listed at the beginning of the Notes, p. 213, apply also to the bibliographical references in this section.

The first reference after the title of each tale hereinunder indicates the original publication of the tale, and the usual abbreviation is employed to indicate the collection in which it now appears. Tales marked "UT," never reprinted by Hawthorne, now appear in the "Uncollected Tales" section of volume 11 of the Centenary Edition.

In addition to the specific references hereinunder, a general reference is indicated to three very useful books: Neal Frank Doubleday, *Hawthorne's Early Tales: A Critical Study* (DUP, 1972); Robert L. Gale, *Plots and Characters in the Fiction and Sketches of Nathaniel Hawthorne* (Archon Books, 1968; MIT Press, 1972); Lee Bertani Vozer Newman, *A Reader's Guide to the Short Stories of Nathaniel Hawthorne* (G. K. Hall, 1974).

ALICE DOANE'S APPEAL (*Token*, 1835; first reprinted in *Sketches and Studies* HM, 1883; "UT"), like *Fanshawe* never acknowledged by Hawthorne, is about as wild a concoction of Gothic sensationalism, comprising murder, jealousy, incest, an extravagant array of evil graveyard ghosts, and a wizard who may or may not have controlled the action as any great writer's reputation ever had to contend against. We do not have the story as originally composed; for attempts to reconstruct its history, see Seymour L. Gross, in *NCF*, 10 (1956), 232–36, and Robert H. Fossum, in *NCF*, 26 (1968), 294–303. As it stands, it has an elaborate frame, in which its putative author reads the story to two girls on Gallows Hill, where the witches were hanged, in an attempt to make their flesh crawl. Parts of the story are not told but only summarized; there are both inconsistencies and scattered effects; and one is never quite sure whether Hawthorne's real interest is in telling a tale or pondering the problems of fiction. For so poor a piece of work, "Alice Doane's Appeal" has inspired a surprising amount of commentary, partly because many of the things Hawthorne does badly in it, he was to do superbly later on and partly because its very shortcomings give a certain type of critic a chance to read his own ideas into it without making any serious attempt to show that Hawthorne shared them. There have also been attempts to read the tale as a unified work of art; among the more sensible examples are the articles by Nina Baym and Stanley Brodwin in *NHJ* 1974. Hawthorne's unsparing condemnation of the witchcraft trials in which his ancestors were involved, highly creditable to him as a man, reflects one of his lifelong agonies, but his imputation of primary responsibility to Cotton Mather is unhistorical.

THE AMBITIOUS GUEST (*New-England Magazine,* June 1835; *TTT*), brief and simple though it is, is a powerful study in irony. There have been many fruitless speculations as to its meaning; actually it has no philosophy; it simply presents a natural calamity such as unfortunately occurs from time to time, and to which we must adjust ourselves as best we can, without understanding. Like "The Great Carbuncle," it connects with Crawford's Notch in the White Mountains, where the Samuel Willey family was destroyed by an avalanche on August 28, 1826; see B. Bernard Cohen, *BPLQ,* 4 (1952), 221–24, and John H. Sears, *AL,* 54 (1982), 354–67. The young man who arrives on the night of the disaster, just in time to share the fate of the loving family which receives paying guests, cherishes "a high and abstracted ambition." Though he could contentedly die unknown, he craves posthumous fame and is convinced that he cannot die until he has achieved his destiny. The tale is crowded with omens, and despite the guest's obsession, he is made attractive to the reader. He and the grown daughter are at once drawn to each other, and since both are rushing toward the same doom, the contrast between his restless ambition and her quiet, home-loving nature is painful and finally terrible. Hawthorne made effective changes in the actual accounts of the disaster. The avalanche skipped the house to destroy the refuge to which the family had fled in both history and fiction, but the actual traveler did not arrive until the morning after, while Hawthorne has him buried with the family, their bodies never found, his identify unknown, even his presence on the fatal night not clearly established. See C. Hobart Edgren, "H's 'The Ambitious Guest': An Interpretation," *NCF,* 10 (1955), 151–56, and, for an interesting anomaly in Hawthorne criticism, James Grossman, "Vanzetti and H," *AQ,* 22 (1970), 902–7, on the resemblances between the tale and Vanzetti's famous last statement.

THE ANTIQUE RING (*Sargent's New Monthly Magazine*, February 1843; "UT") was first reprinted by Mrs. Hawthorne in 1876 in *The Dolliver Romance and Other Pieces*. Edward Caryl, a New England writer of emerging fame, gives his fiancée, Clara Pemberton, an antique ring, which she enjoins him to fit with a legend and read it to her friends. He relates how the Earl of Essex, facing execution, entrusted to the Countess of Shrewsbury, a love token Queen Elizabeth had given him, to be used as a claim upon her mercy in case of need. The Countess betrays both Essex and the Queen by failing to deliver the ring, and Essex is beheaded. All this is cheap, undistinguished, for Hawthorne eminently uncharacteristic historical fiction of the kind the story papers bought by the yard. The ring, which traced back to Merlin, was inhabited by a demon and brought blessing to true lovers but only misfortune to others. Its post-Elizabethan fortunes are traced briefly until it is purified by being donated to charity in the collection box at a Sunday evening service in a Boston church. This part is somewhat better, but the only touch really worthy of Hawthorne comes at the end, where Clara, puzzled how to pin down the "moral" of the tale, is told by Edward, "You know that I can never separate the idea from the symbol in which it manifests itself." The plot of "The Antique Ring" is essentially the same as that of Louis Mercanton's play for Sarah Bernhardt, *Queen Elizabeth*, whose celluloid version was imported into the United States in 1912 by Adolph Zukor to launch his Famous Players film company. The tale gets more attention than it deserves from Angus Fletcher in *Allegory: The Theory of a Symbolic Mode* (Cornell University Press, 1964), and in *NEQ*, 46 (1973), 622–26, John J. McDonald developed the weird notion that Edward Cary represents Longfellow, which, for some reason, Lea Newman seems to accept.

THE ARTIST OF THE BEAUTIFUL (*US Mag*, June 1864; *MOM*) is probably the story in which Hawthorne most deeply ponders the nature of the artist and his relations with society, but whether he makes completely clear just what he wishes to say about these things has occasioned considerable disagreement. The germ of the idea is in an 1840 notebook entry: "To represent a man as spending life and the intensest labor in the accomplishment of some mechanical trifle . . ." and sources have been sought in Spenser ("Muiopotmos"), Swift, Edmund Burke, Mary Shelley (*Frankenstein*), Isaac D'Israeli, Edward Taylor, Emerson ("The Poet"), and Hugh Blair's *Rhetoric*, and outside of literature too, as in Hawthorne's friendship with Thoreau and in Fanny Kemble's reference to a mechanical bird that achieved "the realization of fairyland through machinery." Owen Warland is anything but a trifler however. His search is for a completely nonutilitarian beauty "that should attain to the ideal which Nature has proposed to herself, in all her creatures, but has never taken pains to realize." He is opposed by Peter Hovenden, the hardheaded old watchmaker to whom he was once apprenticed; Hovenden's daughter Annie, whom he idealizes out of all semblance of reality and supposes himself to love, but makes no attempt to win; and the blacksmith Robert Danforth, the completely decent, practical, efficient man of this world, who marries Annie. The end of the story is pure Platonism. After almost superhuman toil and devotion, Owen creates a mechanical butterfly that is more beautiful and in a sense more "real" than any natural butterfly and presents it to Annie as a belated wedding present, but when it is grasped and crushed by her vigorous small son, its creator is quite unmoved. He now knows not only that "the reward of all high performance must be sought within itself, or sought in vain," but also that when an artist has risen "high enough to achieve the beautiful, the symbol by which he made it perceptible to mortal senses became of little value in his eyes." In a sense all this is profoundly true, but it ignores the fact that art is communication, thus robbing it of any social significance and virtually isolating the artist. It is not surprising therefore that Owen should have acquired such warm defenders as Richard Harter Fogle (*H's Fiction: The Light and the Dark*) and James W. Gargano ("H's 'The Artist of the Beautiful,' " *AL*, 35 [1963], 225–30), and also inspired such attacks as that of Rudolph von Abele, in *The Death of the Artist* (Nijhoff, 1955). Only a writer as painfully aware as Hawthorne was of the dangers by which the artist is beset could have been so scrupulously fair in his presentation of the opposing forces in this story. Peter Hovenden is a repellent figure, but Robert Danforth is not, and though Annie has her limitations of intelligence and imagination, she strongly resembles a number of young women in other stories whom the author obviously admired. By his reiterated emphasis upon Owen's smallness, sensitiveness, paleness, and timidity, Hawthorne deliberately refrained from making him a heroic figure. It is somewhat surprising too that a writer so unsympathetic toward science and technology (Owen is actually sickened by the sight of a steam engine) should have chosen even so nonutilitarian a mechanic as Owen to represent the artist. That the divided sympathies with which the reader may finish this tale are due to a blurred focus is nevertheless unlikely. However important art may be and however superior the artist to his less imaginative fellows, it still remains true that his gift involves limitations as well as privileges. Both Millicent Bell, *H's View of the Artist* and John Caldwell Stubbs, *The Pursuit of Form* present admirably balanced views of this matter; see also two recent, thoughtful articles in *ESQ*, by Sheldon W. Liebman, in vol. 22 (1976), 85–95, and by June Howard, in vol. 28 (1982), 1–10. Two stories by Walter de la Mare, "The Connoisseur" and especially "Lispet, Lispett, and Vaine," are interesting to compare with Hawthorne's tale.

THE BATTLE OMEN (Salem *Gazette*, November 2, 1830; "UT") is a brief anecdote, conjecturally Hawthorne's, about two young men returning home from what seems to have been a skirmish with Indians shortly before the American Revolution. Discussing the signs and wonders vouchsafed to their Puritan ancestors but no longer to them, they pause in the shadow of a great rock while one tells the other how, some fifty years ago, "a benighted fisherman had heard a sound of martial music in the air above him, coming from the direction of Canada," and while they talk the phenomenon is repeated. See Donald C. Gallup, "On H's Authorship of 'The Battle Omen,' " *NEQ*, 9 (1936), 690–99.

THE CANTERBURY PILGRIMS (*Token*, 1833; *SI*) and THE SHAKER BRIDAL (*Token*, 1838; *TTT*) are both stories about the Shakers, followers of Mother Ann Lee, who withdraw from the world and "the world's people" to live celibate in their own communities. Though Hawthorne's first impression of the Shakers, after visiting their settlement at Canterbury, New Hampshire, in 1831 seems to have been favorable, both tales emphatically reject the Shaker attitude and way of life. In the first, Josiah and Miriam, leaving the settlement to give themselves to "carnal love," encounter a disappointed poet, a ruined merchant, and a family who have not only suffered an inability to "make good" in the world but have also seen their love for each other grow cold, on their way to join it. Yet at the end the renegades decide that "We will not go back. The world never can be dark to us, for we will always love one another." The tone of "The Shaker Bridal" is considerably more hostile. Here authorial comment brands the Shakers as "generally below the ordinary standard of intelligence." The aged retiring head of the community, Father Ephraim, has been "a dissolute libertine" in his youth and is now not only antiworld but antilife, looking forward to the time "when children shall no more be born and die, and the last survivor of mortal race . . . shall see the sun go down, never more to rise on a world of sin and sorrow!" Worst of all, Martha, who had been content to allow Adam, whom she had once hoped to marry, to make their decision for them, has enough normal feeling left in her heart so that she collapses and perhaps dies at his feet during the ceremony that was intended to install them as the new heads of the community. It is interesting to compare these stories with Howells's two novelettes about the Shakers, *A Parting and a Meeting* and *The Day of Their Wedding* (both 1896). See Seymour L. Gross, "H and the Shakers," *AL*, 29 (1958), 457–63, and John Lauber, "H's Shaker Tales,"

NCF, 18 (1963), 82–86. There is a long, excellent commentary on "The Canterbury Pilgrims" in Hyatt H. Waggoner, *H: A Critical Study,* pp. 64–78

THE CELESTIAL RAILROAD (*US Mag,* May 1843; *MOM*), one of the most brilliant of Hawthorne's minor tales, has often been called a parody, but is more properly speaking a pastiche. Hawthorne brings one of his very favorite books, Bunyan's *Pilgrim's Progress,* up to date, with devastating satirical effect, aimed not at Bunyan but at the religious modernists, including the New England Unitarians and transcendentalists. Guided by Mr. Smooth-it-away, the narrator travels to the Celestial City (though he wakes up before he gets there) in a comfortable railroad coach, whose engine is operated by Apollyon, and where the burden Christian carried on his back is comfortably deposited in the baggage car. The Slough of Despond has been filled in with non-Christian scriptures and the lucubrations of contemporary French and German philosophers, and the menacing giants, Pope and Pagan, have been displaced by Giant Transcendentalism, who feeds pilgrims "smoke, mist, and moonshine" and whose utterances are unintelligible. The Valley of the Shadow is now lighted by gas. Vanity Fair is well churched with the Reverend Messrs. Shallow-deep, Stumble-at-Truth, This-to-day, Bewilderment, Clog-the-spirit, and Wind-of-doctrine as shepherds. But whether the pasteboards Evangelist sells at the ticket office will be accepted at the Celestial City is still unknown. The American Sunday School Union and other Evangelical organizations reprinted "The Celestial Railroad" as a tract, but before we enroll Hawthorne as a Fundamentalist, we should remember that he is more concerned with laodiceanism in religion and in life than with the shortcomings of any particular body. The fact that he respected the stamina and earnestness of his Puritan ancestors does not mean that he accepted all the tenets upon which, for them, these qualities rested. Concord's own Giant Transcendentalism, Emerson, must have recognized this when, despite his general contempt for Hawthorne's work, he saw in this piece "a serene strength which we cannot afford not to praise in this low life." See W. Stacy Johnson, "H and 'The Pilgrim's Progress,'" *JEGP,* 50 (1951), 156–66, and G. Ferris Cronkhite, "The Transcendental Railroad," *NEQ,* 24 (1951), 306–28.

THE CHRISTMAS BANQUET (*US Mag,* January 1844; *MOM*) describes a feast provided year after year for the ten most miserable people that can be found. All the accoutrements are sepulchral, and a skeleton, reputedly that of the founder of the feast, sits at the head of the table holding a cypress wreath. Year by year, all the guests change except one, Gervayse Hastings, who alone fails to represent a type of recognizable misery. At the beginning he seems to possess all the graces of youth, and as time passes all the rewards life can offer come to him. At his last banquet, now aged eighty, he himself, challenged, states his claim: he has never been able to feel either joy or grief. After he has made his confession, the skeleton collapses, and Hastings's fellow banqueters notice that his shadow has ceased to flicker on the wall. The story is told by Roderick Elliston (cf. "Egotism; or, The Bosom Serpent"). Hawthorne's preoccupation with the dangers of isolation from humanity is one of his pervasive themes, and it is clear that he felt himself in danger of being swallowed up by it before his marriage. Frank Davidson has suggested sources in Voltaire's *Candide* (*BPLQ*, 3 [1951], 244–46) and Johnson's *Rasselas* (*MLN*, 65 [1948], 545–48). Readers of Henry James will recall "The Beast in the Jungle."

DAVID SWAN (*Token*, 1837; *TTT*) is subtitled "A Fantasy." It might almost as well have been called a meditation upon the text announced at the beginning: "We can be but partially acquainted even with the events that actually influence our course through life, and our final destiny. There are innumerable other events . . . which come close upon us, yet pass away without actual results, or even betraying their near approach." While David Swan slumbers beside the road on his way to Boston, he escapes wealth, love, and death. A rich old couple are so taken by him that they ponder the possibility of adopting him. A girl who brushes away a bee that might have stung him could easily have been his ideal mate. A pair of drunkards consider stealing his bundle and even killing him if he wakes up and offers resistance, but are frightened away by a dog. "Sleeping or waking, we hear not the airy footsteps of the strange things that almost happen."

THE DEVIL IN MANUSCRIPT (*New-England Magazine*, 1835; *SI*) is more interesting for its reflection of Hawthorne's state of mind when he was, as he himself put it, the most obscure man of letters in America and for the hero's comments on the difficulties of book publication than it is as a story. Oberon, one of the names Hawthorne sometimes used, despairing of recognition, burns his manuscripts. There is only one incident, but it is a "clincher." The papers start a conflagration, so that, at long last, Oberon's brain "has set the town on fire!"

DR. HEIDIGGER'S EXPERIMENT (*Knickerbocker*, January 1837; *TTT*), like Barrie's *Dear Brutus*, makes the point that human beings would not profit by a chance to live their lives over again, since, still being themselves, they would make the same mistakes as before. Dr. Heidigger gives "four venerable friends"—a ruined merchant, a politician, and a superannuated

rake and belle—water from the Fountain of Youth "which Ponce de Leon
. . . went in search of two or three centuries ago." It works temporarily,
even to the extent of causing them to attempt to repeat the excesses of their
youth, the gentlemen making fools of themselves over the same lady, but
the effect soon wears off, after which, having learned nothing, they resolve
to leave for Florida at once in search of the Fountain. Dr. Heidigger's laboratory is rich in Gothic properties, and the use of the elixir links this story
to Hawthorne's late uncompleted romances. In the 1865 edition of *Twice-
Told Tales*, the author expressed resentment over "an English review" that
had suggested his indebtedness for this story to a novel by Dumas that was
actually written later. This notice is identified and discussed by Victor E.
Gibbons in *MLN*, 60 (1945), 408–9. Both Laurence E. Scanlon, "That Very
Singular Man, Dr. Heidigger," *NCF*, 17 (1962), 253–63, and William T.
Blair, " 'Dr. Heidigger's Experiment': An Allegory of Sin," *NHJ* 1976,
286–91, take a very dim view of Dr. Heidigger, the latter seeing him as "not
only a Devil, but somewhat of a Super-Devil."

DROWNE'S WOODEN IMAGE (*Godey's Lady's Book*, July 1844; *MOM*) is
set in colonial Boston. The painter Copley, who plays a chorus role, left for
England in 1774, and Shem Drowne was a coppersmith, best remembered
for his grasshopper weather vane on Faneuil Hall and the Indian weather
vane on the Province House, now in the Massachusetts Historical Society.
That the basic source of the tale is Ovid's story of Pygmalion is made clear
by Copley's exclamation upon perceiving the vast superiority of the figure-
head Drowne creates for Captain Hunnewell over all his other work: "Who
would have looked for a modern Pygmalion in the person of a Yankee
mechanic!" Drowne does not regard his masterpiece as his own work: the
figure lay "within that block of wood," and it was his business to find it. All
he knows is that "a wellspring of inward wisdom gushed within me as I
wrought upon the oak with my whole strength, and soul, and faith," and in
such a statement the whole Romantic doctrine of "inspiration" as the source
of artistic achievement is involved. But the exact circumstances that became
operative in Drowne's case are left rather maddeningly ambiguous. We are
never told directly that the foreign lady whose image was so perfectly
reproduced secretly posed for Drowne. Captain Hunnewell whispers the
necessary information and instructions "in so low a tone that it would be
unmannerly to repeat what was evidently intended for the carver's private
ear," but Hawthorne does commit himself to the extent of telling us that to
the carver "there came a brief season of excitement, kindled by love." Even
the townspeople realize that a wonder has been wrought, though, being
capable of only a degraded interpretation of it, they ascribe it to witchcraft.

Hawthorne, however, is sure that though Drowne was a real artist only once in his life, "the very highest state to which a human spirit can attain in its highest inspiration, is its truest and most natural state." Perhaps the most enthusiastic admirer of this story is Lea Newman, who sees it as "the clearest statement in all Hawthorne's fiction of how the creative artist operates" and thinks it "may be one of Hawthorne's as yet 'undiscovered' masterpieces." It is well analyzed by Millicent Bell in *Hawthorne's View of the Artist*. See also Bryot K. Tripathy, "H, Art and the Artist: A Study of 'Drowne's Wooden Image' and 'The Artist of the Beautiful,' " *Indian Journal of American Studies*, vol. 1, no. 4 (November 1971), 63–71, and Sarah I. Davis, "H's Pygmalion as William Rush," *SSF*, 19 (1982), 343–49.

EARTH'S HOLOCAUST (*Graham's Magazine*, March 1844; *MOM*) is probably Hawthorne's fullest exposition of his much-discussed attitude toward reform. On "one of the broadest prairies of the West," a vast bonfire is built to rid the world of all that impedes its progress or destroys human happiness. The aim of the conflagration is not only the abolition of such evils as war, drunkenness, crime, and capital punishment but also of all badges of special privilege and even of everything in the arts that no longer serves human needs; indeed the more radical reformers wish to destroy marriage, money, property, and government. In itself the holocaust is completely successful, but the Devil watches it unperturbed because "that foul cavern," the human heart, from which all evils spring, has not been destroyed. The bias of the story is not antireform (the "muttered expostulations" against prohibition proceed from "respectable gentlemen with red noses and wearing gouty shoes"), and its essentially religious message is simply that the human condition cannot be substantially improved except by the redemption of humanity itself. The narrative also contains interesting revelations of Hawthorne's judgment of various writers whose works are cast into the fire and of his respect for religion coupled with his contempt for ritual and ecclesiasticism; thus the Bible survives, but "certain marginal notes and commentaries" are consumed. The nineteenth-century nature cult also comes in for some rough handling. Though not one of his significant works of art, "Earth's Holocaust" ranks with "The Celestial Railroad" as a significant expression of Hawthorne's moral and religious beliefs. See H. H. Waggoner, *Hawthorne: A Critical Study*, 19–23.

EDWARD FANE'S ROSEBUD (*Knickerbocker*, September 1837; *TTT*) is an inconsequential though tender if somewhat morbid tale or sketch, essentially a rather exclamatory meditation over Nurse Toothaker, an aged crone, solacing herself with gin and water, who was once the darling of a faithless lover, now the great Edward Fane. Most of the piece comprises an account of how she married Toothaker without love but nursed him faithfully through a lingering illness. The only incident occurs at the end, when she is summoned to the bedside of the dying Fane.

EGOTISM; OR, THE BOSOM SERPENT (*US Mag*, March 1843; *MOM*) is certainly Hawthorne's most horrible story, especially for readers who have a horror of snakes. The author describes the basic idea in two notebook entries: "A snake taken into a man's stomach and nourished there from fifteen years to thirty-five, tormenting him most horribly. A type of envy or some other evil passion." And: "A man to swallow a small snake,—and it to be a symbol of a cherished sin." Melville was enthusiastic about this story, but though Mildred K. Travis (*ESQ*, 63 [1971], 13–18) has plausibly suggested it as a possible source for "The Jolly Corner," more recent readers seem more inclined to agree with Henry James that its development is "stiff and mechanical, slightly incongruous." It has engendered a number of studies, most of which, however, are concerned with possible use or occurrences of the same basic idea in literature, folklore, and theological treatises (see, for example, George Monteiro, "H's Emblematic Serpent," *NHJ* 1973, pp. 134–42, and the references therein cited; also Jackson Campbell Boswell, "Bosom Serpents Before H: Origin of a Symbol," *ELN*, 12 [1975], 179–87). Despite Hawthorne's apparent determination not to commit himself irrevocably to the serpent as either actual or symbolic, the title alone would seem to indicate that the latter is at least the more important aspect. Contradictory as he is, Roderick both rejoices in his horrible idiosyncrasy and seems determined to establish that almost everybody else shares it with him. In his preoccupation with the world within, he is a true Hawthorne protagonist, but the figure employed seems so exaggerated that some readers find it difficult to reach beyond symbol to meaning. The tale comes closest to "The Jolly Corner" in Roderick's salvation through the love of a woman, but Hawthorne's ending is more religious. If the serpent is time or evil, then the fountain into which it may or may not disappear at the end is probably eternity, and Rosina at least is sure that human abnormalities and aberrations can only appear in their true light when viewed in their proper relation to the spiritual world. Both Poe (*PMLA*, 74 [1959], 607–14) and Jones Very (*NEQ*, 42 [1969], 267–75) have been nominated as having furnished possible prototypes for this story. David M. Van Leer's "Roderick's Other Serpent: H's Use of Spenser," *ESQ*, 27 (1981), 73–84, is a detailed study of what he calls "the most extended of the Spenserian analogues and the center of the critical debate over Hawthorne's use of Spenser."

FEATHERTOP: A MORALIZED LEGEND (*International Monthly Magazine of Literature, Science, and Art,* February and March, 1851; *MOM*), Hawthorne's last short story, is an out-and-out fairy tale, with some halfhearted, playful examples at rationalizing or allegorizing, which hardly go far enough to justify James F. Folsom's interpretation of it as "an allegory of the creative process" (*Man's Accidents and God's Purposes: Multiplicity in H's Fiction* [College and University Press, 1963]). Though Percy Matenko (*Ludwig Tieck and America* [UNCP, 1934]) suggests a possible literary source, the basic idea appears in a notebook entry of 1849, where we read of a magician who created a pumpkin-headed scarecrow and sent him out into the world, as "the symbol of a large class," to take in the undiscerning despite the absence of heart, soul, and intellect. In "Feathertop" the magician becomes Mother Rigby, a New England witch, and Feathertop's life principle resides in the tobacco pipe he must continually puff, thus not too happily suggesting a "wild, extravagant, and fantastical impression, as if his life and being were akin to the smoke." The witch sends him to woo Polly Gookin, the rich merchant's daughter, who is taken in by him (only a dog and a small child have apprehended his true nature) until a mirror reveals him for what he is. Feathertop in some aspects suggests both the Scarecrow and Jack Pumpkinhead in L. Frank Baum's Oz books (the latter, like him, is created by a witch), and the mirror suggests another of Baum's stories, *Queen Zixi of Ix* (1905), wherein the witch queen who is more than six hundred years old appears as a beautiful young girl to the world but cannot deceive a mirror, and it may well be that Baum used the tale as a source. Percy MacKaye's play, *The Scarecrow* (1908) was suggested by "Feathertop," and in 1923 Frank Tuttle made the play into a film, bearing the silly title *Puritan Passions,* and starring Glenn Hunter. Produced by a minor company and now almost forgotten, *Puritan Passions* was nevertheless one of the few really fine American fantasy films.

THE GREAT CARBUNCLE (*Token,* 1837; *TTT*) is allied by its subtitle, "A Mystery of the White Mountains," with both "The Ambitious Guest" and "The Great Stone Face," and Hawthorne himself, in his introductory note, credits it to "Indian tradition" and James Sullivan's *History of the District of Maine* (1795), which has not prevented commentators from searching out other possible literary influences. The first paragraph only sets the action "once in the olden time," but later we learn that one of the characters later perished in "the great fire of London," and there are also references to Captain John Smith and pine-tree shillings. The tale is almost straight allegory, and the characters, "each, save one youthful pair, impelled by his own selfish and solitary longing for this wondrous gem," are all types. The merchant Pigsnort represents simple greed; the scientist Doctor Cacaphodel would reduce the Great Carbuncle to its elements for analysis; the Poet seeks inspiration for his poems; and Lord de Vere would add it to the glories of his house. The Seeker and the Cynic are somewhat different. The first is merely a fanatic for whom the long search has become a mania without meaning, and the Cynic, who does not believe in the Great Carbuncle, even when, at last, he stands before it and is stricken blind by its light, is like a proselytizing atheist with his gospel of negativity. Matthew and Hannah, the only characters with whom the author sympathizes, find the Great Carbuncle, but, having learned from the sad fates of their comrades, reject it and resolve never again to "desire more light than all the world may share with us." Raymond L. Haskell, *NEQ*, 10 (1937), 533–35, records a not-unreasonable modern attempt to identify the phenomenon that suggested the legend. See also W. R. Thompson, "Theme and Method in 'The Great Carbuncle,' " *South Atlantic Bulletin*, 21 (1961), 3–10, and Patrick Morrow, "A Writer's Workshop: H's 'The Great Carbuncle,' " *SSF*, 6 (1969), 157–64.

THE GREAT STONE FACE (*National Era*, January 24, 1850; *SI*) was reported by Mrs. Hawthorne as having been downgraded by her husband because of "the mechanical structure of the story, the moral being so plain and manifest." But she was quite right in regarding its hero Ernest as "a divine creation,—so grand, so comprehensive, and so simple." If there is any Hawthorne story that deserves to be called "lovely," it is this one, and if it has been comparatively neglected during recent years, this is not only because it needs comparatively little elucidation but also because loveliness seems to be the last quality that most modern readers of fiction are looking for. In the successive failures of Mr. Gathergold, Old Blood-and-Thunder, Old Stony Phiz, and even the unnamed Poet to be accepted as embodiments of the Great Stone Face, Hawthorne makes a fairly complete rejection of all self-seeking, morally flawed forms of distinction among men (cf. James J. Lynch, "Structure and Allegory in 'The Great Stone Face,' " *NCF*, 15 [1960], 137–46). "The substance of a human face to be formed on the side of a mountain, or in the fracture of a small stone, by a *lusus naturae*" exists in the White Mountains of New Hampshire, but there is no evidence of Hawthorne having seen it before writing his story. Daniel Webster has long been seen as a likely original for Old Stony Phiz and Andrew Jackson for Old Blood-and-Thunder, while Ernest has been thought of as having been influenced by Emerson, Thoreau, and Wordsworth, and even interpreted as a Christ figure (cf. Leo B. Levy, "H and the Sublime," *AL*, 37 [1966], 391–402). Wordsworth has entered the discussion again, in less completely complimentary aspect, as the possible original of the Poet (K. G. Pfeiffer,

"The Prototype of the Poet in 'The Great Stone Face,' " *Research Studies of the State College of Washington,* 9 [1941], 100–108). Finally, "The Great Stone Face" has furnished the "central theme" in the plan of the distinguished novel *Raintree County,* by Ross Lockridge, Jr. (Boyd Litzinger, "Mythmaking in America," *Tennessee Studies in Literature,* 8 [1963], 81–84).

THE HAUNTED QUACK (*Token,* 1831; "UT"), never collected by Hawthorne, was republished with commentary by Frank B. Sanborn in the *New-England Magazine* in 1898. Two years later Horace E. Scudder included it in the Autograph and Old Manse editions, and it is accepted by the Centenary editors. On a canal boat between Schenectady and Utica, the narrator encounters a quack who is on his way to give himself up for having killed a vicious old hag, one Goody Gordon, who expired, cursing and promising to haunt him, after having swallowed one of his nostrums. This undistinguished narrative gains a certain interest as a kind of comic treatment of one of Hawthorne's great themes, the torment of conscience, for, as both the reader and Hippocrates Jenkins himself learn at the end, the old women soon recovered from her fits and her swoon and now craves nothing but more medicine; hence the ghost by which Jenkins has been haunted exists only in his imagination. The treatment of medicine in this tale seems not wholly uncharacteristic of Hawthorne, but it is difficult to believe that he could misquote a familiar passage from *Romeo and Juliet.*

THE HOLLOW OF THE THREE HILLS (Salem *Gazette,* November 14, 1830; *TTT*) is one of the oldest Hawthorne tales extant. Despite Poe's warm praise, it is hardly more than an elaborate exercise in Gothic setting and symbolism. A woman whose sins have destroyed the happiness of her parents, driven her husband mad, and left her son to die consults an aged crone at dusk in the hollow of three hills and dies at the end of what modern psychics would call a "reading." Like the so-called Witch of Endor in the Bible, the crone, though unmistakably evil, seems to function as a medium rather than a witch, and her client's death appears to have been included merely to bring the tale to a conclusion. See C. S. Burhans, "H's Mind and Art in 'The Hollow of the Three Hills,' " *JEGP,* 60 (1961), 286–95. In *NHJ* 1975, pp. 177–81, Prabhat K. Pandeya deals with setting and symbolism. The witchcraft angle is explored by William Bysshe Stein, *H's Faust,* and by Ely Stock in *ATQ,* 14 (1972), 31–33, while Dan F. McCall, in *NEQ,* 42 (1969), 432–35, would establish a connection between the tale and one of Emily Dickinson's poems.

JOHN INGLEFIELD'S THANKSGIVING (*US Mag,* March 1849; *SI*) is, for Haw-thorne, a strangely ineffective and inadequately motivated treatment of his great theme of sin and its effect upon the human soul. The blacksmith's errant daughter returns unannounced to her family's Thanksgiving dinner table and her former lover, from months of "guilt and infamy," is kindly received, and then, quite as abruptly, disappears again into the night, "a smile . . . as of triumphant mockery" gleaming "in her eyes . . . to their sur-prise and grief."

THE LILY'S QUEST (*Southern Rose,* January 18, 1839; *TTT*) is subtitled "An Apologue." Hawthorne himself states the basic idea in an 1836 note— "that there is no place on earth fit for the site of a pleasure-house, because there is no spot that may not have been saddened by human grief, stained by crime, or hallowed by death." It is the lovers Adam Forrester and Lilias Fay who undertake the search, but the place they finally decide upon turns out to be the site of an old tomb, and here Lilias herself is shortly interred. Though this seems a depressing, even morbid, theme, the tale, though of no literary distinction, ends on a triumphant note of hope, based on religious faith, that suggests not only Hawthorne's own story, "The Wedding Knell," but Donne's great sonnet, "Death, Be Not Proud." "Joy! joy!" cries Adam, "on a grave be the site of our Temple; and now our happiness is for Eter-nity." The emphasis upon the vanity of human wishes suggests Samuel Johnson's *Rasselas,* and critics have found echoes and influences from Dante, Bunyan, and the Romantic poets, but the only detailed study is Leo B. Levy's sensitive essay, "The Temple and the Tomb: H's 'The Lily's Quest,' " *SSF,* 3 (1966), 334–42.

LITTLE DAFFYDOWNDILLY (*Boys' and Girls' Magazine,* 1843; *SI*) is an allegorical tale for children, in which the little protagonist runs away from Mr. Toil, the stern schoolmaster, only to find that, in one guise or another, Mr. Toil presides over all aspects of human activity, including even music-making.

THE MAN OF ADAMANT (*Token,* 1837; *SI*) is Hawthorne's reductio ad absurdum of religious independency. Convinced that he alone has found the way of salvation and that all the rest of the world is doomed and damned (in which he rejoices), Richard Digby withdraws to a damp, sepulchre-like cave in the wilderness to read his Bible and pray in solitude, where he drinks only the water that drips from the stalactites above his head and stays there until he dies and turns to stone. Hawthorne's criticism has generally been interpreted as being aimed at the Calvinists, though some think he had the excessive individualism and self-reliance of the Transcendentalists in mind. Some writers find Digby, like Ethan Brand, guilty of the unpardonable sin, yet it is possible that, being insane, he has committed no sin at all (we are told that his heart was already turning to stone before he came to the cave), in which case the story would have little interest save as a clinical study, and it does not go deep enough for that. Hawthorne himself wrote Sophia that "it seemed a fine idea to me when I looked at it prophetically, but I failed in giving shape and substance to the vision which I saw. I don't think it can be very good." The appearance to Digby of his late love, Mary Goffe, either as a ghost or in a dream, in a vain attempt to save him, is characteristic of Hawthorne's attitude toward the *Ewig-Weibliche*, but it is not convincingly handled. There are Biblical references and conceptions, and Spenser's *Faerie Queene*, Scott's *Old Mortality*, and a story by William Austin have all been invoked as possible sources. See John W. Shroeder, "H's 'The Man of Adamant': A Spenserian Source Study," *PQ*, 41 (1962), 744–56, and R. Laman Bland, "William Austin's 'The Man with the Cloaks: A Vermont Legend': An American Influence on 'The Man of Adamant,' " *NHJ* 1977, pp. 139–45.

THE MINISTER'S BLACK VEIL (*Token*, 1836; *TTT*) is perhaps the very best single example in a tale of both Hawthorne's preoccupation as a writer with secret, hidden sin and his use of an object to symbolize a spiritual condition. The Reverend Mr. Hooper appears in his pulpit one Sunday morning wearing a black crape veil, which he thereafter refuses to remove even when he is dying. He loses his betrothed because he will tell her only that it is "a type and a symbol" which may not be removed until the hour "when all of us shall cast aside our veils." Unlike other obsessed eccentrics in Hawthorne, he does not withdraw from society; instead, like Dimmesdale, he becomes a more faithful shepherd of souls than he could otherwise have been. He is "kind and loving, though unloved and feared," and his veil "enabled him to sympathize with all dark affections" and gives him an "awful power over souls that were in agony for sin." Hawthorne himself cites the Reverend Joseph Moody, who wore a veil after accidentally killing a friend as a likely original, but adds that Hooper's veil had "a different import." It could have been assumed as an act of penance for some personal sin (one writer has accused Hooper of murder, and another puts him in a class with Ethan Brand); it might serve as a token of mourning for all the world's evil; but more likely, as Hooper's dying words indicate, it represents the state of fallen humanity, which Hooper shares through the mere fact of sharing human nature. "Why do you tremble at me alone? . . . Tremble also at each other! . . . I look around me, and, lo! on every visage a Black Veil!" Isaiah walked naked through the streets of Jerusalem to typify the coming desolation of his people, and Hosea married a prostitute to indicate that the relationship between Jehovah and Israel resembled that between a faithful husband and an unfaithful wife. Like his illustrious predecessors, Mr. Hooper turns himself into a walking parable, acting out his sermon rather than merely voicing it. "The Minister's Black Veil" is a simple and powerful tale, but it seems to have inspired more wild interpretations than most of Hawthorne's work, for which the basic reason seems to be that commentators, forgetting that art is necessarily much simpler than life, insist upon introducing considerations into it. See Victor Strandberg, "The Artist's Black Veil," *NEQ*, 41 (1968), 567–74; Robert E. Morsberger, " 'The Minister's Black Veil,': 'Shrouded in a Blackness, Ten Times Black,' " *NEQ*, 46 (1973), 454–63; James B. Reece, "Mr. Hooper's Vow," *ESQ*, 21 (1975), 93–102; Lawrence I. Berkove, " 'The Minister's Black Veil': The Gloomy Moses of Milford," *NHJ* 1978, pp. 147–67. But perhaps the warmest and certainly one of the most erudite admirers of the story is Paul Goodman, in *The Structure of Literature* (UCP, 1959).

MR. HIGGINBOTHAM'S CATASTROPHE (*New-England Magazine*, December 1834; *TTT*) has been compared to "Mrs. Bullfrog," as Hawthorne's only other humorous narrative, but though it does not lack a certain tartness, it has nothing like either the disillusion or the burlesque exaggeration of the other tale. Domenicus Pike, a rather silly young tobacco peddler in the small towns of New England, hears that Mr. Higginbotham has been hanged in his orchard by an Irishman and a "nigger," and though the tale as told is obviously self-contradictory, his love of sensation is too strong for him to be able to resist spreading it along his road. It is repeated, believed, contradicted, corroborated, elaborated, modified as to fact, time, and circumstances, achieves local newspaper headlines, makes Pike first a hero and then, when it is authoritatively refuted by the arrival of Higginbotham's niece at Parker's Falls, a subject of public execration. The clever, trick, tongue-in-cheek ending (it turns out that though the crime had not been committed, it had been planned, and Domenicus himself arrives just in time to save the intended victim and be rewarded with the hand of his niece and ultimately his fortune) has led writers determined to have Hawthorne profound even in his most relaxed moods (see James Duban, "The Sceptical Content of 'Mr. Higginbotham's Catastrophe,' " *AL*, 48 [1976], 292–301) to engage in learned speculations, but Daniel G. Hoffman (*Form and Fable in American Fiction*) seems more relevant when he invokes the New England folk tradition and bucolic humor. See also R. R. Brubaker, "H's Experiment in Popular Form: 'Mr. Higginbotham's Catastrophe,' " *Southern Humanities Review*, 7 (1973), 155–66.

MRS. BULLFROG (*Token*, 1837; *MOM*) was virtually repudiated by its author: "The story was written as a mere experiment . . . ; it did not come from any depth within me,—neither my heart nor mind had anything to do with it." This statement may in a measure reflect Mrs. Hawthorne's dislike. It was published before his engagement to her; its treatment is as broadly farcical as a comic valentine; it is the only Hawthorne story that suggests a cynical attitude toward marriage, though, even so, the wife is treated no more severely than the husband. When a carriage accident just after their wedding apprises Bullfrog that his lovely wife is not only a horror without her makeup and accoutrements but an Amazon, a virago, and a tippler, who has fleeced a former admirer in a breach-of-promise suit, he is sorely stricken, but the knowledge that she intends to invest her five thousand dollars in his hardware business makes everything right, and he easily adjusts himself to her view that we cannot expect perfection in this world. Both Johnson's *Rambler* (B. Bernard Cohen, *PQ*, 32 [1953], 382–87) and Le Sage (Darrel Abel, *Notes and Queries*, 198 [1953], 165–66) have been suggested as possible sources; see also John M. Solomon, "H's Ribald Classic: 'Mrs. Bullfrog' and the Folktale," *Journal of Popular Culture*, 7 (1973), 582–88.

THE NEW ADAM AND EVE (*US Mag;* February 1843; *MOM*), like "Earth's Holocaust," is more important for its expressions of Hawthorne's thinking than as a story. Attempts have been made to connect it with one of the minor trends in the literature of its time (see Curtis Dahl, "The American School of Catastrophe," *AQ*, 11 [1959], 380), an interest that seems only more relevant in the atomic age. Written "in a mood half sportive and half thoughtful," it presupposes that all living things have been destroyed on earth but all man's works left standing. The new Adam and Even appear in Boston. They wander into an emporium, a church, a courtroom, a bank, a jewelry store, the Harvard library, Mount Auburn cemetery, etc. They suppose Bunker Hill monument to be an expression of religious devotion, but think the church less conducive to religious feeling than a forest glade. The animal food and alcoholic drinks set out for dinner in the mansion disgust them, and they are shocked by the vulgar display, while the prison with its gallows is almost more than they can bear. Though they see no need of clothing, Adam gets "his first idea of the witchery of dress" when Eve takes "a remnant of exquisite silver gauze and [draws] it around her form," thus anticipating Virginia in Cot's famous 1880 painting, "The Storm." Since Eve comprises "the whole nature of womanhood," she is also attracted by jewels but flings away "inestimable pearls" in favor of flowers. See F. N. Doubleday, "H's Satirical Allegory," *CE*, 3 (1942), 325–37, and Frank Davidson, "H's Hive of Honey," *MLN*, 61 (1946), 14–21. The last paragraph suggests the end of "Eve's Diary," by Mark Twain, and those who find their imaginations stimulated by the contemporary relevance of Hawthorne's tale might find it interesting to compare it with "There Were No More People Upon the Earth," originally in *The World Tomorrow*, 7, February 1924, pp. 58–59, reprinted in *The Collected Short Stories of Mary Johnston*, edited by Annie and Hensley F. Woodbridge (Whitston Publishing Co., 1982).

AN OLD WOMAN'S TALE (Salem *Gazette*, December 21, 1830; "UT") was one of Hawthorne's very first published tales. It is so amorphous that one hesitates over whether it is a story or a sketch, but Hawthorne called it a tale; it contains characters; and it ends with an incident, which is, however, left hanging in the air. Nothing is really vouched for, and various devices are employed to set everything at a distance: the "old woman" tells the narrator a story that somebody else had told her. "All the inhabitants of this village . . . were subject to a simultaneous slumber, continuing one hour's space." "Perhaps" David and Esther, lovers desperately in need of funds if they are to wed, dream together, "one moonlight summer evening," when the village and its inhabitants appear to them as they once were. Aided by the "Squire," a richly and fantastically dressed lady attempts to dig, as if for treasure, "between a walnut tree and the fountain," but without results before the picture fades away and the lovers come to themselves. Perhaps, again, this was intended to cue David, who, in any event, accepts it as such and "had soon scooped a hole as large as the basin of the spring." "Suddenly, he poked his head down to the very bottom of this cavity. 'Oho!—what have we here?' cried David." But since the tale ends here, neither the lovers nor the reader ever finds out, an ending that would be much more satisfying if David's digging too had been part of the dream. Arlin Turner suggested that the story derived from James Thacher's *An Essay on Demonology* (see his *NH: An Introduction and Interpretation* [Holt, 1963], pp. 20–21). "An Old Woman's Tale" is much more satisfying atmospherically than as narrative. Both the atmosphere and the use of the old lady at the beginning strongly suggest the tales of Walter de la Mare, upon whom Hawthorne's work was a strong influence; see especially "The Village of Old Age," in *Eight Tales* (Arkham House, 1971).

PETER GOLDTHWAITE'S TREASURE (*Token*, 1838; *TTT*), though not one of Hawthorne's most profound or meaningful tales, is still an excellent, well-developed piece of narrative. Like some other pieces, it contrasts the man of imagination with the practical, efficient man of business, but this time the first is a fool, while the latter is kindly as well as sensible. Peter Gold-thwaite's imagination, to be sure, is not of an exalted variety. He is a "wild projector," who has never soared higher than crackbrained schemes to achieve glittering fortunes. Long ago he and John Brown were partners, but that partnership was long since dissolved, and when the story begins, Peter dwells in his ruined ancestral mansion, with the old serving woman, Tabitha Porter, whom his granduncle, Peter Goldthwaite I, took from the almshouse as a child, and persists in refusing John Brown's handsome offers for what has become a valuable property, because he has the idea that old Peter had hidden a great treasure within its walls. The action of the story consists in his systematically wrecking the house to find this treasure, beginning with the attic and ending with the kitchen, where a great chest is found, crammed with "old provincial bills of credit, and treasury notes, and bills of land, banks, and all other bubbles of the sort, from the first issue, above a century and a half ago, down nearly to the Revolution," and all now quite worthless. On a stormy night, John Brown happens along just as this discovery has been made and just in time to have his offer at last accepted. Peter already has "a plan for laying out the cash, to great advantage," but Brown resolves to "apply to the next court for a guardian to take care of the solid cash," leaving his old friend free to speculate as much as he likes with the newfound treasure. Two articles in *ESQ* explore different aspects of this story: Sargent Bush, Jr., " 'Peter Goldthwaite's Treasure' and *The House of the Seven Gables*," no. 62 (1971), 35–38, and Samuel Scoville, "H's Houses and Hidden Treasures," no. 71 (1973), 61–73. See also Richard Dorson, "Five Directions in American Folklore," *Midwest Folklore*, 1 (1951), 149–65.

THE PROPHETIC PICTURES (*Token*, 1836; *TTT*) is allied with "The Artist of the Beautiful" and "Drowne's Wooden Image" because artists are prominent in all three and important considerations relating to art are implied or involved. But a comparison is also in order with "Dr. Heidigger's Experiment," which teaches that if we could live our lives over again, we should make the same mistakes we made the first time. This story goes even further, for Hawthorne spells it out in his conclusion that "could the result of one, or all our deeds, be shadowed forth and set before us," most of us would do exactly what we should do anyway. The ultimate source was an anecdote concerning Gilbert Stuart, as recorded by William Dunlap in his *History of the Rise and Progress of the Arts of Design in the United States,* but Hawthorne sets his scene earlier than Stuart's time, for William Burnet was "Governor Burnet" only in 1728–29. The great painter in the tale is able to paint portraits that not only bring out character traits of which their possessors have been ignorant but, though less blatantly than Dorian Gray's portrait in Oscar Wilde's novel, change with the changes that occur in the persons portrayed. When he painted the newly married devoted couple, Walter and Elinor Ludlow, the artist knew that Walter would some time go mad and try to kill Elinor, and when, at the end, he returned to Boston to renew acquaintance with his work, he entered their home just as his insight was about to be verified. Hawthorne's closing statement of his "deep moral" does not cover the case however, for it fails to make adequate allowance for the painter's role and ignores the question of his responsibility. Old-time theologians used to be troubled over whether God's foreknowledge of what would happen to His children involved foreordination; the painter is a kind of god in his own world and in part recognizes himself as such. He "did not possess kindly feelings; his heart was cold," and the "solitary ambition" he cherished exercised the dehumanizing effect upon him that Hawthorne feared and portrayed notably in Ethan Brand. Moreover, there is at least a question whether all the themes and interests of the tale are so handled as to produce a completely unified effect. Millicent Bell's treatment of this tale in *H's View of the Artist* is excellent; see also Mary E. Dichmann, "H's Prophetic Pictures," *AL,* 23 (1951), 188–202. Lee Newman (pp. 251–53) has a good summary of what has been written about possible literary sources, and there are two articles, both in *MLN,* on the possible connection between "The Prophetic Pictures" and Henry James's story, "The Liar": see Robert J. Kane in vol. 65 (1950), 247–58, and Edward H. Rosenberry in vol. 76 (1961), 234–38.

Roger Malvin's Burial (*Token,* 1832; reprinted, *US Mag,* August 1843; *MOM*) begins with two wounded men trying to make their way home after the Indian skirmish known as Lovewell's Fight, near Fryeburg, Maine, on May 8, 1725. In 1938, in *AL,* 10:313–18, G. Harrison Orians established Thomas Symmes's historical account and Thomas C. Upham's ballad, as sources; in 1954, David S. Lovejoy, in *NEQ,* 27, 527–31, added an article by Joseph Bancroft Hill. For Biblical sources, see Ely Stock, "History and the Bible in H's 'Roger Malvin's Burial,'" *EIHC,* 100 (1964), 279–96; for the emphasis upon the right of sepulture, see Joseph T. McCullen, Jr., "Ancient Rites for the Dead and 'Roger Malvin's Burial,'" *Southern Folklore Quarterly,* 30 (1966), 313–22, and Harold Schlechter, "Death and Resurrection of the King: Elements of Primitive Mythology and Ritual in 'Roger

Malvin's Burial,' " *ELN,* 8 (1973), 201–5. After the battle, Reuben Bourne and Roger Malvin, to whose daughter Reuben is betrothed, attempt to struggle home together, but Roger has been so seriously injured it soon becomes clear that he cannot make it and that if Reuben stays with him, both will die. He begs Roger therefore to leave him and try to save himself so that he can make a home for Dorcas, sending help back should it seem practicable but, in any case, returning to bury him, to which Reuben at last reluctantly agrees. Though he faints before reaching his destination, help comes in time to save his life. When he comes out of his delirium, he tries to tell the truth, but is misunderstood by Dorcas, who believes and tells others that he stayed with her father until he died. Recovered, Reuben lacks the courage and moral stamina to tell her or them the truth or to return to the wilderness in search of Malvin's body. He marries Dorcas, but, crushed inwardly by what now seems a double burden of guilt, he fails progressively in his duties as a husbandman, until, after eighteen years, with their only son Cyrus, the couple start out into the hinterland in search of a new homestead. When chance and a strange, undefined inner compulsion lead them to a camping place near the great rock where Malvin died, Reuben and his son go off independently in search of game. Reuben hears a sound near him and accidentally shoots and kills Cyrus. There has been very wide divergence concerning both the "meaning" and the merit of "Roger Malvin's Burial," and the present writer is not among those who consider it a success. The whole first part, describing Reuben's conscientious torment, is vintage Hawthorne, but the tragedy of the final episode is not sufficiently connected with what has preceded it to create a unified effect, and the last two sentences are perilously close to nonsense: "The vow that the wounded youth had made the blighted man had come to redeem. His sin was expiated,—the curse was gone from him; and in the hour when he had shed blood dearer to him than his own, a prayer, the first for years, went up to Heaven from the lips of Reuben Bourne." Many attempts have been made to explain this, including the suggestions that Reuben had gone mad and that Hawthorne was attempting a deep-seated irony, but to my mind most of them make even less sense than what Hawthorne wrote. For an interpretation of the tale as an "unacknowledged masterpiece" and "an allegory of the heart," see Sheldon W. Liebman, *SSF,* 12 (1975), 253–60. Patricia Anne Carlson discusses imagery and structure in *South Atlantic Bulletin,* 41 (1976), 3–9, and E. Arthur Robinson explores the significance of the wilderness setting in *NHJ* 1977, pp. 147–66. Though I am far from agreeing with everything in it, Hyatt H. Waggoner's discussion of the tale in *Hawthorne: A Critical Study,* pp. 78–93, is a very able general study.

THE SEVEN VAGABONDS (*Token*, 1833; *TTT*), derived, in all probability, from one of Hawthorne's own early walking tours, brings the narrator, a writer and tale-teller, obviously Hawthorne's alter ego, into the company of a "grave old showman," who is a puppet master in a covered wagon, "or, more properly, a small house on wheels"; a "sly, prophetic beggar," who is a charlatan and fortune-teller; a "fiddling foreigner" with "a merry damsel" and a mahogany box with a "small round magnifying window" through which one may visit distant cities and see many wonderful sights; a "smart bibliophile" or traveling book peddler; and "a sombre Indian," all bound for the camp meeting at Stamford to ply their trades. The bulk of the piece is devoted to charactery; the only real incident comes at the end, where they meet "a travelling preacher of great fame among the Methodists," who informs them that "the camp-meeting is broke up." Henry James somewhat strangely singled out this story for praise.

THE SHAKER BRIDAL. See THE CANTERBURY PILGRIMS.

THE SNOW-IMAGE (*International Magazine of Literature, Art, and Science,* November 1850; *SI*) relates how two children, Violet and Peony Lindsay, perhaps suggested by Una and Julian Hawthorne, allowed by their mother to go out to play in the snow, make a "snow-image" of a little girl and believe or fancy that she comes alive and plays with them. This is the "Childish Miracle" of the subtitle. Their mother, who has "a strain of poetry" and "a trait of unworldly beauty" in her character, goes along with this, but when their father, an excellent but merely commonsensical hardware merchant, comes home, he insists upon taking the little snow maiden inside and places her beside the stove, where she is soon reduced to a pool of water. Since Hawthorne made "The Snow-Image" the first story in his final collection, he must have thought well of it, and it has also been admired by Henry James and by Q. D. Leavis. Hawthorne's appreciation of childlike sensitivity recalls the child whom Jesus set in the midst of his wrangling disciples, and the distinction he makes between Eyes and No-Eyes, or the imaginative and the materially minded, occurs in many of his stories, but the characterization of the children is so unrealistic as to suggest nineteenth-century Sunday School stories, the narrative is cloyingly sentimental, and the moralizing is heavy-handed. One might also well ask how, if Mr. Lindsey had no imagination, he could mistake the snow maiden for a neighbor's child. Incidentally there is one good touch of humor, when the neighbors wonder "what could possess poor Mr. Lindsey to be running about the garden in pursuit of a snowdrift, which the west wind was driving hither and thither?"

Notwithstanding such objections, Millicent Bell (*H's View of the Artist*, pp. 84–85) has plausibly compared "The Snow-Image" to "Drowne's Wooden Image" as expressing the Romantic conception of inspiration as the source of creativity. See Darrel Abel, " 'A Vast Deal of Human Sympathy': Idea and Device in H's 'The Snow-Image,' " *Criticism*, 12 (1970), 16–32, and, for a different and, to me, unconvincing interpretation, Dennis Berthold, "Anti-idealism in H's 'The Snow-Image,' " *ArQ*, 38 (1982), 119–32.

SYLPH ETHEREGE (*Token*, 1838; *SI*) is an ineffective trifle about a secluded girl, who, betrothed from infancy to a cousin she has never seen, creates a romantic image of him in her own fancy. To cure her of her nonsense, the sardonic intended bridegroom and Sylph's female guardian join in an unbelievable scheme that culminates in suddenly and cruelly undeceiving her, and the girl dies. The only significance of this tale in Hawthorne's oeuvre is as one more illustration of his horror at the idea of any human being attempting to establish dominance over the being of another.

THE THREEFOLD DESTINY (*American Monthly Magazine*, March 1838; *TTT*) is described by Hawthorne himself as such an allegory "as the writers of the last century would have expressed in the shape of an Eastern tale," but James K. Folsom, who points out its resemblance to *Rasselas*, rightly remarks that, strictly speaking, the piece is not an allegory but merely a moral tale. Ralph Cranfield searches the world in behalf of his high destiny, involving love, wealth, and power, "to be confirmed to him by three signs." But, like the children in *The Blue Bird* by Maurice Maeterlinck, who learned that they could only find what they sought at home, he must return to his native village to fulfill his destiny. The girl who alone could make him happy by her love turns out to be the very one with whom he had left a love token before his departure; his treasure must be found through cultivating his native soil; and the sway he sought over human minds can only be achieved teaching the village children. As Lea Newman has remarked, Henry James's interest in this little story may have been sparked by Ralph's resemblance to John Marcher in "The Beast in the Jungle," who, however, did not come to himself in time. Besides Folsom (*Man's Accidents and God's Purposes*), see Buford Jones, "The *Faery Land* of H's Romances," *ESQ*, no. 48 (1967), 106–24.

A VISIT TO THE CLERK OF THE WEATHER (*American Monthly Magazine*, May 1836; "UT") is a mildly entertaining skit about how the narrator was whisked away by an old crone to the cave where the Clerk, who has all kinds of weather in stock, remembers only enough about a mud ball called Earth to resent weather forecasters. Jack Frost and a beautiful maiden called Spring are the other characters.

THE WEDDING KNELL (*Token*, 1836; *TTT*) which was warmly admired by Poe, is remarkable chiefly for Hawthorne's ability to turn even morbid materials into an expression of faith and hope. Mrs. Dabney weds Mr. Ellenwood, the love of her youth, forty years after the breaking of their engagement, filled up, on her part, with two intervening marriages, the first to a man twice her age, to whom she had been an exemplary wife but did not love, and the second to one who treated her badly. The celibate Ellenwood appears at the altar in his shroud, escorted by a funeral party, while the church bells toll drearily. "Come, my bride! the hearse is ready. The sexton stands waiting for us . . . . Let us be married; and then to our coffins!" But the bride, like the author, is equal to the occasion. Admitting both her fault and that "time is no more for both of us," she summons him to wed for eternity: "But let us join our hands before the altar, as lovers whom adverse circumstances have separated through life, yet who meet again as they are leaving it, and find their earthly affection changed into something holy as religion." The wedding knell is then replaced by an anthem of joy over "the union of two immortal souls." John Homan, Jr., "H's 'The Wedding Knell' and Cotton Mather," *ESQ*, 43 (1966), 66–67, finds a source in one of Mather's sermons.

THE WHITE OLD MAID (*New-England Magazine*, July 1835; *TTT*) is a morbid, macabre, semisupernatural tale, obscure as to meaning but rich in atmosphere. It opens with two young women meeting over the corpse of a young man whom both have loved. One had wronged either the dead man or her rival, but we never learn how. They promise to meet again in the same place after many years, during which the sympathetic figure becomes the mysterious "Old Maid in the Winding Sheet" who attends all the funerals in town. The tryst the two women have set up is faithfully kept in a long-deserted mansion, to which they are admitted by the ghost of an ancient black servitor; there both are found dead. Donald R. Barnes has suggested this story as a source for Faulkner: "Faulkner's Miss Emily and H's Old Maid," *SSF*, 9 (1971), 373–78.

THE WIVES OF THE DEAD (*Token*, 1832; *SI*) is a miniature masterpiece, a perfectly told tale of "simple and domestic incidents," set "a hundred years ago, in a principal seaport of the Bay Province," whose plot is arranged and whose properties are set out with almost mathematical exactitude. Mary and Margaret, "the recent brides of two brothers, a sailor and a landsman," sharing a common household, receive on "two successive days . . . tidings of the death of each, by the chances of Canadian warfare and the tempestuous Atlantic." On the same night, both, whose characters have been differenti- ated with admirable clarity considering the brevity of the story, are roused by successive messengers. Each is told that the earlier report of her husband's death was false, and each stifles her first impulse to pass the good news on to her "sister" on the ground that this must make the other's grief harder to bear. Barring what I consider the inadmissible speculations of Bill Christ- oferson (*SSF,* 20 [1983]: 1–6), the only real problem is that suggested by Hans-Joachim Lang, in "How Ambiguous Is H?" in *Freie Gesellschaft,* 1962, pp. 195–230. Lang argued that in the last sentence, "But her [i.e., Mary's] hand trembled against Margaret's neck, a tear also fell upon her cheek, and she suddenly awoke," the "she" indicates Mary, not Margaret, which would mean that Mary at least had dreamed the visit of the messen- ger. I agree with N. F. Doubleday, who rejects this interpretation in *H's Early Tales.*

Notes

For many years the most desirable editions of Hawthorne were the Autograph and Old Manse editions (HM, 1900). These have now been superseded by the Centenary Edition (OSUP, 1964ff.), which includes notebooks and letters. The authorized biography was Julian Hawthorne's *NH and his Wife* (HM, 1884), to which Rose Hawthorne Lathrop's *Memories of H* (HM, 1897) was an important supplement. Outstanding early studies were George Parsons Lathrop, *A Study of H* (HM, 1876); Henry James, *NH* (Macmillan, 1879); and George Edward Woodberry, *NH* (HM, 1902). For some years after 1941, the best modern account was in F. O. Matthiessen's *American Renaissance: Art and Expression in the Age of Emerson and Whitman* (OUP); then, in 1948, came Randall Stewart's *NH: A Biography* (YUP), which commanded the field unchallenged for many years. Recently three additional plethoric biographies have appeared: Hubert H. Hoeltje's *Inward Sky: The Mind and Heart of NH* (DUP, 1962); Arlin Turner's *NH: A Biography* (OUP); and James R. Mellow's *NH in His Times* (HM), both in 1980. If I had to choose one of these books, I should choose Turner's, which summed up the lifetime studies of one of the ranking authorities of our time. Many other books and a far larger number of articles have been cited in the notes which follow; to attempt anything like a comprehensive listing would require a volume in itself. In "Criticism of NH: A Selected Checklist," *SN*, 2 (1970), 519–87, Maurice Beebe and Jack Hardie have provided a very useful guide.

The following abbreviations are employed in bibliographical references in both this section and the appendix:

AL—American Literature
AN&Q—American Notes and Queries
AQ—American Quarterly
ArQ—Arizona Quarterly
ATQ—American Transcendental Quarterly

BPLQ—Boston Public Library Quarterly
BUSE—Boston University Studies in English
CE—College English
DUP—Duke University Press
EIHC—Essex Institute Historical Collections
ELH—English Literary History
ELN—English Language Notes
ESQ—Emerson Society Quarterly
H—Hawthorne
HM—Houghton Mifflin Company
JAmSt—Journal of American Studies
JEGP—Journal of English and Germanic Philology
MLN—Modern Language Notes
MLQ—Modern Language Quarterly
MP—Modern Philology
NCF—Nineteenth Century Fiction
NEQ—New England Quarterly
NH—Nathaniel Hawthorne
NHJ—Nathaniel Hawthorne Journal
OSUP—Ohio State University Press
OUP—Oxford University Press
PMLA—Publications of the Modern Language Association
PQ—Philological Quarterly
SAF—Studies in American Fiction
SAQ—South Atlantic Quarterly
SN—Studies in the Novel
SP—Studies in Philology
SR—Studies in Romanticism
SSF—Studies in Short Fiction
TSLL—Texas Studies in Language and Literature
UCP—University of Chicago Press
UFP—University of Florida Press
UKCR—University of Kansas City Review
UNCP—University of North Carolina Press
UOP—University of Oklahoma Press
YUP—Yale University Press

In the appendix the following abbreviations are also employed:

MOM—Mosses from an Old Manse
SI—The Snow-Image and Other Twice-Told Tales
Token—The Token and Atlantic Souvenir

TTT—Twice-Told Tales
USMag—United States Magazine and Democratic Review
"UT"—"Uncollected Tales"

In the notes to chapter 3 the following abbreviations are also employed:

BR—The Blithedale Romance
HSG—The House of the Seven Gables
MF—The Marble Faun
SL—The Scarlet Letter

Chapter 1. The Life

1. The fullest account of the family history is in Vernon Loggins, *The Hawthornes* (Columbia University Press, 1951).
2. The fullest account of Mrs. Hawthorne and her sisters is in Louise Hall Tharp's entertaining book, *The Peabody Sisters of Salem* (Little, Brown, 1950). Though Henry James never admitted it, Elizabeth in her old age was probably the original of Miss Birdseye in *The Bostonians* (1886).
3. The Wayside was occupied first by the Alcotts, then by the Hawthornes, and then by "Margaret Sidney," author of the "Five Little Peppers" books, and her husband, the publisher Daniel Lothrop. It still stands, now boasting the "Italianate" tower that Hawthorne added to it, near the Emerson house and Orchard House, the later home of the Alcotts. All are literary shrines and open to the public.
4. Hawthorne's attitude toward the Civil War is discussed in Chapter 5 of this volume. See also Randall Stewart, "Hand the Civil War," *SP,* 34 (1937), 91–105.
5. *Hawthorne: A Critical Study* (Harvard University Press, 1955), 229ff. See Arlin Turner, "H's Final Illness and Death: Additional Reports," *ESQ,* 19 (1973), 123–27.
6. See Randall Stewart, "Mrs. Hawthorne's Quarrel with James T. Fields," *More Books,* 21 (1946), 254–63, and " 'Pestiferous Gail Hamilton,' James T. Fields, and the Hawthornes," *NEQ,* 17 (1944), 418–23.
7. Technically Rose Hawthorne Lathrop was "a Dominican of the Third Order, with special permission to wear the habit and live in a community of religious." See Katherine Burton, *Sorrow Built a Bridge* (Longmans, Green, 1937) and Theodore Maynard, *A Fire Was Lighted*

(Bruce, 1948). For Julian Hawthorne, see, besides his books about his parents, *Shapes That Pass* (HM, 1928) and *The Memoirs of Julian Hawthorne*, edited by Edith Garrigues Hawthorne (Macmillan, 1938). For Una Hawthorne, see Raymona E. Hull, "Una Hawthorne: A Biographical Sketch," *NHJ* 1976, pp. 86–119. T. Walter Herbert, Jr.'s article, "NH, Una Hawthorne, and *SL:* Interactive Selfhoods and the Cultural Constructions of Gender," *PMLA,* 103 (1988), 285–297, did not appear until my book was about to go into galley proof. I do not "buy" all its intellectual framework, but it cannot fail to interest deeply all who have responded to this fascinating young woman. Vernon Loggins (cf. note 1) has considerable information on all the Hawthorne children.

Chapter 2. Tales

1. In *Twice-Told Tales,* "Sunday at Home," "Little Annie's Ramble," "A Rill from the Town Pump," "Sights from a Steeple," "The Toll-Gatherer's Day," "The Vision of the Fountain," "Fancy's Show Box," "The Haunted Mind," "The Village Uncle," "The Sister Years," "Snowflakes," "Chippings with a Chisel," "Night Sketches," and "Footprints on the Seashore"; in *Mosses from an Old Manse,* "The Old Manse," "A Select Party," "Fire Worship," "Birds and Bird Voices," "Monsieur de Miroir," "The Hall of Fantasy," "The Procession of Life," "The Intelligence Office," "P's Correspondence," "Passages from a Relinquished Work," "Sketches from Memory," "The Old Apple Dealer," and "A Virtuoso's Collection"; in *The Snow-Image,* "Main Street," "A Bell's Biography," "Old News," and "Old Ticonderoga"; in "Uncollected Tales," "My Visit to Niagara," "Graves and Goblins," "Sketches from Memory," "Fragments from the Journal of a Solitary Man," "Time's Portraiture," "A Good Man's Miracle," and "A Book of Autographs." Some readers might of course classify some of these items differently.
2. See the detailed studies by Hugo McPherson in "H's Major Source for his Mythological Tales," *AL,* 30 (1958), 364–65, and in extenso in his *H as Myth-Maker: A Study in Imagination* (University of Toronto Press, 1969); cf. also Daniel Hoffman, "Myth, Romance, and the Childhood of Man," in R. H. Pearce, ed., *H Centenary Essays* (OSUP, 1964).
3. "H and the Paradise of Children," *Western Humanities Review,* 15 (1961), 161–72.

4. On Hawthorne's Gothicism, cf. Andrew Lang, whose credentials as a folklorist make him an authoritative witness, "H's Tales of Old Greece," *Independent*, 62 (1907), 792–94. Though Lang apparently preferred Kingsley's *The Heroes*, he was not unappreciative of Hawthorne's merits. Cf. Maurice Charney's remarks on the tales in "H and the Gothic Style," *NEQ*, 34 (1961), 36–49. Both McPherson and Helen Collins, "The Nature and Power of Women as Seen through *A Wonder Book* and *Tanglewood Tales*," *Nassau Review*, vol. 3, no. 2 (1976), 16–28, see resemblances between some of the women in the mythological tales and those in the romances.

5. Hathaway remarks acutely that "in creating this land of innocence, Hawthorne was adding his bit to one of the great American myths. That here in this new world civilization was being reborn, purged of its corruptions, a phoenix rising out of the ashes of the past, a new Eden in the wilderness, was an image that determined the framework for much thought about the nature and destiny of America."

6. I agree with Hathaway that Hawthorne's treatment of the Three Gray Women, whom he calls Scarecrow, Nightmare, and Shakejoint is "straight from Disneyland," to which I might add that his remarking after the marriage of Cadmus and Harmonia, that "before many years went by, there was a group of rosy little children (but how they came there has always been a mystery to me) sporting in the great hall" is as good an example of vulgarity masquerading as modesty as Disney's putting brassieres on the mermaids in his cartoon production of *Peter Pan*.

7. See George Dekker, "Sir Walter Scott, the Angel of Hadley, and American Historical Fiction," *JAmSt*, 17 (1983), 221–27.

8. Edward J. Gallagher, "History in 'Endicott and the Red Cross,' " *ESQ*, no. 50, supplement (1968), 62–65. See also John Halligan, "H on Democracy . . . ," *SSF*, 8 (1971): 301–7, and two articles by Sacvan Bercovitch, "Endicott's Breastplate . . . ," *SSF*, 4 (1967), 289–99, and "Diabolism in Salem," *ELN*, 6 (1969), 280–85.

9. Newberry, "The Demonic in 'Endicott and the Red Cross,' " *Papers on Language and Literature*, 13 (1977), 251–59, declares that "the tale unambiguously exposes—and indicts—the demonic cruelty in a predominantly steel-encased Puritan spirit," which he finds both "anti-human" and "anti-Christian," and, not content with this, calls Endicott himself "an emissary from hell," who stands "at odds . . . with everything that might be associated with Christianity." The same tendency toward overstatement appears in another article by Newberry: " 'The Gray Champion': H's Ironic Criticism of Puritan

Rebellion," *SSF,* 13 (1976): 363–70. For Crews, see *The Sins of the Fathers* (OUP, 1966), pp. 41–43. But the fullest expression of the classical Freudian view of Endicott is probably Richard Drinnon's in "The Maypole of Merry Mount," *Massachusetts Review,* 21 (1980), 382–410.

10. See especially G. Harrison Orians, "H and 'The Maypole of Merry Mount,' " *MLN,* 53 (1938), 159–67, and J. Gary Williams, "History in H's 'The Maypole of Merry Mount,' " *EIHC,* 108 (1973), 173–89, which seeks to "clarify and augment" Orians's conclusions.

11. *Form and Fable in American Fiction* (OUP, 1961), p. 139.

12. Taking his cue from Endicott's calling Blackstone "a priest of Baal," Thomas Pribek, "The Conquest of Canaan: Suppression of 'The Maypole of Merry Mount,' " *NCF,* 40 (1985), 345–54, suggests Edward Johnson's *Wonder-Working Providence of Sion's Saviour in New England* (1653) as a more important source than had previously been recognized and builds up an elaborate Biblical background for the tale: "Baal was . . . associated with Asherah [or Astarte], a fertility goddess, for whose worship sacred poles were placed near the altars of Baal." Consequently Endicott's destruction of the maypole "validates God's approval of and support of the New England way," while his welcoming Edgar and Edith into the Puritan community is "a symbolic fulfillment of the prophets' promises to the Children of Israel who repent and return to the Lord." But though this article is of much interest, it would be difficult to prove that Hawthorne intended everything the author finds in his story, and if he knew, as the folklorists have by this time reminded us ad nauseam, that the maypole is a phallic symbol, he made no use of this knowledge in the tale under consideration.

13. Daniel G. Hoffman (*Form and Fable,* pp. 132–34) shows that Milton furnished some of the material that reminded John S. Vickery, "The Golden Bough at Merry Mount," *NCF,* 12 (1957), 203–14, of Sir James Fraser's epoch-making 1890 study, *The Golden Bough.* But Hoffman's own view that Hawthorne was indebted not only to Strutt but also to William Hone's *Every Day Book* (1826) has been questioned by other writers; see Newman, *Reader's Guide,* p. 191.

14. The fullest study is by Sheldon W. Liebman, "H's *Comus:* A Miltonic Source for 'The Maypole of Merry Mount,' " *NCF,* 27 (1972), 345–51. "Corinna's Going a-Maying" has also been, though less definitely, brought into consideration; see Richard H. Deming, "The Use of the Past: Herrick and H," *Journal of Popular Culture,* 2 (1968), 278–91. Another important article by Liebman is "Moral Choice in

'The Maypole of Merry Mount,' " *SSF,* 11 (1974), 173–80.

15. "Transcending the Myth of the Fall in H's 'Maypole of Merry Mount,' " *ESQ,* 20 (1938), 75–99.

16. See note 14. A very different interpretation is offered by Joseph J. Feeney, in "The Structure of Ambiguity in H's 'The Maypole of Merry Mount,' " *SAF,* 3 (1975), 211–15.

17. The child acquired his curious name through having been born in Turkey while his parents were "witnessing" there, and it had been bestowed upon him in gratitude to the sultan, who, unlike contemporary rulers in "Christian" lands, had not persecuted them for their faith. But Agnes McNeill Donohue points out that *Ilbrahim* is not a Turkish name and suggests that possibly Hawthorne intended *Ibrahim,* the Turkish equivalent of Abraham. See " 'The Fruit of the Forbidden Tree': A Reading of 'The Gentle Boy,' " in her *A Case Book on the H Question* (Crowell, 1963).

18. See G. Harrison Orians, "The Sources and Themes of H's 'The Gentle Boy,' " *NEQ,* 14 (1961), 664–78; Frederick Newberry, "H's 'Gentle Boy': The Lost Mediators in Puritan History," *SSF,* 21 (1984), 363–73; James Duban, "H's Debt to Edmund Spenser and Charles Chauncy in 'The Gentle Boy,' " *NHJ* 1976, pp. 189–95. Peter White's attempt to find a source in the nonsense believed about the birth of a monster to a Quaker woman does not seem to me very convincing; see "The Monstrous Birth and 'The Gentle Boy': H's Use of the Past," *NHJ* 1976, pp. 173–88.

19. " 'Wounded Love': NH's 'The Gentle Boy,' " *NHJ* 1978, pp. 47–54. See also Seymour L. Gross, "H's Revision of 'The Gentle Boy,' " *AL,* 26 (1954), 196–208; Louise Daumer, "The 'Case' of Tobias Pearson: H and the Ambiguities," *AL,* 21 (1950), 464–72; William A. Tremblay, "A Reading of NH's 'The Gentle Boy,' " *Massachusetts Studies in English,* 2 (1970), 80–87.

20. Julian Smith, "H's 'Legends of the Province House,' " *NCF,* 24 (1969), 31–44.

21. Jane Donahue Eberwein, "Temporal Perspective in 'The [sic] Legends of the Province House,' " *ATQ,* 14 (1972), 43–45, argues that though only four years actually passed between these two events, Hawthorne makes the time seem much longer, thus impressing the reader with "the crucial difference between the Provincial and the Revolutionary periods."

22. Besides Reed, "The Telling Frame of H's 'Legends of the Province House,' " *SAF,* 4 (1976), 105–11, see Robert H. Fossum, "Time and the Artist in 'Legends of the Province House,' " *NCF,* 21 (1967),

337–48, and Margaret V. Allen, "Imagination and History in H's 'Legends of the Province House,' " *AL,* 43 (1972), 432–37.

23. Two articles in *NHJ* 1974 have a minor bearing on sources. In "The Mischianza Ball and 'Howe's Masquerade' " (pp. 231–35), Fumio Ano cites an actual festivity mounted by Major John André in Philadelphia on May 18, 1778. Readers interested in Poe's reckless assertion that Hawthorne was indebted to his "William Watson" for "Howe's Masquerade" should consult D. M. McKeithan, "Poe and the Second Edition of H's *Twice-Told Tales*" (pp. 257–69).

24. See Seymour L. Gross, "H's 'Lady Eleanore's Mantle' as History," *JEGP,* 54 (1955), 549–55, and for a more elaborate, perhaps less convincing statement, Lawrence Clayton, " 'Lady Eleanore's Mantle': A Metaphorical Key to H's 'Legends of the Province House,' " *ELN,* 9 (1971), 49–51.

25. I find no support in the text for the notion suggested by Sheldon W. Liebman, "Ambiguity in 'Lady Eleanore's Mantle,' " *ESQ,* 58 (1970), 97–101, that the wine Helwyse offers Eleanore at the ball is poisoned and that Dr. Clarke, whom he compares to Baglioni in "Rappaccini's Daughter" and regards as the "fiend" evoked by Eleanore's pride, knows it.

26. Fannye N. Cherry, "A Note on the Source of H's 'Lady Eleanore's Mantle,' " *AL,* 6 (1935), 437–39.

27. "H's Satire in 'Old Esther Dudley,' " *ESQ,* 22 (1961), 31–33.

28. For further comment on symbolism in this tale, see Lewis B. Horne, "The Heart, The Hand, and 'The Birthmark,' " *ATQ,* 1 (1969), 38–41.

29. On Georgiana's share in her own tragedy, see Thomas F. Walsh, Jr., "Character Complexity in H's 'The Birthmark,' " *ESQ,* no. 23 (1961), 12–15.

30. David J. Baxter, " 'The Birthmark' in Perspective," *NHJ* 1975, pp. 232–40, offers a useful survey of "Birthmark" criticism.

31. *NH: Representative Selections* (American Book Company, 1934), pp. 366–67.

32. *H's Fiction: The Light and the Dark* (UOP, 1964), p. 119.

33. *NH and the Truth of Dreams* (Louisiana State University Press, 1979), pp. 112–15.

34. "H's Humanism: 'The Birthmark' and Sir Kenelm Digby," *AL,* 38 (1966), 337–51. See also Karl P. Wentersdorf's excellent article, "The Genesis of H's 'The Birthmark,' " *Jahrbuch für Amerikastudien,* 8 (1963), 171–86, which suggests, among other things, that the mole on Imogen's breast in *Cymbeline* may have contributed to

Georgiana's birthmark and also sees Hawthorne drawing on *The Tempest*. Jane Chambers, "Two Legends of Temperance: Spenser's and H's," *ESQ*, 20 (1974), 295–99, finds another influence in the episode of Guyon and Ruddymane, the infant with bloodstained hands in *The Faerie Queene*, book 2. But Harry C. West's attempt to find a source in Isaac D'Israeli's *Curiosities of Literature*, in "H's 'The Birthmark': From Source to Artifact," *NHJ* 1976, pp. 240–56, seems to me more speculative, and Robert D. Arner, "The Legend of Pygmalion in 'The Birthmark,' " *ATQ*, 14 (1972), 168–71, is more concerned with the differences between the two stories than their similarities.

35. Van Leer, "Aylmer's Library: Transcendental Alchemy in H's 'The Birthmark,' " *ESQ*, 22 (1976), 211–20; Burns, "Alchemy and 'The Birthmark,' " *ATQ*, 42 (1979), 150–57. Van Leer, who discerns Swedenborg in Aylmer's tendency to view the birthmark as a sign of falsity or evil, calls him a "spiritualizing materialist," who is "led by a faulty definition of spirit to act foolishly and finally destructively." Moreover, "the stiff language and cardboard apparatus are not inventions, but part of the historical original, the tone of which Hawthorne has duplicated with extreme care and great facility." According to Burns, Aylmer practices voodoo, not alchemy, upon his wife, forgetting that, according to the alchemists, spirit cannot be separated from matter in this life and that "the perfection of the self must come before any attempt to alter the basic law of nature." See also R. DeHayes, "Charting H's Invisible World," *CEA Critic*, 27 (1965), 94–99; Elizabeth R. Napier, "Aylmer as 'Scheidekünstler': The Pattern of Union and Separation in H's 'The Birthmark,' " *South Atlantic Bulletin*, 41, no. 4 (1876), 32–35; John Gatta, Jr., "Aylmer's Alchemy in 'The Birthmark,' " *PQ*, 57 (1978), 399–411.

36. See Robert B. Heilman, "H's 'The Birthmark': Science as Religion," *SAQ*, 68 (1949), 575–83; Thomas F. Scheer, "Aylmer's Divine Roles in 'The Birthmark,' " *ATQ*, 22 (1974), 108. Says the latter: "As creator, Aylmer can only produce illusions; as savior, he brings only death; and as preserver and sanctifier he works in ignorance and false pride. By the ironic use of divine roles for Aylmer and by portraying his relationship with Georgiana as a near-parody of salvation, Hawthorne criticizes the excessive claims of science and adds another dimension to his plea for sympathetic vision of human imperfection."

37. Aminadab, the character and the name, have drawn considerable commentary, much of it rather farfetched. John C. Rees sums up well in *Names*, 28 (1980), 171–82, and adds the conjectural influence of

The Tempest and *She Stoops to Conquer* upon Hawthorne's choice of name.

38. See Jules Zanger, "Speaking of the Unspeakable: H's 'The Birth-mark,' " *MP*, 80 (1983), 364–71. The "unspeakable" in Haw-thorne's time was menstruation. "The bloody mark on [Georgiana's] cheek represents an aspect of feminine sexuality that resists conven-tional male conceptualization and suggests an autonomous female nature." Zanger also suggests that the blight suffered by the plant Aylmer requires Georgiana to pluck during their experiment thus reflects the nineteenth-century notion that the touch of a menstruat-ing woman was injurious to vegetation.

39. See James W. Mathews, "H and the Chain of Being," *MLQ*, 18 (1957), 282–94; also Chester E. Eisinger, "H as Champion of the Middle Way," *NEQ*, 27 (1954), 27–52.

40. "The Early Projected Works of NH," *Papers of the Bibliographical Society of America*, 39 (1945), 119–55. For the opposite view see Kermit Vanderbilt, "The Unity of H's 'Ethan Brand,' " *CE*, 24 (1965), 453–56.

41. Stock, "The Biblical Context of 'Ethan Brand,' " *AL*, 37 (1965), 115–34; White, "H's Eighteen-Year Cycle: Ethan Brand and Reuben Bourne," *SSF*, 6 (1969), 215–18; McElroy, "The Brand in 'Ethan Brand,' " *AL*, 43 (1972), 633–37; Klingel, " 'Ethan Brand' as H's *Faust*," *SSF*, 19 (1982), 74–76); Pedersen, "Blake's Urizen as H's Ethan Brand," *NCF*, 12 (1958), 304–14; Brown, "H, Melville, and 'Ethan Brand,' " *AL*, 3 (1931), 72–74. On the notebook entry, see Bliss Perry, "H at North Adams," in *The Amateur Spirit* (HM, 1904).

42. Richard Allan Davison, "The Villagers and 'Ethan Brand,' " *SSF*, 4 (1967), 260–62; Cyrill A. Reilly, "On the Dog's Chasing His Own Tail in 'Ethan Brand,' " *PMLA*, 68 (1953), 975–80, which is valuable also for its analysis of how Hawthorne used his notebooks as mate-rial for fiction.

43. On the term, see Leonard C. Butts, "Diorama, Spectroscope, or Peepshow: The Question of the Old German's Showbox in NH's 'Ethan Brand,' " *SSF*, 20 (1983), 320–22.

44. For a different interpretation of this incident, see Alfred J. Levy, " 'Ethan Brand' and the Unpardonable Sin," *BUSE*, 5 (1961), 185–90.

45. See B. A. Sokoloff, "Ethan Brand's Twin," *MLN*, 73 (1958), 73–74; Jerry A. Herndon and Sidney P. Moss, "The Identity and Significance of the German Jewish Showman in H's 'Ethan Brand,' " *CE*, 23

(1962), 362–63; Brother Joseph, "Art and Event in 'Ethan Brand,' " *NCF* (1960), 249–57. The quotations in the text are from Herndon-Moss. Marc Hennelly, "H's *Opus Alchymicum:* 'Ethan Brand,' " *ESQ,* 22 (1976), 96–106, proposes an entirely novel "alchemical reading" of the tale.

46. See his chapter on "Ethan Brand" in *H's Fiction: The Light and the Dark* (UOP, 1965), especially pp. 49–52.

47. " 'Ethan Brand' and the Unpardonable Sin," *BUSE,* 5 (1961), 185–90.

48. One such was the late eighteenth-century English poet, William Cowper, whom nobody could convince that, whatever the Unpardonable Sin was, he had committed it. Cowper resembled Ethan Brand only in his stubbornness. See Gamaliel Bradford's trenchant portrait of him, which is one of his best, in his *Bare Souls* (Harpers, 1924); also Michael J. Quinland, "William Cowper and the Unpardonable Sin," *Journal of Religion,* 23 (1943), 109–16.

49. The most important articles on this point are James E. Miller, Jr., "H and Melville: The Unpardonable Sin," *PMLA,* 70 (1955), 91–114; Joseph X. Brennan and Seymour L. Gross, "The Origin of H's Unpardonable Sin," *BUSE,* 3 (1957), 123–29; Joseph T. McCullen, Jr., and John G. Guilds, "The Unpardonable Sin in H: A Reconsideration," *NCF,* 15 (1960), 221–37; Sheila Dwight, "H and the Unpardonable Sin," *SN,* 2 (1970), 444–47; and Alfred J. Levy's article cited in note 57. See also Father Leonard J. Fick's discussion in *The Light Beyond: A Study of H's Theology* (Newman Press, 1955), pp. 135–40.

50. Christopher Brown, " 'Ethan Brand': A Portrait of the Artist," *SSF,* 17 (1980), 171–74, sees the kiln as "a general symbol of the creative process." Ethan's attitude toward and manipulation of other human beings resembles an author's treatment of his characters. When he flings himself into the kiln, he "makes himself the subject of his art."

51. Joseph Schwartz, " 'Ethan Brand' and the Natural Goodness of Man: A Phenomenological Inquiry," *ESQ,* no. 39 (1965), 79–81. Ethan "expressed his *self* without qualifications" and "emancipated himself completely, but did not find that doubt, conflict, and evil disappeared, as Emerson had promised." His "contempt for others" resulted at last in "contempt for himself," as expressed in his suicide.

52. James W. Mathews, "H and the Chain of Being," *MLQ,* 18 (1957), 282–94.

53. See Sheila Dwight, as cited in note 47, especially pp. 453–55.

54. The result was the book called *Damaged Souls* (HM, 1923).

55. Liebman, " 'Ethan Brand' and the Unpardonable Sin," *ATQ*, 24 (1974), supplement 2, pp. 9–14; Klingel, as cited as note 41.

56. In the coy but amusing introduction to the tale, in which Hawthorne pretends to be translating from a second-rate French writer, M. de l'Aubépine, he does however call it "Beatrice; ou la Belle Empoison-neuse."

57. See Bernard McCabe, "Narrative Technique in 'Rappaccini's Daughter,' " *MLN*, 74 (1959), 213–17.

58. Lloyd Spencer Thomas, " 'Rappaccini's Daughter': H's Distillation of his Sources," *ATQ*, 38 (1978), 177–91.

59. For a good review of criticism and additional bibliography, see Nicholas Ayo, "The Labyrinthine Ways of Rappaccini," *Research Studies of Washington State University*, 42 (1974), 56–67. His "bio-graphical speculation" (pp. 63–64, n. 10) is highly suggestive and put forward with becomingly tentative modesty.

60. Cf. Sidney P. Moss, "A Reading of 'Rappaccini's Daughter,' " *SSF*, 2 (1965), 145–56, and Richard L. Prodmore, Jr., "The Hero's Test in 'Rappaccini's Daughter,' " *ELN*, 15 (1978), 284–91.

61. Walter Rawle, "H's 'Rappaccini's Daughter,' " *Explicator*, 15 (1957), item 15.

62. Cf. Frank Davidson, "H's Hive of Honey," *MLN*, 61 (1946), 14–21; Herbert A. Leibowitz, "H and Spenser: Two Sources," *AL*, 30 (1959), 459–66; Thomas F. Walsh, Jr., "Rappaccini's Literary Gardens," *ESQ*, no. 19 (1960), 9–13. See also Werner Peterich, "H and the *Gesta Romanorum*: The Genesis of Rappaccini and Ethan Brand," in Hans Galinsky and Hans-Joachim Lang, eds., *Kleine Be-iträge zur Amerikanischen Literaturgeschichte* (Heidelberg: Carl Winter, 1961), pp. 11–18; Roy R. Male, *H's Tragic Vision* (Univer-sity of Texas Press, 1957), especially pp. 68–69.

63. Cf. Gabriella La Regina, " 'Rappaccini's Daughter': The Gothic as a Catalyst for H's Imagination," *Studi Americani*, 17 (1971), 29–74; Burton S. Pollin," 'Rappaccini's Daughter': Sources and Names," *Names*, 14 (1966), 30–35.

64. On Shelley, see Oliver Evans, "Allegory and Incest in 'Rappaccini's Daughter,' " *NCF*, 19 (1964), 185–95; Robert L. White, " 'Rappac-cini's Daughter,' *The Cenci*, and the Cenci Legend," *Studi Americani*, 14 (1968), 63–86; Martin F. Kearney, "H's Beatrice Rappaccini: Unlocking her Paradoxical Nature with a Shelleyan Key," *CLA Jour-nal*, 29 (1986), 309–17. On Keats, see Julian Smith, "Keats and H: A Romantic Bloom in Rappaccini's Garden," *ESQ*, no. 42 (1966),

8–12, and Norman A. Anderson, "Rappaccini's Garden: A Keatsian Analogue," *PMLA*, 83 (1968), 271–83; Hubert I. Cohen, "Hoffmann's 'The Sandman': A Possible Source for 'Rappaccini's Daughter,'" *ESQ*, no. 68 (1972), 148–53; Jeannine Dobbs, "H's Dr. Rappaccini and Father George Rapp," *AL*, 43 (1971), 427–30; Richard Clark Sterne, "A Mexican Flower in 'Rappaccini's Garden': Madame Calderon de la Barca's *Life in Mexico* Revisited," *NHJ* 1974, pp. 277–79.

65. Alsen, "The Ambitious Experiment of Dr. Rappaccini," *AL*, 43 (1971), 430–31; Inge, "Dr. Rappaccini's Noble Experiment," *NHJ* 1973, pp. 200–211. Isadore H. Becker, "Tragic Irony in 'Rappaccini's Daughter,'" *Husson Review*, 4 (1971), 89–93, who reads the story as a classical tragedy, also defends Rappaccini. M. D. Uroff, "The Doctors in 'Rappaccini's Daughter,'" *NCF*, 27 (1972), 61–70, connects the tale with the controversy in Hawthorne's Boston between allopaths (Baglioni) and homeopaths (Rappaccini). See also Edward H. Rosenberry, "H's Allegory of Science: 'Rappaccini's Daughter,'" *AL*, 32 (1960), 39–46.

66. Curtis Dahl, "The Devil Is a Wise One," *Cithara*, vol. 6, no. 2 (1967), pp. 52–58, and Sheldon W. Liebman, "H and Milton: The Second Fall in 'Rappaccini's Daughter,'" *NEQ*, 41 (1968), 521–35, both defend Rappaccini and condemn Baglioni. "The Case of the Fatal Antidote," *ArQ*, 11 (1955), 38–43, by Arthur L. Scott, is a clever skit in which Poe's M. Dupin presents a detective's case against Baglioni as a murderer. But the fullest consideration of the character and his role in the story is that of Robert L. Gale, "Rappaccini's Baglioni," *Studi Americani*, 9 (1963), 83–87.

67. Hawthorne himself calls Beatrice "the poor victim of man's ingenuity." See also Kent Bales, "Sexual Exploitation and the Fall from Natural Virtue in Rappaccini's Garden," *ESQ*, 24 (1978), 133–43.

68. See Richard Branzo, "Beatrice Rappaccini: A Victim of Male Love and Horror," *AL*, 48 (1976), 152–64; Frederick L. Gwynn, "H's 'Rappaccini's Daughter,'" *NCF*, 7 (1952), 217–19; Sherwood H. Price, "The Heart, The Head, and 'Rappaccini's Daughter,'" *NEQ*, 27 (1954), 399–403.

69. "Fideism and the Allusive Mode in 'Rappaccini's Daughter,'" *NCF*, 28 (1973), 25–37.

70. Aside from all other considerations, it is not necessary therefore to go along with David Lyttle, "Giovanni! My Poor Giovanni!" *SSF*, 9 (1972), 147–56, who argues that the garden and Beatrice "are not the expression of the doctor's character, but of Giovanni's" and that

"the story is about Giovanni's sexual fantasy . . . from which he is saved by common sense." It is true that as narrator Hawthorne refuses to vouch for the objective reality of everything Giovanni thinks he sees, but in the terms of the story, the poisoned garden and the poisoned girl are both real enough on the common, everyday level of reality, though in her case there is also something much more important about her that Giovanni fails to grasp; consequently he is not "saved by common sense" nor anything else. Cf. Morton L. Ross's excellent article, "What Happens in 'Rappaccini's Daughter'?," *AL*, 43 (1971), 336–45. Without mentioning any of the special considerations adduced by Daly, both Hyatt H. Waggoner (*H: A Critical Study*) and Roy R. Male (*H's Tragic Themes*) present studies basically in harmony with his. They are opposed by the Freudian critic, Frederick C. Crews (*The Sins of the Fathers*).

71. Though Beatrice needs no vindication for any intelligent reader, William Rossky is the critic who provides it more fully, more irrefutably, and in greater detail than any other, in "Rappaccini's Garden, or, The Murder of Innocence," *ESQ*, no. 19 (1960), 98–100.

72. *NH: Representative Selections*, p. 367. Oliver Evans, "The Cavern and the Fountain: Paradox and Double Paradox in 'Rappaccini's Daughter,' " *CE*, 24 (1963), 461–63, replies to Warren; see also Alfred J. Kloeckner, "The Flower and the Fountain: H's Chief Symbols in 'Rappaccini's Daughter,' " *AL*, 38 (1966), 323–36.

73. *H's Tragic Vision*, p. 60.

74. In "The Vision of Goodman Brown: A Source and Interpretation," *AL*, 35 (1963), 218–25, E. Arthur Robinson remarks of Beatrice, "Her spirit could lead Giovanni upward, as Brown thought to follow Faith, but her physical beauty, which resembles the gorgeous but fatal plant, is deadly unless he can assimilate sufficient poison to join her upon equal terms. The moral is old and complex: woman, albeit of finer spiritual quality than man, possesses physical attributes that lure man to evil, although the evil may not be within her power or will."

75. "Rappaccini's Garden," *AL*, 30 (1958), 37–49. Margaret Halliday's "H's Venomous Beatrice," *SSF*, 19 (1982), 231–39, is also valuable for its discussion of what was known or believed about poisons. I find no evidence however to support Richard B. Hovey's view, in his "Love and Hate in 'Rappaccini's Daughter,' " *UKCR* 20 (1962), 137–43, that Beatrice's "emotional nature has been distorted—and consequently her sexuality affected" by her father's attempt to keep her to himself. In "Deadly Innocence: H's Dark

Women," *NEQ*, 43 (1968), 163–79, Gloria C. Erlich has much comparison of "Rappaccini's Daughter" to *The Scarlet Letter.*

76. Stanton, "Secondary Studies on H's 'Young Goodman Brown,' 1845–1975: A Bibliography," *Bulletin of Bibliography*, 33 (1976), 33–44, 52; Leavis, "H as Poet," *Sewanee Review*, 59 (1951), 179–205, 426–58; Abcarian, "The Ending of 'Young Goodman Brown,' " *SSF*, 3 (1966), 343–45; Gallagher, "The Concluding Paragraph of 'Young Goodman Brown,' " *SSF*, 12 (1975), 29–30; Humma, " 'Young Goodman Brown' and the Failure of H's Ambiguity," *Colby Library Quarterly*, series 9 (1971), 425–31. Thomas E. Connolly edited a volume of reprinted essays on "Young Goodman Brown" (Merrill, 1968).

77. Sheldon W. Liebman, "The Reader in 'Young Goodman Brown,' " *NHJ* 1975, pp. 156–69, offers an excellent review of criticism. Liebman gives F. O. Matthiessen the credit for having first expressed the hallucination theory in his *American Renaissance.*

78. Chapter 8 in Daniel G. Hoffman's *Form and Fable in American Fiction* and the references therein cited furnish a good starting place for the study of this subject. On spectral evidence specifically, see David Levin, "Shadows of Doubt: Spectre Evidence in H's 'Young Goodman Brown,' " *AL*, 34 (1962), 344–52, and Michael J. Colacurcio, "Visible Sanctity and Spectre Evidence: The Moral World of H's 'Young Goodman Brown,' " *EIHC*, 110 (1974), 259–99. Other studies in this field, some of which introduce ideas not considered here, are Thomas E. Connolly, "H's 'Young Goodman Brown': An Attack on Puritan Calvinism," *AL*, 28 (1956), 370–75; Paul W. Miller, "H's 'Young Goodman Brown': Cynicism or Meliorism?" *NCF*, 14 (1959), 255–64; James W. Mathews, "Antinomianism in 'Young Goodman Brown,' " *SSF*, 3 (1965), 73–75. In "H's Use of Evidence in 'Young Goodman Brown,' " *EIHC*, 111 (1975), 22–34, James W. Clark, Jr., attempts a detailed examination of the historical background with as much reference to Hawthorne's biography as to the tale. In *Frontier: American Literature and the West* (Princeton University Press, 1965), Edwin Fussell attempts an entirely different approach, in which Brown represents young America. I am not convinced by Terence J. Matheson's argument that Brown draws back from the Black Mass because he fears social ostracism; see " 'Young Goodman Brown': H's Condemnation of Conformity," *NHJ* 1978, pp. 137–40.

79. E. Arthur Robinson, "The Vision of Goodman Brown: A Source and Interpretation," *AL*, 35 (1963), 218–25.

80. "Deodat Lawson's *Christ's Fidelity* and H's 'Young Goodman Brown,' " *EIHC*, 104 (1968), 349–70. Cohen suggests that Lawson's appendix to his second edition, 1704, "could have suggested to Hawthorne the psychological basis of his story with its dream-like atmosphere so suitable to the mental aberrations involved in spiritual experiences. Above all, some details cited by Lawson may have provided Hawthorne the master psychological and structural symbol of his story: the pink ribbons."

81. Herbert A. Leibowitz, "H and Spenser: Two Sources," *AL*, 30 (1959), 459–66.

82. B. Bernard Cohen, "*Paradise Lost* and 'Young Goodman Brown,' " *EIHC*, 94 (1958), 282–96.

83. The most extensive study of Hawthorne's relationship to Goethe is of course William Bysshe Stein, *H's Faust: A Study of the Devil Archetype* (UFP, 1953). But see also John F. Krumpelmann, "H's 'Young Goodman Brown' and Goethe's *Faust*," *Die Neueren Sprachen*, Neue Folge, 1956, pp. 516–21. Krumpelmann, who points out many parallels between the two works, believes that Hawthorne "probably became acquainted with Goethe's work in translation, and, under the spell of the same, conceived his 'Young Goodman Brown.' "

84. Fannye N. Cherry, "The Sources of 'Young Goodman Brown,' " *AL*, 5 (1934), 342–48, goes so far as to find Cervantes the main source. She also cites an article on "Witch Ointment," published in the *American Magazine*, July 1836, more than a year after the first appearance of "Young Goodman Brown," which she thinks Hawthorne may have written, and which gives the same recipe for flying as does Goody Cloyse in the tale. Cervantes makes his witch refer to the opinion "that we do not go to these orgies except in imagination," and there seems to be some evidence to support the view that the formula cited could produce a hallucination of flying.

85. *NH* (William Sloane Associates, 1949), p. 78.

86. *American Renaissance*, p. 484.

87. Hurley, "Young Goodman Brown's 'Heart of Darkness,' " *AL*, 37 (1966), 410–19; Davis, "H's 'Young Goodman Brown,' " *NHJ* 1973, pp. 198–99; Carpenter, "H's Polar Explorations: 'Young Goodman Brown' and 'My Kinsman, Major Molineux,' " *NCF*, 24 (1969), 45–56; Abel, "Black Glove and Pink Ribbon: H's Metonymic Symbols," *NEQ*, 42 (1969), 163–80. See also Leo B. Levy, "The Problem of Faith in 'Young Goodman Brown,' " *JEGP*, 71 (1975), 375–87.

88. Shriver, "Young Goody Brown," *Etudes Anglaises*, 30 (1966), 407–19. See also William R. Haller, "Hail, Wedded Love," *ELH*, 13 (1946), 79–97, and (with Malleville Haller), "The Puritan Art of Love," *Huntington Library Quarterly*, 5 (1942), 255–72; and cf. chapter 5, "Milton and Eve," in the present writer's *The Personality of Milton* (UOP, 1970).

89. Cf. Robert W. Cochran, "H's Choice: The Veil or the Jaundiced Eye," *CE*, 23 (1962), 342–48, with Thomas E. Connolly's rebuttal (24:153) and Cochran's reply (24:153–54). For Liebman, see "The Reader in 'Young Goodman Brown,'" *NHJ* 1975, pp. 156–69, and for Paulits, "Ambivalences in 'Young Goodman Brown,'" *AL*, 41 (1970), 577–84.

90. "The Woe That Is Madness: Goodman and the Face of the Fire," *NHJ* 1973, pp. 177–82.

91. "'Young Goodman Brown' and H's Theory of Mimesis," *NCF*, 23 (1969), 393–412. James L. Williamson's argument, in "'Young Goodman Brown': H's 'Devil in Manuscript,'" *SSF*, 18 (1981), 155–62, that the narrator is himself of the Devil's party was too far off the beam even to deserve Karen Hollister's effective refutation in 19 (1982), 381–84.

92. Cf. Norman H. Hostetler, "Narrative Structure and Theme in 'Young Goodman Brown,'" *Journal of Narrative Technique*, 12 (1922), 221–28.

93. The best single example from Hawthorne's own writings is ingeniously cited by Alison Ensor in "'Whispers of the Bad Angel': A *Scarlet Letter* Passage as a Commentary on 'Young Goodman Brown,'" *SSF*, 7 (1970), 467–68. In chapter 5 of the novel Hester is tempted to project her own sin upon others as Brown does, but, unlike him, she resists the temptation, and Hawthorne's editorial comment makes his own attitude unmistakable: "O Fiend, whose talisman was that fatal symbol [i.e. the scarlet letter], wouldst thou leave nothing, whether in youth or age, for this poor sinner to reverse?—such loss of faith is ever one of the saddest results of sin."

94. McKeithan, "H's 'Young Goodman Brown': An Interpretation," *MLN*, 67 (1952), 93–96; Walsh, "The Bedeviling of Young Goodman Brown," *MLQ*, 19 (1958), 331–36; Davidson, "'Young Goodman Brown'—H's Intent," *ESQ*, 31 (1963), 68–71; Whelan, "H Interprets 'Young Goodman Brown,'" *ESQ*, 62 (1971), 2–4.

95. One critic has plausibly suggested that Hawthorne may have feared that his unadmiring presentation of the colonial "patriots" in

"Molineux" might give offense. See Nelson F. Adkins, "H's Democratic New England Puritans," *ESQ*, 44 (1966), 66–72.

96. Many of the topics touched upon in this paragraph are more fully explored in P. L. Abernathy, "The Identity of Major Molineux," *ATQ*, 31 (1976), 5–8; Alexander W. Allison, "The Literary Contents of 'My Kinsman, Major Molineux,' " *NCF*, 23 (1968), 304–11; Jesse Bier, "H's 'My Kinsman, Major Molineux,' " *Explicator*, vol. 38, no. 4 (1980), 40–41; Arthur J. Broes, "Journey into Moral Darkness: 'My Kinsman, Major Molineux' as Allegory," *NCF*, 19 (1964), 171–84; Mario D'Avanzo, "The Literary Sources of 'My Kinsman, Major Molineux: Shakespeare, Coleridge, Milton," *SSF*, 10 (1972), 121–36; James Duban, "Robin and Robinarchs in 'My Kinsman, Major Molineux,' " *NCF*, 38 (1983), 271–88; Robert C. Grayson, "The New England Sources of 'My Kinsman, Major Molineux,' " *AL*, 54 (1982), 545–59; Stanley J. Kosckowski, " 'My Kinsman, Major Molineux' as Mock-Heroic," *ATQ*, 31 (1976), 20–21; Roy Harvey Pearce, "H and the Sense of the Past, or, The Immortality of Major Molineux," *ELH*, 21 (1964), 327–49; Marilyn Gaddis Rose, "Theseus Motif in 'My Kinsman, Major Molineux,' " *ESQ*, no. 47 (1967), 21–23; Peter Shaw, "Fathers, Sons, and the Ambiguities of Revolution in 'My Kinsman, Major Molineux,' " *NEQ*, 49 (1976), 559–76; Julian Smith, "Coming of Age in America: Young Ben Franklin and Robin Molineux," *AQ*, 17 (1965), 550–58, but cf. A. B. England, "Robin Molineux and Young Ben Franklin: A Reconsideration," *JAmSt*, 6 (1972), 181–88, and Dennis Murphy, "Poor Robin and Shrewd Ben: H's Kinsman," *SSF*, 15 (1978), 185–90; Dwayne Thorpe," 'My Kinsman, Major Molineux': The Identity of the Kinsman," *Topic*, 18 (1969), 53–63; Richard Van Der Beets and Paul Witherington, "My Kinsman, Brockden Brown: Robin Molineux and Arthur Mervyn," *ATQ*, 1 (1969), 13–15.

97. Raymond Benoit, "H's 'My Kinsman, Major Molineux,' " *ATQ*, no. 14, part 1 (1972), 8–9, interprets this character in terms of symbolism. See also J. C. Nitzsche, "House Symbolism in H's 'My Kinsman, Major Molineux,' " *ATQ*, no. 38 (1976), 167–76.

98. See Franklin B. Newman, " 'My Kinsman, Major Molineux': An Interpretation," *UKCR*, 21 (1955), 203–12; Robert E. Abrams, "The Psychology of Cogitation: 'My Kinsman, Major Molineux,' " *PQ*, 58 (1979), 336–46; also Sheridan Baker's reply, opposing the dream hypothesis, "H's Evidence," *PQ*, 61 (1982), 481–83.

99. See Simon O. Lesser, *Fiction and the Unconscious* (Random House, 1957); Thomas E. Connors, " 'My Kinsman, Major Molineux': A

Reading," *MLN*, 74 (1959), 299–302; Roy Harvey Pearce, "Robin Molineux on the Analyst's Couch: A Note on the Limits of Psychoanalytical Criticism," *Criticism*, 1 (1959), 83–90; Bartlett C. Jones, "The Ambiguity of Shrewdness in 'My Kinsman, Major Molineux,' " *Midcontinent American Studies Journal*, vol. 3, no. 2 (1962), 42–47; T. R. Sharma, "Diabolic World and Naive Hero in 'My Kinsman, Major Molineux,' " *Indian Journal of American Studies*, vol. 1, no. 1 (1969), 35–43; Sanford Pinsker, "H's Double-faced Fellow," *NHJ* 1972, pp. 255–56.

100. Cf., for various views, Joseph D. Adams, "The Societal Initiation and H's 'My Kinsman, Major Molineux': The Night Journey Motif," *English Studies Colloquium*, 1 (1976), 1–19; Nathan A. Corvo, "The Gargouille Anti-Hero: Victim of Christian Satire," *Renascence*, 22 (1970), 69–77; Carl Dennis, "How to Live in Hell: The Bleak Vision of H's 'My Kinsman, Major Molineux,' " *University Review*, 37 (1971), 350–58; Seymour L. Gross, "H's 'My Kinsman, Major Molineux': History as Moral Adventure," *NCF*, 12 (1957), 97–109; Sheldon W. Liebman, "Robin's Conversion: The Design of 'My Kinsman, Major Molineux,' " *SSF*, 8 (1971), 443–57; Edwin Haviland Miller, " 'My Kinsman, Major Molineux': The Playful Art of NH," *ESQ*, 24 (1978), 145–51; Roger P. Wallins, "Robin and the Narrator in 'My Kinsman, Major Molineux,' " *SSF*, 12 (1979), 173–79; Robert Zajkowski, "Renaissance Psychology and H's 'My Kinsman, Major Molineux,' " *NHJ* 1978, pp. 159–67. Gross's careful and detailed reading provides a good guide to the entire story, and Liebman offers a valuable study of characterization, structure, and imagery, as well as of the special subject under consideration here.

101. See John Russell, "Allegory and 'My Kinsman, Major Molineux,' " *NEQ*, 40 (1967), 432–40.

3. Romances

1. See Anthony Trollope, "The Genius of NH," *North American Review*, 274 (1879), 203–22.

2. "H on the Romantic: His Prefaces Related and Examined," *MP*, 53 (1955), 17–24. See also Charles H. Foster, "H's Literary Theory," *PMLA*, 57 (1942), 241–54; Robert Kimbrough, " 'The Actual and the Imaginary': H's Concept of Art in Theory and Practice," *Transactions of the Wisconsin Academy of Sciences, Arts, and Letters*, 50 (1961), 277–93; John C. Stubbs, "H's *SL:* The Theory of the Romance and the Use of the New England Situation," *PMLA*, 83

(1968), 1439–47, also his book, *The Pursuit of Form, A Study of H and the Romance* (University of Illinois Press, 1970); Leo B. Levy, "The Notebook Source and the 18th Century Context of H's Theory of Romance," *NHJ* 1973, pp. 120–29; Evan Carton, "H and the Province of Romance," *ELH*, 47 (1980), 331–54.

3. Roy Harvey Pearce gives the best account of these matters in his introduction to *Fanshawe* in *The Centenary Edition of the Works of NH*, III, 310ff.

4. "*Fanshawe*: H's World of Images," *SN*, 2 (1970), 440–48. Carl Bode's "H's *Fanshawe*: The Promising of Greatness" is in *NEQ*, 23 (1950), 235–42. See also Robert Eugene Gross, "H's First Novel: The Future of a Style," *PMLA*, 78 (1963), 60–68; Nina Baym, "H's Gothic Discards: *Fanshawe* and 'Alice Doane,' " *NHJ* 1974, pp. 105–15; James G. Janssen, "*Fanshawe* and H's Developing Comic Sense," *ESQ*, 22 (1976), 24–27.

5. Philip E. Burnham, "H's *Fanshawe* and Bowdoin College," *EIHC*, 80 (1944), 131–38.

6. Goldstein, "The Literary Source of H's *Fanshawe*," *MLN*, 60 (1945), 1–8; Stein, *H's Faust* (UFP, 1953); Sattelmeyer, "The Aesthetic Background of H's *Fanshawe*," *NHJ* 1975, pp. 200–209.

7. See N. F. Doubleday, "H and Literary Nationalism," *AL*, 12 (1941), 447–53; Randall Stewart, "H and *The Faerie Queene*," *PQ*, 12 (1933), 196–206; and W. S. Johnson, "H and *The Pilgrim's Progress*," *JEGP*, 50 (1951), 156–66.

8. See G. Harrison Orians, "Scott and H's *Fanshawe*," *NEQ*, 11 (1938), 388–94.

9. It is only fair to add that "The Custom House" has inspired a rather amazing number of studies, many of which invest what I cannot but regard as an enormous amount of misplaced ingenuity attempting to establish a closer relationship between the introduction and the story than I can perceive or even read the sketch as containing the key to the meaning of the romance. Cf. Larzer Ziff, "The Ethical Dilemma of 'The Custom House,' " *MLN*, 83 (1958), 338–44; Sam S. Baskett, "The (Complete) *SL*," *CE*, 22 (1961), 321–28; Earl H. Rovit, "Ambiguity in H's *SL*," *Archiv*, 198 (1961), 76–88; Frank McShane, "The House of the Dead: H's Custom House and *SL*," *NEQ*, 35 (1962), 94–101; Marshall Van Deusen, "Narrative Tone in 'The Custom House' and *SL*," *NCF*, 21 (1966), 61–84; Dan McCall, "The Design of H's 'The Custom House,' " *NCF*, 21 (1967), 356–58; David Stouck, "The Surveyor of the Custom House: A Narrator for *SL*," *Centennial Review*, 15 (1971), 309–29; J. A. Ward, "Self-

Revelation in *SL*," *Rice University Studies*, vol. 1, no. 1 (1975), 141–50; James M. Cox, "*SL:* Through the Old Manse and the Custom House," *Virginia Quarterly Review*, 51 (1975), 432–47; John Franzosa, " 'The Custom House,' *SL*, and Hawthorne's Separation from Salem," *ESQ*, 24 (1978), 57–71; Robert L. Berner, "A Key to 'The Custom House,' " *ATQ*, 41 (1979), 33–43; Calenda Green, "The Custom House: H's Dark Wood of Error," *NEQ*, 53 (1980), 184–95; John G. Bayer, "Narrative Technique and the Oral Tradition in *SL*," *AL*, 52 (1980–81), 250–63. See also the discussion of this matter in Joel Porte, *The Romance in America* (Wesleyan University Press, 1969) and Michael T. Gilmore, *The Middle Way: Puritanism and Ideology in American Romantic Fiction* (Rutgers University Press, 1977). The quotation from Daniel Hoffman is from his *Form and Fable in American Fiction* (OUP, 1961).

10.   For the publication data cited, see William Charvat's introduction to *SL* in the Centenary Edition of H's writings (*OSUP*, 1962), Hubert H. Hoeltje's "The Writing of *SL*," *NEQ*, 27 (1954), 326–46, is concerned largely with H's dismissal from the custom service and the attendant circumstances.

11.   Harry Thurston Peck's essay in *Studies in Several Literatures* (Dodd, Mead, 1909) was the pioneer discussion of this point. In 1892 Richard Mansfield appeared in an unsuccessful dramatization; see William Winter, *Life and Art of Richard Mansfield* (Moffat, Yard, 1910). There have been operas by Walter Damrosch, Vittorio Giannini, and others. In 1926 the great Swedish director Victor Sjöström made a film for M-G-M with Lillian Gish as Hester, Lars Hanson as Dimmesdale, and Henry B. Walthall as Chillingworth. But at least one critic has argued, I think rightly, that the novel suggests a series of lantern slides rather than the fluidity of a film. In *Studi Americani*, 5 (1959), 339–50, Robert W. Mann, "Afterthoughts on Opera and *SL*," discusses what he regards as the operatic character of *SL* and adds his own libretto (pp. 351–81).

12.   For a defense of H's accuracy see Ernest W. Baughman, "Public Confession and *SL*," *NEQ*, 40 (1967), 532–50. There is a vigorous statement of the other point of view in Nina Baym's "Passion and Authority in *SL*," *NEQ*, 43 (1970), 209–30.

13.   Cowley, "Five Acts of *SL*," *CE*, 19 (1957), 11–16; MacLean, "H's *SL*: 'The Dark Problem of This Life,' " *AL*, 29 (1955), 12–25; Gerber, "Form and Content in *SL*," *NEQ*, 17 (1944), 25–55; Roper, "The Originality of H's *SL*," *Dalhousie Review*, 30 (1950), 63–79; Tanselle, "A Note on the Structure of *SL*," *NCF*, 17 (1962), 283–85;

Warren, "*SL:* A Literary Exercise in Moral Theology," *Southern Review,* n.s. 1 (1965), 22–45. There are more minute analyses of structure in Leland Schubert, *H, the Artist* (UNCP, 1944) and Charles Ryskamp, "The New England Sources of *SL,*" *AL,* 31 (1959), 257–79, and Hyatt H. Waggoner diagrams the plot in "NH: The Cemetery, the Prison, and the Rose," *UKCR,* 14 (1948), 175–90. Mona Scheuermann, "The American Novel of Seduction: An Explanation of the Omission of the Sex Act in *SL,*" *NHJ* 1978, pp. 105–15, has the fullest consideration of why H made the adultery antecedent to the action of the novel. In "From Allegory to Romance: H's Transformation of *SL,*" *MP,* 80 (1982), 145–50, Watson Branch analyzes the novel on the assumption of a hypothetical revision after Fields had seen the first draft, his clues being survivals of what he regards as the older version, resulting in "equivocal" characterizations of all the principals.

14. "*SL* and its Modern Critics," *NCF,* 7 (1953), 251–64. On symbolism see also Stephen A. Black, "*SL:* Death by Symbols," *Paunch,* 24 (1964), 51–71, and, for a different approach, Millicent Bell, "The Obliquity of Signs: *SL,*" *MR,* 23 (1982), 9–26; also Lawrence E. Scanlon, "The Heart of *SL,*" *TSLL,* 4 (1962), 190–213, and M. L. Lasser, "Mirror Imagery in *SL,*" *English Journal,* 56 (1967), 274–77. In "The Landscape Modes of *SL,*" *NCF,* 23 (1969), 377–92, Leo B. Levy sees "the traditions of the sublime and the picturesque" in painting and literature that prevailed in Hawthorne's time as "determining the structure and meaning" of the novel. Mistress Hibbens is a historical character who was actually hanged for witchcraft, though she was probably guilty of nothing worse than bad temper. For a masterly interpretation of this figure against the background of Puritan beliefs, see Earl F. Wentersdorf, "The Element of Witchcraft in *SL,*" *Folklore,* 83 (1972), 232–53.

15. "H versus Hester: The Ghostly Dialectic of Romance in *SL,*" *TSLL,* 24 (1982), 47–67.

16. On some of the problems created by these paradoxes, cf. Walter Shear, "Characterization in *SL,*" *Midwest Quarterly,* 12 (1971), 437–54.

17. Hutchinson's "Antiquity and Mythology in *SL:* The Primary Sources" may be read in *ArQ,* 36 (1980), 197–210, or in *Hartford Studies in Literature,* 13 (1981), 92–110. Todd's "The Magna Mater Archetype in *SL*" is in *NEQ,* 45 (1972), 421–29.

18. Stanton, "H, Bunyan, and the American Romances," *PMLA,* 71 (1956), 155–65; Autrey, "A Source for Roger Chillingworth," *ATQ,*

no. 26, supp. (1975), 24–26; Maybrook, " 'Bearings Unknown to English Heraldry' in *SL*," *NHJ* 1977, pp. 173–214; Darnell, "*SL: H's Emblem Book*," *SAF*, 7 (1979), 153–62; Robert and Marijane Osborn, "Another Look at an Old Tombstone," *NEQ*, 46 (1973), 278–79, and Robert L. Brant, "H and Marvell," *AL*, 30 (1958), 366.

19. Reid's *The Yellow Ruff and "SL"* was published by UFP in 1955, and Reid edited *Sir Thomas Overbury's Vision . . . And Other English Sources of H's "SL"* for the same in 1957. H is known to have consulted references in the Salem Athenaeum from which he could have learned of the Overbury affair. There is an excellent brief account in the Norton critical edition of *SL*; for a fuller account see William McElwen, *The Murder of Sir Thomas Overbury* (OUP, 1942). There are also two absorbing novels: *My Tattered Loving*, by George R. Preedy (Herbert Jenkins, 1927) and *The King's Minion*, by Rafael Sabatini (HM, 1930). Kenneth Serb's "A Note on H's Pearl" is in *ESQ*, no. 39 (1965), pp. 20–21, and Donna Allen Wright's "The Meeting at the Brook-Side: Beatrice, the Pearl Maiden, and Pearl Prynne" in *ESQ*, 28 (1982), 114–120. "*SL* and Revolutions Abroad," by Larry J. Reynolds, is in *AL*, 57 (1965), 44–67.

20. See Louis Owens, "Paudling's 'The Dumb Girl' A Source for *SL*," *NHJ* 1974, 240–49; Francis E. Kearns, "Margaret Fuller as a Model for Hester Prynne," *Jahrbuch für Amerikastudien*, 10 (1965), 191–97. The most detailed study of the possible influence of Ann Hutchinson is Michael J. Colacurcio, "Footsteps of Ann Hutchinson: The Context of *SL*," *ELH*, 39 (1972), 459–94, who also sees possible reflections of John Cotton in Dimmesdale. See also Charles Boewe and Murray G. Murphey, "Hester Prynne in History," *AL*, 32 (1960), 202–4. In "Hester Prynne's Grave," *Descant*, vol. 5, no. 2 (1961), 29–33, John J. McAleer calls attention to the presence in King's Chapel burying ground of the grave of "Hannah ye Wife of Adam Dinsdale," who died in 1710. On the general subject of this paragraph see Charles Ryskamp, "The New England Sources of *SL*," *AL*, 31 (1959), 257–72; cf. Michael T. Gilmore, *The Middle Way*, pp. 86–91.

21. See D. C. Gallup, "On H's Authorship of 'The Battle Omen,' " *NEQ*, 9 (1936), 690–99. I must confess however that the parallels between *SL* and another tale of doubtful authorship seem to me less significant than Gerald R. Griffin finds them in " 'The New England Village': Internal Evidence and a New Genesis of *SL*," *EIHC*, 107 (1971), 268–79.

22. See Edward Stone, "The Antique Gentility of Hester Prynne," *PQ*, 36 (1957), 90–96. Frederick Newberry, "Tradition and Disinheritance in *SL*," *ESQ*, 23 (1977), 1–17, places the Puritans against the background of their English inheritance. For a different consideration of this from a more specialized and more theological point of view, see Ronald J. Gervais, " 'A Papist among the Puritans': Icon and Logos in *SL*," *ESQ*, 25 (1971), 11–16.

23. For a considered reply to James, see Terence Martin, "Adam Blair and Arthur Dimmesdale: A Lesson from the Master," *AL*, 34 (1962–63), 274–79.

24. Mona Scheuermann (see n. 13) points out that in fiction the conventional end for the seduced and violated woman was death. But Hester "withstands the social and psychological pressures which the Puritan world exerts." See also Gary Lane, "Structural Dynamics and the Unknowable in *SL*," *NHJ* 1977, pp. 323–29. It is true that at one time Hester is so discouraged that she considers infanticide and suicide, but Hawthorne passes this over in a sentence, and I doubt that she was ever in great danger of activating this impulse.

25. Frank Neal Doubleday, "H's Hester and Puritanism," *PMLA*, 54 (1939), 825–28, protests against seeing Hester's "consecration" in the forest scene as expressing H's own point of view. On the contrary, she had turned, or been turned, away from what he calls "the normal life of a woman."

26. The quotation from Hart is from "*SL* One Hundred Years After," *NEQ*, 23 (1969), 381–95, the Brodhead from his *H. Melville, and the Novel* (UCP, 1976), p. 43. See also Rosemary Stephens's over-subtle but suggestive article, "*A* is for *Art* in *SL*," *ATQ*, 1 (1969), 23–27.

27. See Gilmore, *The Middle Way*, p. 105, and the references there indicated.

28. Important exceptions are Seymour L. Gross, " 'Solitude, and Love, and Anguish': The Tragic Design of *SL*," *CLA Journal*, 3 (1960), 154–65, and Allan Austin, "Hester Prynne's Plan of Escape: The Moral Problem," *UKCR*, 28 (1962), 317–18. Austin goes so far as to defend Hester's action as moral under the circumstances and even sees Dimmesdale's confession as satisfying nothing "except his own morbid ego."

29. Frederick C. Crews, *The Sins of the Fathers*, doubts even this. To him Hester at the end is "selfless and humble . . . not because she believes in Christian submission but because all passion has been spent." See

also two amusing articles by a somewhat like-minded critic, Frederic Ives Carpenter: "Puritans Preferred Blondes: The Heroines of Melville and H," *NEQ,* 9 (1936), 253–72, and "Scarlet A Minus," *CE,* 5 (1944), 172–80. Carpenter believed that H created Hester as a transcendental idealist and then imposed his own "moralistic" judgment upon her from the outside. Darrel Abel replied in "H's Hester," *CE,* 13 (1952), 303–9, a sane and balanced consideration of the moral responsibilities of all three of the persons concerned and of the society in which they lived. Abel's own position is that Hester "typifies romantic individualism, and in her story Hawthorne endeavored to exhibit the inadequacy of such a philosophy." Though "more a victim of circumstances than a wilful wrong doer, she is nevertheless to be held morally responsible." See Carpenter's reply in *CE,* 13, pp. 457–58, and Abel's rejoinder in 14 (1952), 34. See further James G. Janssen, "Pride and Prophecy: The Final Irony of *SL,*" *NHJ* 1975, pp. 241–47. Dan Vogel, "H's Concept of Tragedy," *NHJ* 1972, pp. 183–93, probably stands alone in seeing Hester as "melodramatically . . . conceived" and too "morally obtuse" to be a tragic heroine.

30. Davidson, "Dimmesdale's Fall," *NEQ,* 36 (1963), 358–70; Houston, "Hester Prynne as Eternal Feminine," *Discourse,* 9 (1966), 230–44; Dillingham, "Arthur Dimmesdale's Confession," *Studies in the Literary Imagination,* vol. 2, no. 1 (1969), 21–26; Nolte, "H's Dimmesdale: A Small Man Gone Wrong," *NEQ,* 32 (1965), 168–86.

31. "*SL* as Dialectic of Temperament and Idea," *SN,* 2 (1970), 474–86.

32. Darrel Abel's very important article is "H's Dimmesdale, Fugitive from Wrath," *NCF,* 11 (1956), 81–105. On the Election sermon and its consequences, see further Thomas F. Walsh, "Dimmesdale's Election Sermon," *ESQ,* 44 (1966), 64–65; Terence Martin, "Dimmesdale's Ultimate Sermon," *ArQ,* 27 (1971), 230–40; Robert F. Haugh, "The Second Secret in *SL,*" *CE,* 17 (1966), 269–71. Bruce Ingham Granger, "Arthur Dimmesdale as Tragic Hero," *NCF,* 19 (1964), 192–203, suggests that the minister's change of heart was inspired by the *writing* of his sermon. See also Donald Ringe, "H's Psychology of Head and Heart," *PMLA,* 65 (1950), 120–32, and C. R. O'Donnell, "H's Dimmesdale: The Search for the Realm of Quiet," *NCF,* 14 (1960), 317–32. Frederick C. Crews offers a Freudian interpretation of Dimmesdale in "The Ruined Wall: Unconscious Motivation in *SL,*" *NEQ,* 38 (1965), 312–20.

33. The fullest account of whom is Raymona E. Hull's "Una Hawthorne: A Biographical Sketch," *NHJ* 1976, pp. 86–119.

34. "Pearl: Symbolic Link Between Two Worlds," *Ball State University Forum*, vol. 13, no. 1 (1972), 60–67.

35. "Pearl, 1850–1955," *PMLA*, 72 (1957): 689–99.

36. Eisinger, "Pearl and the Puritan Heritage," *CE*, 12 (1951), 323–29; Newberry (see n. 22); May, "Pearl as Christ and Anti-Christ," *ATQ*, no. 24, supp. 1 (1974), pp. 8–11. For Reynolds, see n. 11.

37. *The Power of Blackness: H, Poe, Melville* (Knopf, 1958), p. 78.

38. "The Character of Flame: The Function of Pearl in *SL*," *AL*, 27 (1956), 537–55. See also Darrel Abel, "H's Pearl: Symbol and Character," *ELH*, 18 (1951), 50–66; Richard Emmet Whelan, Jr., "Hester Prynne's Little Pearl: Sacred and Profane Love," *AL*, 38 (1967), 488–505; Leland S. Person, Jr., "*SL* and the Myth of the Divine Child," *ATQ*, no. 44 (1979), 295–309. Grace Pleasant Wellborn strengthens the case for this interpretation by what she writes about H's red and gold symbolism in "The Golden Thread in *SL*," *Southern Folklore Quarterly*, 29 (1965), 167–78, and especially by showing, in "Plant Lore and *SL*," vol. 27 (1963), 160–67, that the flowers associated with Pearl are symbols of grace. See also the same writer's articles in *South Central Bulletin*: "The Mystic Seven in *SL*," vol. 21 (1961), 23–31, and "The Symbolic Three in *SL*," vol. 23 (1963), 10–17.

39. William Bysshe Stein has a point when he sees "the dramatic movement of the plot" in *SL* controlled by Chillingworth, "the devil archetype." In a sense this allies *SL* with the *Othello*-type of tragedy, in which the action is initiated not by the hero but by the opposition.

40. Abel, "The Devil in Boston," *PQ*, 32 (1953), 366–81; Vogel, "Roger Chillingworth: The Satanic Paradox of *SL*," *Criticism*, 5 (1963), 272–80; Munger, "Notes on *SL*," *Atlantic Monthly*, 93 (1904), 521–35, reprinted in *Essays for the Day* (HM, 1904); Lefcowitz, "Apologia pro Hester Prynne, A Psychological Study," *Literature and Psychology*, 24 (1974), 34–45.

41. In "The 'Many Morals' of *SL*," *NHJ* 1977, pp. 215–37, which considers H's whole attitude toward morality and moralizing fiction against the background of literary criticism in his time. Charles Child Walcutt's "*SL* and Its Modern Critics," *NCF*, 7 (1953), 251–64, is an interesting review of representative critics to date. David Leveranz's "Mrs. Hawthorne's Headache: Reading *SL*," *NCF*, 37 (1983), 552–75, is concerned largely with what the author considers the "unrelieved tensions of the book." H silences Hester "with values he and his audience hold dear" but "makes his readers uncomfortable with those

values." Whether or not the reader accepts these judgments, the author's documented review of criticism is useful.

42. Studies of *SL* are like the sands of the sea in number, and I do not claim to have cited anything like all of them here. A considerable number of articles, along with material from books, have been reprinted in whole or in part in John C. Gerber, ed., *Twentieth Century Interpretations of "SL"* (Prentice-Hall, 1968); Arlin Turner, ed., *The Merrill Studies in "SL"* (Merrill, 1976); and in the Norton critical edition of *SL*, edited by Sculley Bradley, Richmond Croom Beatty, and E. Hudson Long (1962).

43. Cf. Norman Holmes Pearson, "The Pynchons and Judge Pyncheon," *EIHC*, 100 (1964), 235–55.

44. Introduction to the Rinehart edition of *HSG*, 1957.

45. Abel, "H's House of Tradition," *SAQ*, 52 (1953), 561–78; Waterman, "Dramatic Structure in *HSG*," *Studies in the Literary Imagination*, vol. 2, no. 1 April 1969, pp. 13–19; Dillingham, "Structure and Theme in *HSG*," *NCF,* !4 (1939), 55–69. See also Edgar A. Dryden, "H's Castle in the Air: Form and Theme in *HSG*," *ELH*, 38 (1971), 294–317. In "The House of the Seven Deadly Suns," *ESQ*, 19 (1973), 26–33, Carol Schoen takes a hint from L. Etienne in 1857 to argue that the novel is "one of the most carefully structured works in American literature" around the framework of the seven suns. Abel's is the most elaborate study of structure and defense of the unity of the novel; his article also contains an excellent discussion of H's conception of romance.

46. *Inward Sky,* 353.

47. Swanson's "On Building *HSG*," *Ball State University Forum*, vol. 10, no. 1 (1960), pp. 43–50, is the best and fullest treatment of sources. For relevant suggestions in H's notebooks, Swanson cites Randall Stewart's edition of the *American Notebooks* (YUP, 1932), especially pp. lxxvi–lxxxii. See also William Charvat's introduction to *HSG* in the Centenary Edition. Donald Junkins, "H's *HSG*: A Prototype of the Human Mind," *Literature and Psychology,* 17 (1967), 198–209, tries to establish an autobiographical base for the story.

48. See Thomas Morgan Griffiths, " 'Montpelier' and Seven Gables," *NEQ*, 16 (1943), 432–43. Julian Smith, "A H Source for *HSG*," *ATQ*, 1 (1969), 18–19, points out interesting resemblances between *HSG* and "Legends of the Province House." The parade of dead governors in "Howe's Masquerade" is especially interesting in connection with chapter 18.

49. Mathews, "The House of Atreus and *HSG*," *ESQ*, no. 63 (1971), 31–36; Emry, "Two Houses of Pride: Spenser's and H's," *PQ*, 33 (1964), 91–94; Arac, "The House and the Railroad: *Dombey and Son* and *HSG*," *NEQ*, 51 (1978), 3–22; Beebe, "The Fall of the House of Pyncheon," *NCF*, 11 (1956), 1–17; Jaffe, "The Miniature That Inspired Clifford Pyncheon's Portrait," *EIHC*, 98 (1962), 278–82. Edward Craney Jacobs does not in my judgment make much of a case for what he considers "Shakespearean Borrowings in *HSG*," *NHJ* 1977, pp. 343–48. Nor do the parallels John F. Byers, Jr., "*HSG* and 'The Daughters of Dr. Byers,' " *PMLA*, 89 (1982), 174–77 finds in a factual article in *Graham's Magazine* for 1842 seem very close. In "H's Alembic: Alchemical Immagery in *HSG*," *ESQ*, 26 (1980), 173–83, Jeffrey L. Meikle argues that H "consciously structured" his book as "an alchemical drama."

50. I find Richard F. Platizky overingenious however when he argues in "Hepzibah's Gingerbread Cakes in *HSG*," *AN&Q*, 17 (1979), 106–8, that Ned is not only used as a unifying device but that "even the kinds of cakes he chooses to eat are symbolic of some of the central themes of the work." For much fuller studies of H's symbolism, see Richard Harter Fogle, *H's Fiction: The Light and the Dark* and *H's Imagery: The "Proper Light and Shadow" in the Major Romances* (UOP, 1969); also Hyatt H. Waggoner, *H, A Critical Study, H's Fiction*, pp. 165–67, is interesting on the house itself as a symbol. Waggoner thinks that Clifford's speculations on time and history come closer than anything else to presenting "the chief themes of the novel." See also Harold Orel, "The Double Symbol," *AL*, 23 (1951), 1–6, which is a detailed consideration of chapter 18; Leo B. Levy, "Picturesque Style in *HSG*," *NEQ*, 39 (1966), 147–60; Edward C. Sampson, "Sound-Imagery in *HSG*," *English Review*, vol. 22, no. 2 (1971), pp. 26–29; and Richard P. Flack, "Industrial Imagery in *HSG*," *NHJ* 1976, pp. 273–76. Clark Griffith, "Substance and Shadow: Language and Meaning in *HSG*," *MP*, 51 (1951), 187–95, attempts through a study of language "in which exposition, symbolism, irony, drama, and meaning are subsumed" to demonstrate that "far from being aesthetically slipshod or thematically unsatisfying, *HSG* is, in the main, among H's most effectively executed works of art."

51. See Patrick K. Dooley, "Genteel Poverty: Hepzibah in *HSG*," *Markham Review*, 8 (1980): 33–35.

52. *Rage for Order* (UCP, 1948), p. 102.

53. Smith, "The Morals of Power," in Clarence Gohdes, ed., *Essays on American Literature in Honor of Jay B. Hubbell* (DUP, 1967). For a more elaborate consideration of these matters, see Viola Sachs, "The Myth of America in *HSG* and *BR*," *Kwartalnik Neofilologiczny*, 15 (1968), 268–83, and Richard Clark Sterne, "H's Politics in *HSG*," *Canadian Review of American Studies*, 6 (1975), 74–83. See further Michael T. Gilmore's interesting discussion of H's views on "Manifest Destiny" and other current political issues in *The Middle Way*, pp. 125–30.

54. Alfred H. Marks's article, "Who Killed Judge Pyncheon?: The Role of the Imagination in *HSG*," *PMLA* 71 (1957), 355–69, is an entertaining detective story, which attempts to show that, through mistaking him for a ghost, Judge Pyncheon was frightened to death by Clifford's unexpected appearance in the parlor.

55. The best study of Holgrave is Alfred H. Marks's "H's Daguerreotypist: Scientist, Artist, Reformer," *Ball State Teachers College Forum*, vol. 3, no. 1 (1966), pp. 61–74. Among other things this article gives interesting information about the daguerreotype process and what was believed about it in the 1850s and shows why it furnished a suitable occupation for a man of Holgrave's talents and interests. See also J. Gill Holland, "H and Photography: *HSG*," *NHJ* 1978, pp. 1–10. Two other highly speculative but to my mind less-convincing interpretations are Nina Baym, "H's Holgrave: The Failure of the Artist-Hero," *JEGP*, 69 (1970), 584–98, and Jane Bernadete, "Holgrave's Legend of Alice Pyncheon as a *Godey's* Story," *SAF*, 7 (1979), 229–33.

56. See Mildred K. Travis, "Past versus Present in *HSG*," *ESQ*, 58 (1970), 109–11, and R. A. Yoder, "Transcendental Conservatism and *HSG*," *Georgia Review*, 28 (1974), 33–51.

57. *The Middle Way*, p. 125.

58. Such, for example, as Judith S. Gustafson, whose "Parody in *HSG*," *NHJ* 1976, pp. 294–301, argues that H set out to burlesque in Phoebe the conventional heroine of sentimental fiction. The fact that "Phoebe" was H's pet name for his wife, some of whose traits he gave this character, ought alone to have served to save Ms. Gustafson from this blunder, even if the whole design of *HSG* had not cried out against her. It may very well be that H succeeded better in vivifying characters like Hester, Zenobia, and Miriam than he did with Phoebe, Hilda, and perhaps Priscilla, but it was girls like those of the second trio that he really liked, and if Ms. Gustafson does not know why the first group was easier to do, any competent actress should be able to

tell her. The best and most elaborate defense and appreciation of
Phoebe is Alfred J. Levy's in "*HSG:* The Religion of Love," *NCF,* 16
(1961), 189–203.

59. *The Romance in America,* p. 124.

60. "*HSG:* New Light on Old Problems," *PMLA,* 82 (1967), 579–90;
     see also Battaglia's refutation of the view that H produced his ending
     against the grain to satisfy public taste, "The (Unmeretricious)
     HSG," *SN,* 2 (1970), 468–70, and cf. John Gatta, Jr., "Progress and
     Providence in *HSG,*" *AL,* 38 (1950), 37–48. Though he admits the
     ending is contrived, Richard C. Carpenter, "H's Scarlet Bean Flow-
     ers," *University Review,* 30 (1963), 65–71, shows how "a series of
     horticultural symbols and images which place in opposition the ste-
     rility and decay of the elder Pyncheons and the promise of the young
     couple indicates that the fruitful and optimistic outcome is inevita-
     ble." By commenting on the relevant passage in the *Aeneid,* book 6,
     Elmer A. Havens, "The 'Golden Branch' as Symbol in *HSG,*" *MLN,*
     74 (1959), 2–22, shows that H's use of this symbol forecasts a happy
     future for Phoebe and Holgrave and the reconciliation of their houses,
     and in "The Golden Stain of Time: Ruskinian Aesthetics and the
     Ending of H's *HSG,*" *NHJ* 1973, 143–53, Barton Levi St. Armand
     invokes Ruskin's influence to justify H's meliorism. One of the best
     and most thoughtful discussions of this whole matter is Richard H.
     Brodhead's in his *H, Melville, and the Novel.* For an excellent review
     of various interpretations of the meaning of the ending to date, see
     Brook Thomas, "*HSG:* Reading the Romance of America," *PMLA,*
     97 (1982), 195–209, who also considers what he thinks the "political
     and social implications" of the novel.

61. See Joel R. Kebler, "*HSG:* House, Home, and H's Psychology of
     Habitation," *ESQ,* 21 (1975), 142–55. E. Kleiman's "The Wizardry
     of NH: *Seven Gables* as Fairy Tale and Parable," *English Studies in
     Canada,* 4 (1978), 289–304, is a fine study. A good many studies of
     HSG are reprinted or extracted in Seymour L. Gross's Norton crit-
     ical edition of the novel (1967) and in Roger Asselineau, ed., *The
     Merrill Studies in HSG* (1970).

62. H's specific statement in his preface that he used the community only
     as "a theatre, a little removed from the highway of ordinary travel,
     where the creatures of his brain may play out their phantasmagorical
     antics" and his disclaimer of "the slightest pretensions to illustrate
     a theory, or elicit a conclusion, favorable or otherwise, in respect
     to socialism" have not prevented critics from considering back-
     grounds. See Darrel Abel, "H's Scepticism about Social Reform, with

Especial Reference to *BR*," *UKCR*, 19 (1953), 181–93; Gustaf Van Cromphout, "Emerson, H, and *BR*," *Georgia Review*, 25 (1971), 471–78; Allen Flint, " 'Essentially a Day-dream, and Yet a Fact': H's *Blithedale*," *NHJ* 1972, pp. 75–83; and John G. Hirsh, "The Politics of Blithedale: The Dilemma of the Self," *SR*, 11 (1972), 138–46. Two articles in *Kwartalnik Neofilologiczny* deal with *Blithedale* as an "exemplification of the collapse of the American dream" or "an archetypal American experience in the New World." The first, by Viola Sachs, is cited in note 53; the other, by Grażyna Branny, "H's 'Cold Arcadia': The Collapse of the American Dream in *BR*," is in vol. 26 (1979), 477–87. H's own statement however is quite correct. The tragedies that occur at Blithedale are due to the character of those involved and have nothing to do with socialism or communism. As Nicholas Canady, Jr., puts it in "Community and Identity at Blithedale," *SAQ*, 71 (1972), 30–37: "What seems most clear looking backward to Blithedale is that this ideal community was not really a community in any meaningful sense of that term, and thus the benefits to be derived from a communal relationship were lost from the beginning . . . . Nothing can be more detrimental to brotherhood or destructive of a community than the impulse which is symbolized by putting on a mask." In "H's Fallen Puritans: Eliot's Pulpit in *BR*," *SN*, 18 (1986), 283–90, Byron L. Stay sees this property as a symbol of "Puritan strength in order to contrast the Blithedalers with their seventeenth-century counterparts."

63. John D. Winslow, "New Light on Miles Coverdale," *Journal of Narrative Technique*, 7 (1977), 189–97, conjecturally attempts to determine the changes H made and the alterations of emphasis in the novel thus determined.

64. See Roy Harvey Pearce's introduction to the Centenary Edition of *BR* (1964).

65. Howells was indebted to *BR* for *The Undiscovered Country* (1880) and James for *The Bostonians* (1886). On the latter see Robert Emmet Long, "The Society and the Masks: *BR* and *The Bostonians*," *NCF*, 19 (1964), 105–22.

66. Browning is merely recorded as having told its author that *Blithedale* was his favorite H book. For George Eliot, see James W. Rust, "George Eliot on *BR*," *BPLQ*, 7 (1958), 207–15, who accepts the British novelist's authorship of the "mixed" notice in the *Westminster Review*, October 1852.

67. *NH*, pp. 188–91.

68. " 'Romance' in *BR*," *AN&Q*, 9 (1971), 72–73.

69. To Robert Emmet Whelan, Jr., "*BR:* The Holy War in H's Mansoul,"
    TSLL, 13 (1971), 91–109, and Robert Stanton, "The Trial of Na-
    ture: An Analysis of *BR,*" *PMLA,* 76 (1961), 528–38, the novel is as
    much an allegory as if Bunyan had written it. Whelan calls the
    characters "personified abstractions," and both writers work out
    their correspondences in masterly fashion, though the balance of pros
    and cons Stanton achieves at the end seems to me worthy of Cover-
    dale himself. Crews's "New Reading of *BR*" is in *AL,* 29 (1957),
    147–70.
70. "H: Pastoral and Politics," in Howe's *Politics and The Novel* (Ho-
    rizon Press, 1957).
71. Kelley Griffith, Jr., "Form in *BR,*" *AL,* 40 (1968), 15–26. See also
    Richard VanDeWeghe, "H's *BR:* Miles Coverdale, His Story," *NHJ*
    1977, pp. 289–302, and Allen Flint, as cited in note 62.
72. Kay, "Five Acts of *BR,*" *ATQ,* 13 (1972), 25–28 (cf. Maurice A.
    Crane, "*BR* as Theatre," *Notes and Queries,* 203 [1958], 84–86);
    Lentz and Stein, "The Black Flower of Necessity: Structure in *BR,*"
    Essays in Literature, 3 (1976), 86–96; Stubbs, *The Pursuit of Form,*
    p. 122; Hill, "Narrative Form in *BR,*" *English Studies in Canada,* 7
    (1981), 388–401; Auchincloss, "*BR:* A Study of Form and Point of
    View," *NHJ* 1972, pp. 53–58.
73. Much of this material has been conveniently gathered into the Norton
    critical edition of *BR,* edited by Seymour Gross and Rosalie Murphy,
    1978. See also Arlin Turner, "Autobiographical Elements in H's
    BR," *University of Texas Bulletin,* no. 3526, July 8, 1935, and the
    references there cited; also Lisa Böhmer, *Brookfarm and H's "BR"*
    (Jena, Gustav, Neuenhahan, 1936).
74. See Peter J. McGuire, "Dante's Inferno in *BR,*" *ELN,* 18 (1980),
    25–27. John O. Rees, Jr., Shakespeare in *BR,*" *ESQ,* 19 (1973),
    84–93, points out what he thinks are echoes of Shakespeare, espe-
    cially from *Antony and Cleopatra, The Tempest,* and *As You Like It.*
75. Shroeder, "Miles Coverdale's Calendar; or, A Major Literary Source
    for *BR,*" *EIHC,* 103 (1967), 353–64. Spenser is also involved in
    Buford Jones, "H's Coverdale and Spenser's Allegory of 'Mutabil-
    ity,' " *AL,* 39 (1967), 215–19, and, less importantly, in Leo B. Levy's,
    "*BR:* H's 'Voyage Through Chaos,' " *SR,* 8 (1966), 1–15. For the
    Bible, see Joan Magretta, "The Coverdale Translation: *Blithedale*
    and the Bible," *NHJ* 1974, pp. 250–56.
76. Waggoner, *H: A Critical Study,* p. 175; Swann, "A Note on *BR,* or
    'Call Him Fauntleroy,' " *JAmSt,* 10 (1978), 103–4. Edward G. Lued-
    ers, "The Melville-H Relationship in *Pierre* and *BR,*" *Western Hu-*

manities Review, 4 (1950), 323–34, finds resemblances between the two novels which he tries to connect with the personal contacts between their authors.

77. Murray, "Mythopoesis in *BR*," *PMLA* (1960), 591–96; Stanton, as cited in note 69; Hirsh, "Zenobia as Queen: The Background Sources to H's *BR*," *NHJ* 1971, pp. 182–90; Whitford, "*BR*: H's Reveries of a Bachelor," *Thoth*, vol. 15, no. 1 (1974–75), pp. 19–28. In "*Blithedale* and the Androgyne Myth," *ESQ*, 18 (1972), 141–45, Gustaf Van Cromphout considers Zenobia in this connection, with which he thinks H must have been familiar through Charles Fourier and Margaret Fuller.

78. Justus, "H's Coverdale: Character and Art in *BR*," *AL*, 47 (1975), 21–36; Smith, "Why Does Zenobia Kill Herself?" *ELN*, 6 (1968), 37–39. Without quite denying the possibility of suicide, Mary Suzanne Schriber suggests that Zenobia may have drowned accidentally or been murdered by Hollingsworth! See her "Justice to Zenobia," *NEQ*, 55 (1982), 61–78.

79. "Feminism and Femininity in *BR*," *NHJ* 1976, pp. 215–26. This and Carl Dennis's article, "*BR* and the Problem of Integration," *TSLL*, 15 (1973), 93–110, are among the best studies that have been made of Zenobia and, in the second instance, of the other characters also. Nancy Joyner, "Bondage in Blithedale", *NHJ* 1975, pp. 227–31, is another good commentary on the characters from a more specialized point of view.

80. Rahv, "The Dark Lady of Salem," *Partisan Review,* 8 (1941), 362–81; Kaul, *The American Vision: Actual and Ideal Society in Nineteenth Century American Fiction* (YUP, 1963).

81. "Some Rents in the Veil: New Light on Priscilla and Zenobia," *NCF*, 21 (1966), 263–75. See also R. H. Fogle, "Priscilla's Veil," *NHJ* 1972, pp. 57–65.

82. See Marilyn Geddes Rose, "Miles Coverdale as H's Persona," *ATQ*, 1 (1969), 90–91.

83. *H's Tragic Vision,* p. 151.

84. Smith, "*BR*: H's Testament of Failure," *Personalist*, 49 (1968), 540–49; Bales, "*BR*: Coverdale's Mean and Subversive Egotism," *Bucknell Review*, vol. 21, no. 2 (1973), 60–82. For further discussion of some of these points see William Van O'Connor, "Conscious Naïveté in *BR*," *Revue des langues vivants*, 20 (1954), 37–45; W. L. Hedges, "H's *Blithedale*: The Function of the Narrator," *NCF*, 14 (1960), 303–16; Rita K. Gollin, " 'Dream-Work' in *BR*," *ESQ*, 19 (1973), 74–83; Lyle H. Justus, "H's Coverdale: Character and Art in *BR*,"

AL, 47 (1975), 21–36; Irvin Stock, "H's Portrait of the Artist: A Defense of *BR*," *Novel*, 11 (1978), 244–56; Judy Sharf Anhorn, " 'Gifted Simplicity of Vision': Pastoral Expectations in *BR*," *ESQ*, 28 (1982), 135–53; and Keith Carabine, " 'Bitter Honey': Miles Coverdale as Narrator in *BR*," in A. Robert Lee, ed., *NH: New Critical Essays* (Barnes and Noble, 1982). John C. Stubb's note in *The Pursuit of Form*, p. 126, has useful comment on some of these items. Among other articles, less centered upon Coverdale, see Frank Davidson, "Toward a Re-evaluation of *BR*," *NEQ*, 25 (1952), 374–83; James F. Ragan, "The Irony in H's Blithedale," *NEQ*, 35 (1962), 239–46; Nina Baym, "*BR*: A Radical Reading," *JEGP*, 67 (1968), 545–69; Alfred H. Marks, "Ironic Inversion in *BR*," *ESQ*, 55 (1969), 95–102; Kent Bales, "The Allegory and the Radical Romantic Ethic of *BR*," *AL*, 46 (1974), 41–55.

85. Morgan, "The Veiled Lady: The Secret Love of Miles Coverdale," *NHJ* 1971, pp. 169–81; Ross, "Dreams and Sexual Repression in *BR*," *PMLA*, 66 (1971), 1014–17. See also Claire Sprague, "Dream and Disguise in *BR*," *PMLA*, 84 (1969), 596–97.

86. The principal study of "The Structure of *MF*" is by Merle E. Brown, *AL*, 28 (1956), 302–13, who saw all four characters undergoing transformation. Amendments to Brown's interpretation were offered by Sheldon W. Liebman, "The Design of *MF*," *NEQ*, 40 (1967), 61–78, and by Charles R. Smith, Jr., "The Structural Principle of *MF*," *Thoth*, 3 (1982), 32–38, who preferred a seven-part division. Gene A. Barrett worked out a time-scheme in "H's Italian Calendar," *ESQ*, 43 (1966), 68–70. In "Optimism and Pessimism in *MF*," *BUSE*, 2 (1956), 95–112, Bernard J. Paris saw the main plot as "the maturation and humanization of Donatello" and the subplot as "the maturation, in a somewhat different sense, and humanization of Hilda." Taking his cue from the questionable observation that sculpture is more important than painting in *MF*, Harry Levin (*The Power of Blackness*) called the "approach" of the book "sculptural," with "its movement . . . reducible to a sequence of standstills or *tableaux vivants*," and with the characters striking attitudes and engaging in colloquies: "duets, trios, and quartets in varying combinations." But, as we have already seen, *MF* is not the only Hawthorne novel of which this is characteristic.

87. "Point of View in *MF*," *Die Neueren Sprachen*, 1961, pp. 218–24. Cf. Murray Krieger, *The Play and Place of Criticism* (Johns Hopkins Press, 1967), p. 85.

88. See Gary J. Scrimgeour, "H's Faery Land," *AL*, 36 (1964), 271–87.

89. A good early example of such allegorical interpretation is the un-signed article, "*MF:* An Allegory with a Key to Its Interpretation," *New Englander,* 19 (1861), 160–70, reprinted in 56 (1892), 26–36. Perhaps the wildest of recent interpretations is Paul A. Lister's "Some New Light on H's *MF,*" *NHJ* 1978, pp. 79–92, in which Kenyon is God the Father; Donatello, Christ; Hilda, the Holy Spirit; Miriam, Humanity; and the model, Satan. Obuchowski's "Character and Theme in *MF*" is in *CLA Journal,* 24 (1980), 26–41. For a modified and modernized allegorical interpretation see Darrel Abel, "A Mas-que of Love and Death," *UTQ,* 23 (1953), 9–25. On symbolism and imagery, see, besides the two books by R. H. Fogle, already cited, Marjorie J. Elder, *NH, Transcendentalist Symbolist* (Ohio University Press, 1969) and cf. Josefina T. Mariano, "NH's Symbolism of Black and White as a Synthesis of Permanence and Change in *HSG* and *MF,*" *Diliman Review,* 18 (1970), 268–83, and, for a related theme, Joseph Schwartz, "Myth and Ritual in *MF,*" *ESQ,* no. 25 (1961), pp. 26–29. John W. Bickell, "*MF* Reconsidered," *UKCR,* 20 (1954), 193–99, and Marga C. Jones, "*MF* and a Writer's Crisis," *Studi Americani,* 16 (1970), 81–123, speak, the latter at wearisome length, for those who find the novel a failure.

90. See Patrick Brancaccio, "Emma Abigail Salomons: H's Miriam Iden-tified," *NHJ* 1978, pp. 94–103; Donald G. Darnell, " 'Doctrine by Example': The Emblem and *MF,*" *TSLL,* 15 (1973), 301–10; David B. Kesterson, "Journey to Perugia: Dantean Parallels in *MF,*" *ESQ,* 19 (1973), 24–35.

91. Fogle, "Coleridge, Hilda, and *MF,*" *ESQ,* 19 (1973), 105–11; Ber-covitch, "Hilda's 'Seven-branched Allegory' " *Early American Liter-ature Newsletter,* vol. 1, no. 2 (1966), pp. 5–6, and "Miriam as Shylock," *Forum for Modern Language Studies,* 5 (1969), 385–87. Paul A. Miller's article, "A New Review of the Career of Paul Akers (1825–1861)," *Colby Library Quarterly,* series 7 (1966), 227–52, though principally concerned with the artist himself, has some bear-ing on the use Hawthorne makes of his work in *MF.* H. H. Hoeltje's *Inward Sky,* pp. 501ff., has an excellent discussion of the sources of characters and incidents in *MF* in the author's own life, thought, and earlier writings.

92. Nathalia Wright's "H and the Praslin Murder," *NEQ,* 15 (1942), 5–14, covers the case very nicely so far as *MF* is concerned. There is a full and admirable account of this affair in Stanley Loomis, *A Crime of Passion* (Lippincott, 1967). There are also two very inter-esting modern novels: Joseph Shearing's *Forget-Me-Not* (1932),

which in this country was called first *Lucile Cléry, A Woman of Passion* and then *The Strange Case of Lucile Cléry,* and Rachel Field's *All This and Heaven Too* (1938). We have already met Joseph Shearing under another pseudonym, George R. Preedy, in note 19. She was Margaret Gabrielle Long, who published some 150 fascinating books, mostly as Marjorie Bowen. Of Henriette she took a dim view, and it is a pretty safe guess that the latter's kinswoman, Rachel Field, was prompted by her work to rush to the defense. *All This and Heaven Too* was filmed in 1940 with Bette Davis and Charles Boyer.

93. The Romantic glorification of Beatrice Cenci was facilitated by the fact that the nineteenth-century believed that her father had either forced incestuous relations upon her or attempted to do so. Francesco Cenci was a brute who had treated his family with extreme cruelty, but the accusation of incest was introduced into the case at a late stage by Beatrice's lawyer and is no longer regarded as possessing validity. Beatrice also had a lover, who was drawn into the crime. It is now regarded as very doubtful that the much-reproduced portrait is a picture of of Beatrice Cenci; some have even doubted that it is by Guido. Antonio Bertolozzi was the first important Cenci revisionist in the 1870s; the authoritative modern book is Corrado Ricci's *Beatrice Cenci,* which is based on an exhaustive study of the original documents. Morris Bishop and Henry Logan Stuart translated it into English; the result was published in two sumptuous volumes in 1926 by Heinemann in London and by Boni and Liveright in New York, unfortunately without the exhaustive documentation that appears in the Italian.

94. Haselmayer's "H and the Cenci" is in *Neophilologus,* 47 (1942), 59–65, and Hall's "Beatrice Cenci: Symbol and Vision in *MF*" in *NCF,* 25 (1970), 85–95. See also Roland A. Duerksen, "The Double Image of Beatrice Cenci in *MF*," *Michigan Academician,* vol. 1, nos. 3–4, pp. 47–55; Diane Long Hoeveler, "La Cenci: The Incest Motif in H and Melville," *ATQ,* 44 (1979), 247–59; and Louise K. Barnett, "American Novelists and the 'Portrait of Beatrice Cenci,' " *NEQ,* 53 (1980), 168–83, which concerns *MF, Pierre,* and two novels by Edith Wharton, *The House of Mirth* and *The Mother's Recompense.* Hall comments that "the painting becomes a kind of nexus between Miriam and Hilda, a 'symbolic mirror' in which each recognizes her own identity and which thus reflects the inexorable bond of common humanity which links the two women together," and links them too with Beatrice, who, as a woman, becomes a kind of "sister."

The quotation from Randall Stewart is from his edition of Hawthorne's *American Notebooks* (YUP, 1932), p. xcv.

95. *"MF:* 'A Frail Structure of Our Own Rearing,' " *Essays in Literature,* 7 (1980), 54–65.

96. Goldman, "The Plot of H's *MF,*" *JAmSt,* 18 (1984), 383–404; Moss, "The Symbolism of the Italian Background in *MF,*" *NCF,* 23 (1968), 332–36; for Scrimgeour, see note 88. A number of other studies have been made in this area. See Christof Wegelin, "Europe in H's Fiction," *ELH,* 14 (1947), 219–45; John A. Huzzard, "H's *MF,*" *Italica,* 35 (1958), 119–24; Nathalia Wright, "The Influence of Italy on *MF,*" *Tennessee Studies in Literature,* special number, 1961, pp. 141–49; Gene A. Barnett, "H's Italian Towers," *SR,* 3 (1964), 252–56; Edward Ciefelli, "H and the Italian[s]," *Studi Americani,* 14 (1968), 87–96. Conrad Shumaker, " 'A Daughter of the Puritans': Hilda in H's *MF,*" *NEQ,* 57 (1984), 65–85, supplements these studies of the Italian backgrounds by viewing Hilda as the product of her American inheritance and as representing Hawthorne's "final commentary on the course he believed American history should take," and Cushing Stewart, "H's International Novel," *NCF,* 24 (1969), 169–81, stresses the contrasts developed between American and European standards.

97. Perhaps the fullest and most thoughtful discussion of the artistic backgrounds of *MF* is Leo B. Levy's *"MF:* H's Landscape of the Fall," *AL,* 42 (1970), 139–56; for a much less sympathetic presentation, see David Downing, "The Feminine Ideal and the Failure of Art in *MF,*" *Recovering Literature,* 9 (1981), 5–14. Rita K. Gollin's "Painting and Character in *MF*" is in *ESQ,* 21 (1975), 1–10. Dennis Berthold, "H, Ruskin, and the Gothic Revival: Transcendent Gothicism in *MF,*" *ESQ,* 20 (1974), 15–32, and Marjorie J. Elder, "H's *MF:* A Gothic Structure," *Costerus,* 1 (1972), 81–88, bring out Hawthorne's affinity with Ruskin's views. Other articles dealing with these and related themes include Harry Levin, "Statues from Italy: *MF,*" in Roy Harvey Pearce, ed., *H Centenary Essays;* G. A. Barnett, "Art as Setting in *MF,*" *Transactions of the Wisconsin Academy of Sciences, Arts, and Letters,* 54 (1965), 231–47; Jay Bochner, "Life in a Picture Gallery: Things in *The Portrait of a Lady* and *MF,*" *TSLL,* 11 (1969), 761–77; Robert Emmet Whelan, "Rome as H's Mansoul," *Research Studies of Washington State University,* 40 (1972), 163–75, and "God as Artist in *MF,*" *Renascence,* 34 (1982), 144–66; Jonathan Auerbach, "Executing the Model: Painting, Sculpture, and Romance-Writing in H's *MF,*" *ELH,* 47 (1980), 103–20.

Paul Brodtkorb, Jr., "Art Allegory in *MF*," *PMLA*, 77 (1962), 254–67, is the only article I recall ever to have read that concludes with the author's observation that perhaps there may be nothing in his argument after all! For a good book-length treatment of the whole subject indicated, see Millicent Bell, *H's View of the Artist*.

98. *The American Novel, 1789–1930* (Macmillan, 1940).

99. Goldfarb, "*MF* and Emersonian Self-Reliance," *ATQ*, 1 (1969), 19–23; Zivkovic, "The Evil of the Isolated Intellect," *Personalist*, 43 (1962), 202–13. Waggoner launches his broadside on pp. 202–7 of *H: A Critical Study*.

100. In an interesting article, "Of Wise and Foolish Virgins: Hilda *versus* Miriam in *MF*," *NEQ*, 41 (1968), 281–86, Sacvan Berkovich moves toward justifying Hilda's behavior in the light of Christ's parable in Matthew, chapter 5, and Calvinistic commentary thereupon, finding her actuated "on some half-conscious level" by humility and Christian compassion.

101. See Walter V. Gavigan, "H and Rome," *Catholic World*, 135 (1935), 555–59; Gilbert P. Voight, "H and the Roman Catholic Church," *NEQ*, 19 (1946), 394–97, and especially Henry G. Fairbanks, "H and the Catholic Church," *BUSE*, 1 (1955), 148–65.

102. On this point see Joseph C. Pattison, "The Guilt of the Innocent Donatello," *ESQ*, 31 (1963), 66–68, who protests against confusing Donatello with a true innocent like Melville's Billy Budd.

103. John C. Guilds seems to have written the only article on Miriam that strikes a distinctively religious, perhaps even fundamentalistic, note. It is "Miriam of *MF*: H's Subtle Sinner," *Cairo Studies in English*, 1960, pp. 61–68. To Guilds her portrait is "a complex study of the insidious manner in which despair can seize the heart of a well intentioned individual lacking in self-knowledge and faith in God's mercy." She "understands, even overestimates, her responsibility to fellow man, but remains woefully ignorant of her proper relationship with God."

104. Nina Baym, "*MF*: H's Elegy for Art," *NEQ*, 44 (1971), 355–76, is the only recent writer I have read who echoes Whipple's complaint, though without mentioning him. Curtis Dahl, "When the Deity Returns: *MF* and *Romola*," *Papers on Language and Literature*, 5 supplement (1968), 82–99, an illuminating comparative study of the two novels, remarks of the model that "he is more an idea than a man." It is interesting that Father Fick, in *The Light Beyond*, p. 88, expresses the opinion that "it is highly probable that neither Miriam nor Donatello is guilty of 'formal, deadly sin.' "

105. Paris himself (see note 86) accepts the last view and summarizes the
      others. There is another useful review of criticism in Peter G. Beidler,
      "Theme of the Fortunate Fall in *MF*," *ESQ*, no. 17 (1967), 56–62,
      who points out that four questions are involved: (1) Does Donatello
      rise as a result of his experience? (2) Is sin the only means of edu-
      cation? (3) Was Donatello's experience worth what it cost? (4) Was
      Adam's fall part of a Divine plan? He believes that Hawthorne an-
      swers the first question yes, the second and fourth no, and refrains
      from giving a definite answer to the third, seeing both gain and loss
      in Donatello's experience. There is an odd variation of the debate in
      Daniel J. Schneider, "The Allegory and Symbolism of H's *MF*," *SN*,
      1 (1967), 38–50, who believes that "we must learn to accept our
      shortcomings and sins as a part of life." Cf., in this connection, James
      G. Janssen, "The 'Grim Identity' in H's *MF*," *SN*, 15 (1983), 108–
      21. Other articles worth consulting include Richard H. Fogle, "Sim-
      plicity and Complexity in *MF*," *Tulane Studies in English*, 2 (1950),
      103–20; Sidney P. Moss, "The Problem of Theme in *MF*," *NCF*, 18
      (1964), 393–99; David Howard, "The Fortunate Fall in H's *MF*," in
      Ian Fletcher, ed., *Romantic Mythologies* (Routledge & Kegan Paul,
      1967).
106. "Suggestions for Interpreting *MF*," *AL*, 13 (1941), 224–39.
107. See Arthur O. Lovejoy, "Milton and the Paradox of the Fortunate
      Fall," *ELH*, 4 (1937), 161–79.
108. Frederick W. Turner III, "H and the Myth of Paradise," *Serif*, vol. 3,
      no. 3 (1960), 9–12, probably stands alone in finding art, which he
      seems to equate with knowledge, as the cause of Donatello's "descent
      into experience" and consequent loss of innocence.
109. A number of critical studies of *MF* have been reprinted by David
      Kesterton in *The Merrill Studies in "MF"* (Charles E. Merrill Pub-
      lishing Co., 1971). See also his own article, "*MF* as Transformation
      of Author and Age," *NHJ* 1978, pp. 67–77.

4. Experiments

1. *H's Last Phase* was published by YUP in 1949, *H's Doctor Grim-
    shawe's Secret*, edited, with an introduction and notes, by Edward H.
    Davidson, by HUP in 1954. See also Davidson's article, "The Unifin-
    ished Romances," in Roy Harvey Pearce, ed., *H Centenary Essays*
    (OSUP, 1964). If Crews's *The Sins of the Fathers: H's Psychological
    Themes* does not satisfy a reader's Freudian appetite, he might be

referred to John H. Lamont, "H's Unfinished Works," *Harvard Medical Alumni Bulletin*, 36 (1962), 13–20. There is a considerably less extreme psychoanalytical interpretation in Robert Shulman's "H's Quiet Conflict," *PQ*, 47 (1968), 215–38.

2. It is interesting to speculate as to whether Hawthorne might have handled "The Ancestral Footstep" more successfully if he had set to work on it when the idea first occurred to him.

3. Una Hawthorne has been much praised for her conscientious editing of *Septimius Felton*, and all this praise has been justly earned. For a young lady not yet thirty who had had no training whatever in this field, she did an excellent job; obviously her intelligence was quite equal to her beauty and her character. But I do not feel that the comparisons that have been made between her work on *Septimius* and that of her brother Julian on *Doctor Grimshawe's Secret* are wholly fair to him. Obviously she came much closer to what modern standards of scholarship require, but some allowance must be made for the fact that he faced a much more difficult problem. Comparing his edition of *Grimshawe* to what Albert Bigelow Paine and F. A. Duneka did when they made the 1916 edition of Mark Twain's *The Mysterious Stranger*, I should say that his liberties were rather less daring and that he was franker in revealing what he had done; see his "A Glimpse into H's Workshop," *Century*, 25 (1883), 433–48, and also "NH's 'Elixir of Life' Manuscripts," serially in *Lippincott's Magazine*, 45 (1890), 66–76 and subsequently. His selling H's manuscript piecemeal to collectors was something else of course. For that matter, the publication of any of these materials after H's death was contrary to his wishes, as all members of his family knew. About this all I have to say is that any writer of eminence who does not wish to share his scraps and shavings with the world had better destroy them while he is still alive.

4. It seems incredible that both F. O. Matthiessen, *American Renaissance*, p. 355, and George Snell, *The Shapers of American Fiction* (Dutton, 1947), p. 129, should have judged *Footstep* the most promising of the last manuscripts.

5. Good examples of contemporary comment are Thomas Wentworth Higginson, "H's Last Bequest," *Scribner's Monthly*, 5 (1872), 100–105; George P. Lathrop, "History of H's Last Romance," *Atlantic Monthly*, 30 (1872), 452–60; John Addison Porter, "The 'Dr. Grimshawe' Manuscripts," *New Englander*, 42 (1883), 339–53.

6. *AL*, 39 (1968), 506–16.

7. The reference of course is to the Civil War.

8. *H as Myth-Maker: A Study in Imagination* (University of Toronto Press, 1969), pp. 204ff.

9. Stein's "A Possible Source of H's English Romance" is in *MLN,* 61 (1952), 52–55. Lundblad's *NH and European Literary Tradition* was a University of Upsala dissertation, which avowed its indebtedness to Schonbach's "Beiträge zur Charakteristik NHs," in *Anglia,* 1886. The American edition was published by Harvard in 1947. As its title indicates, John A. Kouwenhoven's "H's Notebooks and *Doctor Grimshawe's Secret,*" points out resemblances between passages in the notebooks and in the story. Since it appeared in *AL,* 5 (1934), 349–58, it was of course written without benefit of Davidson's researches and the materials thus made available. Christof K. Lohmann, "The Agony of the English Romance," *NHJ* 1972, pp. 219–29, makes an interesting attempt to trace the development of what he thinks began as a plan to "transform the accumulated materials of [the] English notebooks into a light, satirical treatment of a confrontation between the Old and the New World." Lawrence S. Hall, *H, Critic of Society* (YUP, 1944) concerns himself with the social and political implications of H's themes, as does Thomas D. Calhoon, from a very different point of view, in "H's Gothic: An Approach to the Four Last Fragments: 'The Ancestral Footstep,' *Doctor Grimshawe's Secret, The Dolliver Romance, Septimius Felton,*" *Genre,* 3 (1970), 220–41. As Calhoon sees it, Hawthorne "wanted to write a novel about the ancestry, the heritage, of America—or an American. He also wanted to write a novel about immortality: the elixir of life, or the future of America—or an American. These themes are really asking a similar question from different points of view. Where did we come from? Where are we going?"

10. *NH: Identity and Knowledge* (Southern Illinois University Press, 1967), especially pp. 138–43.

11. Darrel Abel, "Immortality and Mortality in *Septimius Felton:* Some Possible Sources," *AL,* 27 (1956), 566–80, points out striking resemblances between Hawthorne and both Swift and Orestes Brownson and, somewhat less convincingly, Shakespeare. Alexander Cowie, *The Rise of the American Novel* (American Book Company, 1948) compares *Septimius* to Cooper's *Lionel Lincoln.* In 1854 an English gardener gave Mrs. Hawthorne "a purple everlasting flower" as a souvenir of her visit to Eaton Hall. According to Rose Hawthorne Lathrop, Aunt Keziah or Nashoba was based on Mrs. Peters, a black servant of the Hawthornes in Lenox, but H's aunt, Mrs. Richard

Manning, had a sister named Kezia, and Nashoba was the name of a settlement of Christianized Indians near Concord.

12. For further discussion of this aspect, see Rita K. Gollin, *NH and the Truth of Dreams*, pp. 211–12.

13. See Davidson, *H's Last Phase* and the Centenary Edition, vol. 13.

5. The Man

1. Randall Stewart, "Mrs. Hawthorne's Quarrel with James T. Fields," *More Books*, 21 (1946), 254–63, and " 'Pestiferous Gail Hamilton,' James T. Fields, and the Hawthornes" *NEQ*, 17 (1944), 418–23.

2. Cf. Taylor Stoehr, *H's Mad Scientists: Pseudoscience and Social Science in Nineteenth Century Art and Letters* (Shoe String Press, 1978).

3. Not that it is relevant here, but simply to make it clear that nothing is being suppressed, let it be noted that in 1681 Nicholas Manning, brother of Hawthorne's great-great-grandfather on his mother's side, was guilty of incest with two sisters. This may well have given Hawthorne another phase of inherited guilt to add to the shame he felt for the cruelty of his ancestors toward Quakers, Indians, and alleged witches. Philip Young seems to have done a scholarly job in digging out the relevant documents, but the conclusion to which he jumped in *H's Secret: An Untold Tale* (David R. Godine, 1984), that Hawthorne himself committed incest with his sister Elizabeth and that this was the "secret" over which he brooded, does not seem to have convinced many.

4. "The Centenary of H," in *Park-Street Papers* (HM, 1908), pp. 102–3.

Index of Names

Note: In the Index of Names I have attempted to include all the names mentioned in Chapters 1–5, excluding characters of fiction but including critics and commentators. In the Appendix and Notes, on the other hand, critics have been indexed only in a comparatively few instances, where I believed the reference might be especially helpful. In the Index of Hawthorne's Writings, page references in the Appendix and Notes have been given along with those referring to the main text. Hawthorne's nonfictional writings have been included in the index only as referred to in the text, though page 236 contains a complete list of the sketches and essays included in *Twice-Told Tales, Mosses from an Old Manse,* and *The Snow-Image and Other Twice-Told Tales.*

Index of Hawthorne's Writings